JOHN
THE MAVERICK GOSPEL

JOHN
THE MAVERICK GOSPEL

REVISED EDITION

ROBERT KYSAR

Westminster John Knox Press
LOUISVILLE • LONDON

Scripture quotations from the Revised Standard Version of the Bible are copyright 1946, 1952, ©1971, 1973 by the Division of Christian Education of the National Council of the Churches of Christ in the U.S.A. and are used by permission.

Scripture quotations from the New Revised Standard Version of the Bible are copyright ©1989 by the Division of Christian Education of the National Council of the Churches of Christ in the U.S.A. and are used by permission.

The chart on pages 34–35 is adapted with the permission of Charles Scribner's Sons, an imprint of Macmillan Publishing Company, from *The Foundations of New Testament Christology* by Reginald H. Fuller. Copyright © 1965 Reginald H. Fuller.

Book design by Carol Dukes Eberhart

Published by Westminster John Knox Press
Louisville, Kentucky

This book is printed on acid-free paper that meets the American National Standards Institute Z39.48 standard. ♾

PRINTED IN THE UNITED STATES OF AMERICA

9   8   7

Library of Congress Cataloging-in-Publication Data

Kysar, Robert.
   John, the maverick Gospel / Robert Kysar.—Rev. ed.
      p.   cm.
   Includes bibliographical references.
   ISBN 0–664–25401–2 (alk. paper)
   1. Bible. N.T. John—Criticism, interpretation, etc.   I. Title.
BS2615.2.K93   1993
226.5'06—dc20   93–17159

Dedicated with gratitude to
Edward P. Blair

CONTENTS

CONTENTS

PREFACE

This book is addressed to the beginning student of New Testament literature. It pretends to be neither technical nor scholarly, but aspires to introduce the reader to the thought and symbolism of the Fourth Gospel as those matters are increasingly understood among contemporary New Testament scholars. Thereby, I hope to lead the reader into the Fourth Gospel and bring him or her abreast of the way this Gospel is understood by a number of more advanced students.

Among the various introductions to the Fourth Gospel available, I hope this volume will accomplish a number of distinctive things. First, I hope to stress the uniqueness of the Fourth Gospel among the literature of the early Christian movement. Second, and at the same time, I want to set the thought and symbolism of the Gospel in a much broader context, namely, that of the universal human religious quest. The Gospel of John, this volume proposes, represents an exemplary piece of religious literature that poses questions that transcend Christianity alone to stand within the context of religion in general. The third peculiar feature of this introduction is its effort to keep the reader involved in the text of the Gospel itself. Too often reading an introduction to the New Testament or some specific portion of it draws the reader away from the document itself and into a concentration on secondary literature. So, the following pages are punctuated with insertions entitled "Reader's Preparation." These suggestions for reading in the Gospel will, I hope, make the task a triangular discussion—a conversation among the Gospel, the reader, and the ideas of this book. The degree to which the reader is kept involved with the other two parties of this triad is the degree of the success of the book itself.

It has often been said that creativity is the art of forgetting the source of one's ideas. That is surely the case with the ideas of this book. While I have tried to acknowledge the sources of my major ideas when I am conscious of them, I am sure that in many cases forgetfulness alone accounts for what may appear to be creativity. Still, this sort of book should not be burdened with footnotes. So, I ask the indulgence of my colleagues in Fourth Gospel criticism and implore the reader to take seriously the fact that the book is heavily indebted not only to the volumes listed in the bibliography but to a multitude of readings and conversations.

A history of this book would entail nothing short of an autobiography, since it represents my own lifelong struggle with the Gospel of John. The old saying "If it ain't broke, don't fix it" is good advice. Reactions to the first edition of this volume seem to indicate that it "worked." Therefore, when I began a revised edition, it was risky to tamper with that which seems to have accomplished its original purpose. Still, my own struggle with the Fourth Gospel had continued in the years since I had written the first edition. Those years have seen many changes in the scholarly study of the Gospel of John as well as in my own views of it. And books, after all, should change and grow even as people do.

There are ways, too, in which the first edition did not deal with all that the reader had the right to expect of an introduction to the religious thought of the Fourth Gospel. Some additions were called for, especially with regard to a discussion of salvation. Supplementary subjects are also discussed in the appendixes of this edition so as not to intrude on the basic approach of the book but still to provide readers with discussions of topics of current interest.

There are a host of important people in the history of this book to whom I owe thanks. First and most prominent among them are my students over the years. The ideas of this book reflect numerous efforts to interpret the Gospel to groups of beginning students and to respond with some degree of clarity to their concerns. Some were young, some old, some within an academic (both undergraduate and graduate) setting, some within a church setting. The chapters actually originated in my preparation for a lay Bible study group in a congregation. Since then they have been revised numerous times for other groups and in response to new insights I gained from learners.

I am indebted to all who have offered critical remarks concerning the original edition. Those remarks have become the basis for the changes made in this edition. I am grateful also to my colleagues in the field of Johannine studies who, like my students, persistently refuse to allow me to become content with all that I once thought was true!

Most important, I thank my spouse, the Reverend Dr. Myrna C. Kysar. Her theological perception and her understanding of human nature have taught me a great many things, and without her encouragement of my literary efforts this volume would not exist. Another individual who has shaped the whole of my career is Edward P. Blair, Professor Emeritus of Garrett-Evangelical Theological Seminary. It is with gratitude for all that he taught me that I dedicate this volume to him.

INTRODUCTION

There is a delightful little film about a small boy who learned to walk on his hands instead of his feet. The story is done in animation and stresses the pressures toward conformity in our society. The little boy's strange behavior had the most pleasant results for him. Walking on his hands gave him a radically different perspective on the world. He could smell the fragrance of the flowers without bending down. He was close to the earth so that he could see vividly the beauty of grass, and he met the butterfly eyeball to eyeball as it skimmed along the ground. But his parents were deeply distressed. Their darling child was a misfit! And so they took him first to a medical doctor, then a psychiatrist, and then a social worker. All of the newest theories were employed to change the little boy's behavior. Gradually he was made to learn to walk like all other humans—on his feet. The parents were relieved; the doctors, social workers, and others who had helped were proud of their success. But now the little boy began to see the world as others saw it: dirty, ugly, polluted, and filled with persons obediently doing what was expected of them. His short-lived posture that had enabled him to appreciate more easily the beauty of the world was ended. Now he was like everyone else!

The little parable illustrates the manner in which conformity is given high priority in our society. It also suggests the way in which nonconformist positions in religion are made to fit into the mainstream of traditional thought. Religions must by their nature be homogeneous, lest their claim to the truth about human existence and the cosmos seem compromised. Sometimes a religious tradition is flexible enough that it somehow manages to encompass variations of interpretation within its midst. Hinduism is an example. Other religious traditions more characteristically tend to abort those movements which are heterodox. The history of Christianity is dotted with such events, most especially the fragmentation of Protestantism. One way or another, religions must deal with the nonconformists—those who appear to walk on their hands.

Early Christianity soon developed a tendency to view its origins from a single perspective. The belief that the earliest years of Christianity saw the emergence of one harmonious community was very quickly adopted. Read the account of the earliest church in the Acts of the Apostles and then compare it with the letters of the apostle Paul. It is obvious that already the author of Acts was presenting a view of the church that smoothed out the differences among the first believers. By 80–90 C.E. the author of Luke was already attempting to propagate an understanding of the earliest church as

1

having been without significant rift! Paul's letters, on the other hand, would seem to suggest that there were important differences at least between him and certain other Christian leaders. (That is especially evident in Galatians.)

It is not surprising, therefore, that the history of the interpretation of the Fourth Gospel has tended to stress its similarities with the other three canonical Gospels. The so-called harmonies of the Gospels popular in previous centuries struggled to fit the account of the ministry of Jesus found in the Gospel of John into the pattern presented by the first three Gospels. For example, Jesus is represented as cleansing the Temple early in his ministry in the Fourth Gospel (2:13–22) but in the very final week of his ministry in the other Gospels (Matthew 21:12–13; Mark 11:15–19; Luke 19:45–46). The harmonizers solved the problem with the suggestion that Jesus cleansed the Temple not once but twice! Let's all walk on our feet!

Given this tendency to harmonize the four Gospels, the uniqueness of each of the Gospels is overlooked. This is true especially of the Fourth Gospel. To make it conform with the first three Gospels is to rob it of its vitality and its contribution to our understanding of the origins of the Christian movement. The very title now given to the first three Gospels among students of the New Testament stresses the peculiarity of the fourth. They are called the *Synoptic* Gospels. This means that they have a common point of view, that they see their subject in a similar fashion. The Fourth Gospel is not synoptic, then, but sees its subject in a way that stands quite apart from its three colleagues in the Christian canon. If you will, the Fourth Gospel is a maverick among the Gospels. It runs free of the perspective presented in Matthew, Mark, and Luke. It is the nonconformist Gospel of the bunch. No wonder that many of the heretical movements in the history of the Christian church have used the Gospel of John as their authority in the New Testament.

I want to stress at the beginning of this introduction to the religious thought of the Fourth Gospel that it represents a unique form of early Christian thought. It is a heterodox form of Christianity, at least when compared with other literature in the New Testament. With this understanding of the maverick character of the Gospel in mind, let us examine a number of preliminary matters concerning it. The issues that we must briefly address are three: (1) the relationship of the Fourth Gospel and the Synoptics; (2) the literary structure of the Fourth Gospel; and (3) a collection of subjects, including the purpose of the Fourth Gospel, its date and destination, and its historical environment. What follows are really assertions of my opinion on these matters. They will supply the context within which we will go on to examine the religious thought of the Gospel. You are invited to test my opinions with the evidence in the Gospel itself as we proceed.

Reader's Preparation: Read quickly through the Fourth Gospel. Note its language and style. Get in mind a general outline of the book.

THE RELATIONSHIP BETWEEN
THE FOURTH GOSPEL AND THE SYNOPTICS

Since I want to stress the peculiarities of the Fourth Gospel as compared with the Synoptics, we will examine first of all the *differences* between them. Having done so, we shall point out the similarities between it and the Synoptics.

> *Reader's Preparation*: (1) Read Matthew 1–2, Mark 1:1–11, and Luke 1–2 and compare them with John 1:1–18. (2) Read and compare Luke 11:14–20 and John 5:10–24. (3) Read one of the parables from the Synoptic Gospels (e.g., Luke 10:29–37) and one of the metaphorical speeches in John (e.g., 10:1–18). (4) Compare Matthew 6 with John 8. (5) Compare Matthew 9:18–26 with John 11.

The reader gets no further than the introductory chapters of the Gospels before the uniqueness of the Fourth Gospel stands out. The Gospels of Matthew and Luke each in its own way presents the reader with an account of the birth of Jesus and a genealogy. The Gospel of Mark dives right into the ministry of Jesus; the author gives no account of Jesus' birth but begins with the preaching of John the Baptist. The Fourth Evangelist, like Matthew and Luke, has a preface to the account of the preaching of the Baptist, but what a distinctive preface it is! No birth narrative! No virgin conception! No genealogy! Rather, the reader steps onto the stage of the cosmos. We begin "In the beginning." The attention is upon the "Word" and its activity. It is with God in the beginning: it participates in creation; it becomes flesh. The Baptist is introduced as one distinct from this incarnate Word but as one who bears witness to it.

The reader is struck by the cosmic setting of the Gospel. If the authors of Matthew and Luke stress the role of God in the origin of the subject of their Gospels, John stresses the eternal status of that subject. Jesus is not born—not even by the intervention of the Holy Spirit in a wondrous way. He has always existed. He is but the incarnate appearance of the eternal Word. Hence, the Fourth Gospel begins by making the highest possible claim for the person of Jesus—his divine nature.

The Prologue to the Fourth Gospel (1:1–18) suggests, too, the differences of style and language between the Gospel and the Synoptic Gospels. Did you note the use of the words life, light, darkness, true, world, Father, and son? These are among some of the favorite expressions of the writer of the Fourth Gospel. Others are knowing, seeing, and the Jews. This Evangelist likes to have Jesus introduce his utterances with the expression, "Amen, amen" (translated, for instance, "Very truly"). Moreover, Jesus often speaks with an emphatic "I am." (We will examine these statements in chapter 1.) While most of these terms can be found in the Synoptic Gospels, they do not play such a featured role in the sayings of Jesus there. For example, those scholars who have time to do so have counted the number of times Jesus is made to refer to God as Father in the Synoptic Gospels and in the Fourth Gospel. Their findings are instructive: Father refers to God 64 times in the first three Gospels and 120 times in the Fourth Gospel.

Moreover, some of the more prominent terms in the Synoptic Gospels are relegated to a secondary role in John. "The kingdom of God" ("kingdom of heaven" as the Gospel of Matthew would have it), repent, apostles, scribes, Pharisees, tax collectors, adultery, demon, and inherit are examples of words often used in the Synoptics found rarely if at all in the Fourth Gospel.

What may we conclude? Simply that the writer of the Fourth Gospel has a unique vocabulary. It is one that is rich and profound, but above all distinctive.

time

A third kind of distinctiveness about the Fourth Gospel we might call chronological (the order of events). An apparently small detail that nonetheless may have great significance is the number of references to the Passover feast. In the Synoptic Gospels there is but one such reference. That is the occasion of Jesus' trip to Jerusalem that culminated in his arrest, trial, and crucifixion. In the Fourth Gospel, however, there are three Passover occasions cited (2:13; 6:4; 11:55). These chronological references imply that Jesus spent more of his ministry in Judea than in Galilee. This is quite in contrast with the Synoptics where Jesus spends the bulk of his time in Galilee and travels on only one occasion to Jerusalem for the celebration of Israel's escape from bondage, the Passover.

Perhaps more important than the simple difference in geography is the fact that this change of the locale of Jesus' ministry in the Gospel of John means a radical departure from the basic pattern of the Synoptic Gospels. Their structure (perhaps originating with the Gospel of Mark and followed by the Gospels of Matthew and Luke) divides the ministry of Jesus into two parts—one in Galilee and one in Judea. The author of John in no way adheres to such a pattern and has Jesus moving freely back and forth between the two areas.

If we were to take the chronology of the Fourth Gospel quite literally, we would interpret Jesus' ministry as spanning three years—one year for each of the references to the Passover season. The Synoptic chronology would suggest that Jesus' ministry encompassed one year. It is likely that the chronology of the Fourth Gospel has theological significance. This Evangelist may have wanted to stress the Passover in relation to Jesus' ministry, because that ministry represented for the Johannine community a new exodus and the opportunity for a new Passover celebration. But such suggestions must await further exploration.

Another difference in chronology is evident to the careful reader. According to the Synoptics, Jesus' last meal with his disciples before his arrest, trials, and eventual crucifixion occurs at the very time other Jews are celebrating the Passover meal. But in the Fourth Gospel that last meal occurs in effect twenty-four hours earlier, and his crucifixion and burial are completed before the meal. The relationship between these events in Jesus' life and the Passover observance in the Synoptics and John is shown in figure 1.

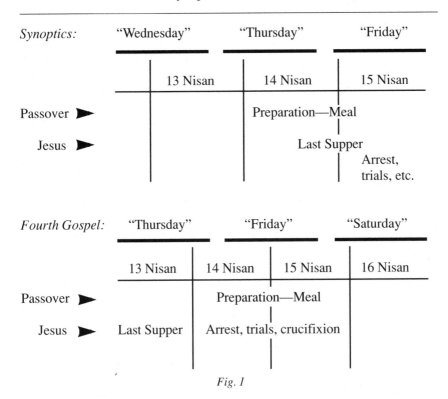

Fig. 1

Let us note a couple of things about this comparison before we dismiss too lightly an apparently insignificant deviation between the Synoptics and the Fourth Gospel. First, the implication of the Synoptic account is that the Last Supper with the disciples was a Passover celebration. The institution of the sacrament of the Last Supper is then to be understood in the context of Jewish Passover observance. But the Fourth Gospel loses that significant association of the Last Supper and the Passover by placing the event one day earlier in the week. So, in the Fourth Gospel there is no formal institution of the Last Supper (see chapter 4) and, further, the occasion of the last meal is not associated with the Passover meal proper.

Second, note the results of the deviation in the Gospel of John from the other Gospels regarding the relationship of the crucifixion to the Passover. According to the Fourth Gospel, Jesus was crucified at the very time the arrangements for the Passover meal were being made. That activity included, of course, the slaughter of the Passover lambs and their preparation for the subsequent meal. Jesus is slain at the same time the Passover lambs are slain! A coincidence? Or, are we to understand the parallel to be a deliberate allusion to the nature of Jesus' death? Are we to associate this parallel with the witness of the Baptist to Jesus, "Here is the Lamb of God who takes away the sin of the world!" (1:29)?

Actually this slight variation of the dating of the last meal raises a whole series of questions (which we cannot consider here): Was the last meal Jesus shared with his disciples a Passover observance? Did the Fourth Evangelist employ a Jewish calendar different from that of the majority of the Jews of the time and for that reason date the occasion differently from the Synoptics? Is the variation an intentional historical observation on the part of the author, or a casual slip? Are we to read some symbolic significance into this dating of the crucifixion? Could it be that the Fourth Evangelist intended us to find a theological significance in the parallel between Jesus' crucifixion and the killing of the Passover lamb? Which of the two accounts (if either)—the Synoptics or the Fourth Gospel—is historically accurate?

We have already mentioned the different place of the Temple cleansing in the Fourth Gospel. It is interesting that in the Synoptic Gospels that event is the last public act of Jesus. It is the "last straw" as far as his opponents are concerned. They are represented as setting about to seek a means of ridding themselves of this troublemaker immediately *after* he had done this brazen deed (Mark 11:18). So, in the Synoptics the Temple cleansing is the pivotal event in the plot of the last days of Jesus' life. But the Fourth Evangelist presents this as the *first* public act of Jesus (excluding the wedding at Cana as a public occasion). The pivotal public act that leads to the plot on Jesus' life in the Johannine account is the raising of Lazarus. Ironically, this gracious act of restoring a dead person to life stimulates Jesus' antagonists to seek ways of destroying him (11:47–54). We cannot here explore the reasons for the difference except to note that again there is a symbolic role given the Temple cleansing in the Fourth Gospel. Standing as it does at the beginning of Jesus' ministry, it seems to suggest that his ministry was in general designed to cleanse Judaism.

Enough has been said of the chronological differences between the Synoptics and John. Let us consider next the differences in the portrayal of Jesus. First, we must note the silence of the Fourth Gospel with regard to a series of very important events in the Synoptic scheme of things. Missing from the Fourth Gospel are the following: (1) Jesus' baptism by John the Baptist (the Baptist is nothing more or less than a witness to the Christ); (2) the temptation in the wilderness (Jesus is never subjected to temptation in the Fourth Gospel and seems far above such difficulties); (3) the confession at Caesarea Philippi where Jesus evokes from Peter the declaration, "You are the Messiah" (Mark 8:29, cf. John 6:66–71); (4) the transfiguration; (5) the agonizing struggle in the garden of Gethsemane (12:27); (6) the institution of the Last Supper; (7) the cry of derelition from the cross ("My God, my God, why have you forsaken me?"—Mark 15:34–35 and Matthew 27:46— the only words of Jesus from the cross recorded in those two Gospels).

On the other hand, note a few examples of events found in the Fourth

Gospel about which we hear nothing in the Synoptics: (1) the wedding at Cana; (2) the conversation with Nicodemus; (3) the encounter with the woman of Samaria; (4) the raising of Lazarus; (5) the washing of the feet of the disciples.

There are related deviations. In the Synoptics the ministry of Jesus does not begin until John the Baptist is arrested (Mark 1:14; Matthew 4:12; Luke 3:19–20). But in the Fourth Gospel Jesus has a concurrent ministry with that of the Baptist. In stark contrast to the Gospel of Luke, especially, Jesus does not have to pray, according to the Fourth Gospel (11:41–42). In the Synoptics we get the picture of Jesus, the rabbi. He argues with the teachers of the day over such issues as the observance of the Sabbath (Mark 2:23–28), fasting (Mark 2:18–22), and divorce (Matthew 19:3–9). The impression one gains is that of a teacher and interpreter of the Hebrew Bible—although a radical one, to be sure. However, his rabbinic character is far less prominent (but not entirely missing) in the Fourth Gospel. Granted, Jesus has disputes with the leaders of Judaism, but the controversy is always over the issue of Jesus' own identity. It involves the interpretation of Torah only insofar as that is relevant to a proper understanding of who Jesus is. (See John 5:21–29 for an example.) Furthermore, the Synoptic Gospels (especially Mark) contain the fascinating feature of what has been called the "messianic secret." For the most part it has to do with Jesus' practice of exhorting those whom he has healed to remain silent and tell no one of Jesus' wonders (e.g., Mark 1:43–44). That whole matter is entirely missing in the Fourth Gospel, and the only thing that we might claim to be comparable is the manner in which Jesus is constantly misunderstood by those around him (e.g., 8:27).

The impression these differences leave on the reader is that the Johannine Jesus is clearly a divine, heavenly being. The Jesus of the Fourth Gospel is openly and clearly extrahuman. He knows who he is and speaks constantly of it. If the Synoptics hint at any sort of hesitancy on the part of Jesus to identify himself, the Fourth Gospel has obliterated that hesitancy. Moreover, Jesus' extraordinary powers are emphasized in the Fourth Gospel. We will see this in the wondrous acts attributed to him when we discuss that subject below. For now it suffices to observe that the Johannine portrait of Jesus is through and through a marvelous one! This man does not have to pray. He knows the thoughts of others before they speak (1:47; 2:25). He walks through the midst of a hostile crowd without having a hand laid on him, because "his hour had not yet come" (7:30; 8:20). I do not want to say that the portrait of Jesus in the Synoptic Gospels lacks an extrahuman dimension; for that is surely not the case. Nor do I want to say that the Jesus of the Johannine Gospel is pure spirit with no human dimension, for that is surely not the case (e.g., 11:35; 19:28; 21:9–13). Nevertheless, the Johannine Jesus is extrahuman in a manner that exceeds the portrayal in the Synoptic Gospels.

The speeches of Jesus in the Synoptics and Fourth Gospel offer another contrasting feature of the two portrayals of the Galilean. I want to generalize from evidence of the kind you sampled in reading the speeches of Jesus from the Synoptics and John. The speeches of Jesus in the Synoptic Gospels seem to be of two kinds: Succinct sayings and parables. The extended speeches in the Synoptics (such as the Sermon on the Mount in Matthew 5–7) clearly appear to be collections of short, pithy sayings. The parables are sometimes extended, sometimes brief. Sometimes they are story parables (e.g., Luke 15:3–32), sometimes simple comparisons (e.g., Matthew 5:13).

In the Gospel of John the words of Jesus are quite different. First, the story parable is entirely missing. There are comparisons made, but they take on the form of elaborate images and lose the simplicity of their counterparts in the Synoptics. (But see 12:24 for a Synoptic-like metaphor.) Moreover, the subject shifts. The subject of the metaphorical speeches in the Fourth Gospel is always the same—the identity of Jesus (see 8:12; 10:1–18; 15:1–10). The subject of the parables in the Synoptics, in contrast, is consistently the kingdom of God (e.g., Matthew 25:1). Those short, pithy sayings of Jesus in the Synoptics are missing as well, for the most part. Instead, Jesus' speeches are long, extended discourses—perhaps even wearisome in their length. Jesus is made to go on and on (like a college professor, one might insert). From the point of view of good communication, he is prone to repetition and obscurity. The logic of these discourses is not at all clear. If one wanted to speak of them as logical at all, it would have to be said their logic is like a spiral rather than a lineal development. As with the parabolic comparisons, the discourses of Jesus have but one subject—his identity, his origin, his relation with the Father. Finally, I should add that in the Synoptics many of those terse sayings are found at the conclusion of brief encounters and discussions (usually with the opponents of Jesus). An example is the famous saying about the Sabbath Day (Mark 2:23–28). There is a dialogical character to many of the discourses in the Gospel of John. But the partners in the dialogue with Jesus do little more than mutter their disagreement and entirely and curiously misunderstand him. This simply occasions Jesus' taking up the subject again to go on at some further length.

The discourses of Jesus in the Fourth Gospel suggest a different understanding of the Christ figure and a different view of his teaching. He is above all the revealer whose words are the essential knowledge needed for human salvation. He stands apart from human teachers, for he is the proclaimer whose proclamation is one with his person. That is, the revelation contained in the words of the Johannine Jesus has to do with the identity of the proclaimer.

We are led finally to look at the differences between the Synoptics and the Fourth Gospel in their representation of the wondrous works of Jesus. There are four observations to be made. First, the most common form of wondrous deed attributed to Jesus in the Synoptic Gospels is the exorcism—driving out demons and overcoming the demon possession of persons. Exorcisms dominate the wondrous works of Jesus especially in the Gospel of Mark (see 1:23–28; 5:1–10; 7:25–30; 9:19–27). But, oddly enough, they are conspicuous only by their absence in the Gospel of John. Jesus is said to have a demon (8:48), but he never exorcises demons.

Second, it is a fair generalization to say that the marvelous quality of Jesus' acts are heightened in the Fourth Gospel. The healings accomplished by the Johannine Jesus are even more remarkable than those claimed by the Synoptics. The illnesses cured are longer. Often they are infirmities known by the patient from birth (e.g., 9:1). There is possibly a sense in which the wondrous deeds done in relationship to nature are more extreme. That is, those cases in which Jesus works marvelously with nature as opposed to persons are more startling. Examples include the transformation of water into wine (John 2:1–10) and the extraordinary catch of fish (John 21:1–11).

The most telling is the comparison of the raising of persons from the dead. You were asked to compare the account of the raising of the daughter of the ruler in Matthew 9 with the resurrection of Lazarus in John 11. In the Matthean account the girl's condition is questionable. Jesus insists, "The girl is not dead but sleeping" (Matthew 9:24). This is in spite of the father's statement that she is dead (v. 18). With Lazarus there is no question about it—he is dead. He has been in the grave four days (John 11:39). This fact would have suggested to the original readers that his spirit (his life breath) had departed. (Jewish thought of the day seems to have held that the life spirit of the deceased hovered about the grave for three days before departing entirely.) The mourners are reluctant to remove the stone from the grave because the body has already begun to decompose and the odor will be frightful. Lazarus is dead—no question about it. Hence, this is no mere resuscitation as might be the case in the Synoptic stories. This is a genuine resurrection from the dead.

Our third observation is a way of qualifying the emphasis upon the extension of the wondrous quality of the acts of Jesus. For in spite of what we have just said, it must be pointed out that the number of wondrous deeds attributed to Jesus in the Fourth Gospel is significantly fewer than in the Synoptics. The wonders of Jesus dominate the Gospel of Mark. But the Fourth Gospel records only seven (or eight) wondrous works:

1. The marriage at Cana (2:1–11)
2. Healing of the nobleman's son (4:46–54)
3. Healing at the pool of Bethesda (5:2–9)
4. The feeding of the multitude (6:1–15)
5. Walking on the water and the wondrous landing (6:16–21)
6. Healing of the man blind from birth (9:1–7)
7. Raising of Lazarus (11)
8. The miraculous catch of fish (21:1–7)

Chapter 21 is regarded by most as a later addition to the Gospel. Hence, we may say the Gospel originally contained only seven accounts of marvelous deeds. Few but forceful they are!

The exorcisms common to the Synoptics are strikingly missing in John. The wondrous acts in John are heightened by their marvelous quality, although they are few in number. Finally the wondrous deeds of Jesus in the Fourth Gospel clearly have a different function from their counterparts in the first three Gospels. As you read in the Gospel of Luke, the casting out of demons was significant, for it signaled the advent of the reign of God (11:14–20). Set as they are in the context of Jesus' proclamation of the beginning of the kingdom of God (Mark 1:14), the wonders done by the Synoptic Jesus point to the reality of that newly asserted dominion of God in the world. These deeds point beyond Jesus, one might say, to the presence of the kingdom inaugurated by his ministry. Not so with the wonders performed by the Johannine Jesus. They point not to the reign of God. (There is little talk of the kingdom at all in the Fourth Gospel.) Rather they point to the identity of the performer himself. They are in fact called "signs" in a number of passages (see 2:11; 4:54; 20:30–31) and are understood as indications of the true identity of the performer. They are intended to evoke a believing response to the claims of the one who does them. Thus the wonders are given a revelatory character along with the words of Jesus: they reveal the truth about the identity of the revealer. There are more complex problems associated with the function of the signs and works of Jesus in the Fourth Gospel, which must occupy us later. For now we should note only the sense in which the wondrous acts of Jesus are treated so differently in the Fourth Gospel from in the Synoptic Gospels.

So much for the differences between the Fourth Gospel and the Synoptics. That is half of the story (the larger "half," I believe). The other half is the sense in which there are striking *similarities* between the maverick Gospel and its three colleagues. I will only suggest a few examples of the similarities—enough, I hope, to pose more sharply the problem of determining the relationship between the Synoptics and our Gospel.

The most obvious similarity between the Fourth Gospel and the Synoptics is their accounts of the passion story. Along with the Synoptics, the Fourth Gospel records the same basic story of Jesus' separation from the disciples, his arrest, trial before both a religious body and the ruling political chief, his execution, burial, and finally his resurrection. To be sure, each of the Gospels has its own peculiarity somewhere in the account (e.g., the Gospel of Luke reports that Jesus was taken to the high priest's house, but there is no account of the hearing itself before the high priest—see 22:54). John is no exception. In that Gospel Jesus undergoes an examination at the hands of both Caiaphas, the high priest, and Annas, the former high priest and father-in-law of Caiaphas (18:12–24). This is to suggest only one variation in the passion story of the Fourth Gospel, which shares the basic structure of the account with the Synoptics.

Second, you will notice that even with the deviation in chronology, the Fourth Gospel still has a basic structural similarity with the order of the ministry of Jesus recorded in the Gospel of Mark. We believe that the Markan order was the foundation upon which the other two Synoptics were built, and some would propose that the Fourth Gospel is likewise dependent upon the

Markan order. The Fourth Evangelist follows this basic pattern, which parallels Mark.

1. The preaching of John the Baptist (Mark 1:4–8 and John 1:19–36)
2. The movement into Galilee (Mark 1:14f. and John 4:3)
3. The feeding of the crowd (Mark 6:34–44 and John 6:1–13)
4. Walking on the water (Mark 6:45–52 and John 6:16–21)
5. Peter's confession (Mark 8:29 and John 6:68f.)
6. Departure for Jerusalem (Mark 9:30f.; 10:1, 32, 46 and John 7:10–14)
7. The entry into Jerusalem and the anointing (Mark 11:10; 14:3–9 and John 12:12–15, 1–8. (Notice that John reverses the order of the two events.)
8. A last supper (Mark 14:17–26 and John 13:1–17:26)
9. The passion story (Mark 14:43–16:8 and John 18:1–20:29)

(I have summarized the list of parallels offered by C. K. Barrett in *The Gospel According to St. John*.) The parallel is obvious even given the differences we have already noted.

From this point on the similarities are less imposing on the reader, but discernible nonetheless. Compare, for instance, the stories of the healing of the centurion's son in Matthew 8:5–13, the healing of the Syrophoenician woman in Mark 7:24–30, and the healing of the nobleman's son in John 4:46–54. There are some striking similarities even though the stories have different characters. There is a common portrayal of John the Baptist in the Synoptics and the Fourth Gospel: All identify him in much the same way and all have him predicting the appearance of the Messiah.

Finally, one might not expect to find parallels between the speeches of Jesus in the Fourth Gospel and the Synoptics, but such parallels are there. You are invited to compare the following examples:

John	*Synoptics*
"Those who love their life lose it, and those who hate their life in this world will keep it for eternal life" (12:25).	"Those who find their life will lose it, and those who lose their life for my sake will find it" (Matthew 10:39).
"Very truly, I tell you, whoever receives one whom I send receives me; and whoever receives me receives him who sent me" (13:20).	"Whoever welcomes you welcomes me, and whoever welcomes me welcomes the one who sent me" (Matthew 10:40).
[To a paralytic, Jesus says] "Stand up, take your mat and walk" (5:8).	[To a paralytic, Jesus says] "Stand up, take your mat and go to your home" (Mark 2:11).

There are also some comparable metaphors used by Jesus, such as the grain of wheat (John 12:24 and Matthew 5:13 or Mark 3:24). There are even dialogues that follow a pattern similar to those in a Synoptic Gospel, such as John 7:3ff. and Luke 13:31ff. (For further similarities, see C. H. Dodd, *Historical Tradition in the Fourth Gospel*.)

These similarities will have to suffice to convince you that there are striking parallels between the Fourth Gospel and the Synoptics. Sometimes that parallel is exclusively with one of the Synoptics, and sometimes it is with a common Synoptic pattern. We must conclude, then, that the differences between the Synoptics and the Fourth Gospel emphasized above should be tempered by these similarities. Ah, but that is just the problem! The Fourth Gospel could more easily be explained if we had one without the other—that is, either its totally different account of the ministry of Jesus or its fully harmonious account. The way it is, with both differences and similarities, we have a far greater problem.

How shall we explain both these similarities and these differences at once? I propose that there are really three ways of accounting for the relationship of the maverick Gospel to its canonical colleagues: First, it has been argued that the Fourth Evangelist knew at least one or perhaps all of the Synoptic Gospels and was to some degree dependent on it or them. By this theory the author intended to write a "supplementary" gospel. The Gospel assumed the readers had some acquaintance with the Synoptic account of Jesus and offered a meditation, as it were, on that account. By this proposal the Evangelist was trying to write a "theological" or "spiritual" document that would emphasize new aspects implicit in the Synoptic Gospels. This view held sway for a number of years and is still advocated in some circles.

The opposite of this first proposal is that the Fourth Evangelist did not know the Synoptic Gospels at all. The author, it is supposed, wrote to some degree out of a personal knowledge and recollection without the assistance of the witness of the first three Evangelists. The differences are obviously explained by this second theory, but the similarities are a bit more problematic. At the points of parallel with the Synoptic Gospels, our second theory would propose that the Fourth Evangelist is simply reporting memories that happen to be in accord with the Synoptic witnesses.

The third view is the one with which I find myself in agreement. The Fourth Evangelist had access to a tradition that was associated with the Synoptic traditions. That is, the dynamic oral transmission of the words and activities of Jesus took several different forms (as the differences among the Synoptics themselves also suggest). One form of that tradition reached our Evangelist. By the time it came to the author it was quite different from that which was incorporated into the Synoptic Gospels, but it still showed evidence of having been spawned in the same pool of oral transmission with the Synoptic materials. Diagrammatically, this view might by simplified as shown in figure 2.

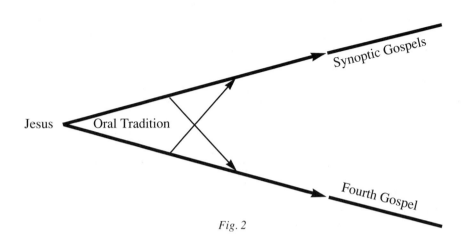

Fig. 2

The oral tradition arising after the crucifixion of Jesus was an ever-expanding and growing body of sayings and narratives. This development resulted from the church's effort to understand and relate to itself the ministry of the historical Jesus. It was also the result of faith that Jesus was still alive and active in the church, speaking through Christian prophets and teachers. Hence, the reservoir of "Jesus material" was not fixed by the simple memories of the eyewitnesses to his ministry but was dynamic and growing. For whatever reason, it appears that two primary segments of that tradition developed. The one is known to us today by virtue of the Synoptic Gospels, and the other is incorporated at least in part in the Fourth Gospel. (We could speak of still a third tradition represented in the letters of Paul.) Perhaps it was geography that accounted for the separation of the traditions; perhaps the difference was due to the peculiar interests and character of the community out of which the Fourth Gospel arose. The two streams of tradition were not entirely independent of one another. In addition to having a common source, there was interchange between them (suggested by the arrows intersecting between the two bodies of tradition; see figure 2). The result was that the two traditions were quite distinct from one another, yet had some parallels and similarities.

The tradition reached our Evangelist in a number of forms. There may have been some written materials which the Evangelist incorporated into the Gospel. More than likely this included a document concerned primarily with Jesus' wondrous acts and which contained narratives of the seven signs of Jesus. In addition there were perhaps some other writings (such as the passion story) passed on to the community of which the Fourth Evangelist was a member. Surely, however, the oral tradition was still very rich and active when our Evangelist worked. This means that much of what the author heard in the life of the Christian community was not yet written down but was handed on by word of mouth for the benefit of succeeding believers.

With the benefit of this rich tradition, our Evangelist—whom we will for convenience continue to call John, but without assuming the author was a male (see Appendix B, "The Women of the Gospel of John")—set about to write the Gospel. This figure wanted at once to be faithful to the traditional materials he or she knew and to be relevant to the community addressed in the document. The Fourth Evangelist was not unlike a good Christian theologian (or preacher) of our own day who tries faithfully to articulate the heritage of her or his religion in response to the burning questions of the day.

THE LITERARY STRUCTURE OF THE FOURTH GOSPEL

Reader's Preparation: Skim the entire Gospel, looking for its major parts and noting how they are related to one another. Ask yourself these questions: (1) What holds the narrative together? (2) What has the author done to make this an engaging and readable story?

Before we probe any further behind the Fourth Gospel for possible answers to some historical questions, we need to examine the text itself. Before we can learn much about the background of another person, we need to get to know that person in the present. A person's history does not make much sense unless we know what that history produced. The same is true of any ancient document. So, we will attempt a brief examination of the present state of the Gospel of John as a basis on which to pursue its background. Our major attention will focus on the way in which the Fourth Gospel's story of Jesus flows, how it is put together, and how the author leads the reader through its sequence. We want to concentrate on how we, the readers, experience the story—how it draws us into the tale and affects our emotions.

As we read the Gospel carefully, we note, first of all, that it begins with a kind of preface. The first eighteen verses of the Gospel seem to be a sort of orientation to the story that will follow. The preface of a book often alerts readers to what they ought to know, keep in mind, and ponder as they proceed with their reading. John 1:1–18 is just such an informative and orienting preface to the Gospel. But it is more. It smacks of the chorus of a Greek tragedy that comes on stage before the actors assume their places and begin the play. In other words, this preface gives us the clue to the drama that is about to unfold before our eyes.

That lets us in on the secret, we soon learn, that many of the characters in the story are trying to discover. Most important, the preface informs us of who the main character really is and where he comes from. He is none other than the Word of God, and his origin is with God from the very beginning. But more! He is himself God (1:1, 18). But still more! We are forewarned in this preface that the divine central figure of the story is responsible for the existence of the world, and yet he is rejected by those who are his very own. Yet to those who accept and do not reject him, this one who is the Word of God bestows a significant benefit: the power to become children of God (1:12).

The identity of Jesus, the likelihood of his rejection, and the benefits of receiving him—these are the bits of vital information entrusted to us before we begin the journey through the story. Those bits will provide the insight that will enable us to grasp what is going on, even while some of the story's characters stumble about in their ignorance. The author gives us a special gift, puts us on the inside—as it were—where we can perceive the story in a much deeper and understanding way.

Then at 1:18 the prologue abruptly ends, and we are plunged into the narrative itself. Through the next eleven chapters we participate in a strange and intriguing drama. We are not surprised that this one who has been identified as the Word of God does some marvelous things. He seems to know what is inside people (1:47; 4:17–19), changes ordinary water into the finest of wines (2:1–11), heals the hopelessly afflicted (5:2–29; 9:1–7), transforms a few loaves and fish into a meal for a crowd (6:1–14), and even raises a dead friend from his tomb (11:1–44).

Nor are we surprised that the hero speaks in strange ways. He sounds like one whose origin was in another realm—like an alien from another planet. His words are puzzling and provocative: "No one can see the kingdom of God without being born from above" (3:3); "The water that I will give will become in them a spring of water gushing up to eternal life" (4:14); "I am the bread of life" (6:35); "I am the light of the world" (8:12); "I am the resurrection and the life" (11:25). There is an air of mystery about this figure—something very peculiar!

So, the controversy he stirs is not unexpected. We know he is a divine creature, and in stories we expect unusual things from divine creatures. We can understand why the public reaction to him is mixed. Right away we sense that this fellow is going to cause trouble for the religious authorities. He disrupts the Temple and claims that he can build such a structure in three days (2:19). He shows no respect for the Sabbath and claims he can work then because his "Father" works on the Sabbath (5:17). The strange words spoken about eating his flesh and drinking his blood in chapter 6 are what really stir up the opposition (6:60), and from that point on there are drastically divided opinions about him (7:12). But worse, there is talk abroad about putting him to death (7:1)! By the time we reach the end of chapter 11 that rumor has become a full-blown plot (11:45–54).

We readers are amazed at this. Sure, we can understand how this weird fellow could incite some controversy. And we remember from the preface how the hero of the story would be rejected. Even though we know the secret of his identity, we too have been put off by some of his claims for himself. But to murder the hero would be a terrible mistake. We sense a tragedy unfolding toward its inevitable conclusion.

We think that the tragedy is about to climax as we begin chapter 12. Jesus interprets his anointing at the hands of Mary as preparation for his burial (12:7). And then we hear, "The hour has come" (12:23). We remember that Jesus has said before that the "hour" was coming (4:21, 23; 5:25, 28), but that it was not yet here (2:4; 7:30; 8:20). This is it! The opponents will make their move. What's our hero going to do? In 12:32 he again speaks of being "lifted up," just as he had in 3:14 and 8:28. But we do not have the foggiest notion what that means. Now perhaps we will learn.

However, the narrative takes a sudden detour in chapter 13. Jesus has been out in public for most of the story. Now he retreats into private (hiding?) with his disciples. Here we are, eagerly waiting to find out if the antagonists will carry through their plan to murder him and how he will respond if they try. Instead of immediately resolving this terrible suspense, the story spends five whole chapters on Jesus' private conversations with his followers.

We are, therefore, tempted to skip to the last page to find out how the whole thing ends. But we must not do so, for the intervening chapters are important. The enigmatic hero does not disappoint us in these conversations. First, there is that puzzling act of washing the feet of the disciples (13:1–20). Then, a great deal of what he has to say sails over our heads, as it does the characters in the story. He talks about being glorified (e.g., 13:32; 16:14; 17:5), and about "going away" (14:28; 16:7), about some "Advocate" (14:16, 26; 15:26; 16:7). The elusive language he has used in public discourse is unchanged: "I am the way, and the truth, and the life" (14:6); "I am the true vine, and my Father is the vinegrower" (15:1). We keep relying on that secret information conveyed in the prologue—the Word in the world, rejection, acceptance. As before, it helps, but it does not solve all our problems.

With the end of Jesus' long prayer in chapter 17 a resolution of the suspense seems near. We are almost relieved when Judas does his dastardly deed and Jesus is arrested. But we are put on hold still again while Pilate deliberates Jesus' fate. It looks as if the tragedy is going to be averted. Pilate is going to close the route the religious authorities have mapped out, for he thinks Jesus is innocent (18:39). But a subtragedy emerges as we watch Pilate struggle between Jesus and "the Jews." The religious authorities are determined. Pilate tries to satisfy them without violating his own conscience (19:1–5), but it does not work. Pilate's fear of his constituency gets the best of him (19:8), and he finally hands Jesus over to them.

We are still thinking that maybe this God-man will snap his fingers and end the whole thing, but he does not. He is crucified. It is true, Jesus dies with dignity, but he dies nonetheless. Still puzzling and provoking us with his words as he hangs on the cross, he "gave up his spirit" (19:30).

The tragic last scene has been played. The world crushes this foreigner. Then comes a sudden reversal in the plot. We should have listened more carefully to his odd assertion that he was the resurrection (11:25). We should have noted more carefully what he did for Lazarus. For now *he* rises from his tomb. He appears first to Mary Magdalene, as she stands weeping at the entrance to the empty tomb, and commands her to announce his resurrection to his other followers (20:11–18). Then he pops in on some of those cowardly followers in their hideaway, not once, but twice (20:19–23 and 24–28). They go fishing to try to get all this sorted out, and he appears to them again on the shore of the lake, serves them breakfast, and has an extended conversation with one of them (21:1–23).

The story ends with the risen Jesus appearing to his followers at unexpected times and places. We are told then that this whole story has been reported in order that we may "believe that Jesus is the Messiah, the Son of God, and that through believing [we] . . . may have life in his name" (20:31). This is not just any story. It is a story intended to make a change in us. We cannot get off the hook by putting down the book and saying, "Well, that was interesting." We must decide whether or not the story is "true" as the author claims (21:24). And if it is true, then we "believe." The narrative is designed to bring us to the same fork in the road to which it has led the characters of the story: whether to believe the central character really is who he claims to be or to side with his opponents.

The Gospel of John tells a fascinating story—predictable in some ways, suspenseful in others. As we disengage ourselves from the story and sit back to consider the whole of it, some patterns become clear. The story seems to divide itself between chapters 11 and 13, with 12 providing a kind of bridge between the two parts. In the first part (chapters 1–11), chapter 6 functions as the decisive turning point—the spot at which the opposition is fueled with energy to develop a plot against the hero. In the second part (chapters 13–21), chapter 18 marks the resumption of the major plot line after an important hiatus in chapters 13–17. In the finale (chapters 20 and 21), the whole plot is turned upside down, but not entirely without warning. We are never told that Jesus would be crucified and then conquer death, but enigmatic hints to that effect are scattered throughout the whole narrative. We begin, for instance, to understand what Jesus means by speaking of his being "lifted up."

Detached from the narrative and able to look back over our experience of reading it, we realize the story has had a distinctive rhythm. The author narrates, first, a public ministry of Jesus; second, a private teaching of his disciples; third, a public trial and execution; and finally, a series of private appearances to his disciples. The rhythm between the public and private work of Jesus is the cadence of the narrative.

The whole of John's story of Jesus might be viewed in a diagram like figure 3.

The Structure of the Gospel of John

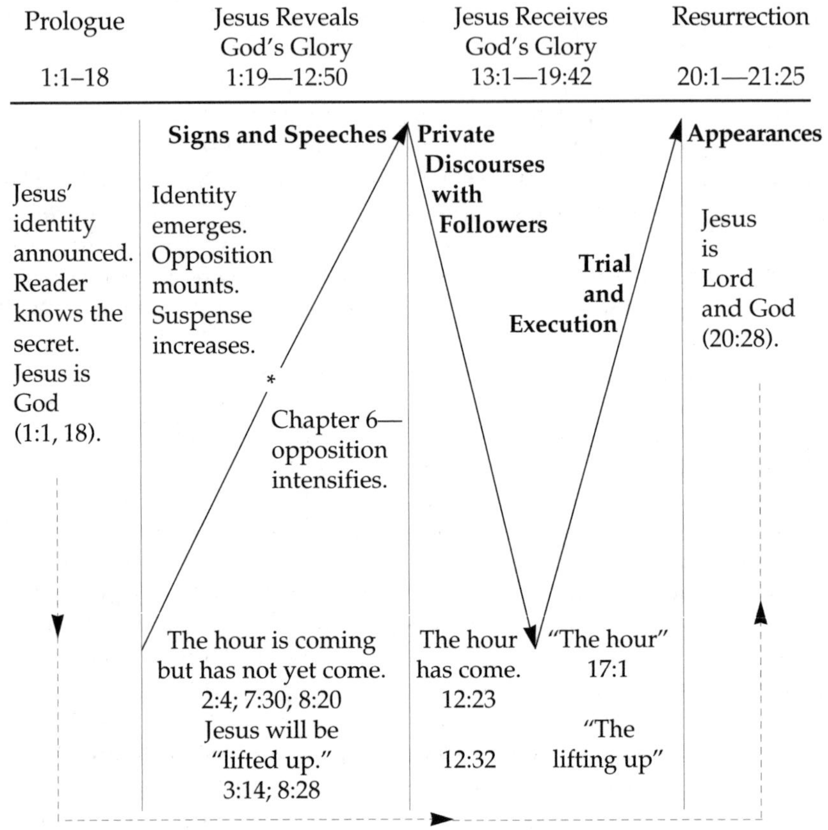

Prologue	Jesus Reveals God's Glory	Jesus Receives God's Glory	Resurrection
1:1–18	1:19—12:50	13:1—19:42	20:1—21:25

Signs and Speeches ▲ **Private Discourses with Followers** ▲ **Appearances**

Jesus' identity announced. Reader knows the secret. Jesus is God (1:1, 18).

Identity emerges. Opposition mounts. Suspense increases.

*

Chapter 6— opposition intensifies.

Trial and Execution

Jesus is Lord and God (20:28).

The hour is coming but has not yet come. 2:4; 7:30; 8:20 Jesus will be "lifted up." 3:14; 8:28

The hour has come. 12:23

12:32

"The hour" 17:1

"The lifting up"

Fig. 3

THE PURPOSE, DESTINATION, HISTORICAL ENVIRONMENT, AND DATE OF THE FOURTH GOSPEL

Reader's Preparation: The following are important passages in the Gospel relevant to the questions with which we are dealing: (1) 20:30–31; (2) chapter 9; (3) 6:22–58.

For what purpose was this skillfully constructed narrative written? Let us move beyond the structure of the text through history to the origin of the Gospel. What was the author trying to accomplish? And precisely to whom was the writing addressed? There are two levels on which we should proceed to deal with this question. First, does the writer make an explicit statement of purpose anywhere in the Gospel? Second, do other passages imply a purpose and destination that might not be explicitly stated?

We have already noted in the discussion of the structure of the Gospel that there seems to be an explicit purpose stated in 20:30–31. What is written in the Gospel is intended to evoke faith on the part of the readers. To convince readers that this Jesus is the Messiah of Jewish expectation (the Christ) and a uniquely divine revealer (Son of God) is what it is all about. According to the reading of these verses, the Evangelist hoped to win new believers to the faith. The goal was to produce a document for use in the missionary enterprise—one that would inspire belief among those who did not yet embrace the faith. The Fourth Evangelist was, then, an *evangelist* in the modern sense of the word—one who proclaims the Christian faith in order to win converts.

However, this explicit statement of purpose for the Gospel is less than adequate in several ways. In the first place, the statement of purpose found in 20:31 is questionable because of a variation in the form of the Greek verb translated "believe." There are some ancient manuscripts that contain a verbal form best translated "may come to believe," as the New Revised Standard Version has it. However, other manuscripts have another form that should be rendered something like, "may continue to believe" (see footnote in the NRSV). The difference between the two Greek words is only a single letter, but the meaning each renders is significant. If preference is given to the first reading, it would suggest the Gospel was written for the purpose of bringing unbelievers to faith. On the other hand, if preference is given to the second reading, the purpose of the Gospel is to sustain those who already are believers. Unfortunately, textual critics are divided on the question of which verbal form better approximates the original, and the usefulness of the passage for determining the purpose of the Gospel is seriously diminished.

Second, when we examine the Gospel as a whole it does not strike us as primarily a missionary document. To be sure, there are parts of it that read as if that was the purpose for which they were written. The prime example of such passages are the so-called signs of Jesus, for they appear to be told in order to evoke faith, just as 20:30–31 suggests. But much of the rest of the Gospel leaves the impression of having another purpose in mind. The discourses of Jesus, for instance, seem too complicated and sophisticated to have been intended for the nonbeliever. To speak analogically for a moment, the signs are the kind of thing a Billy Graham might write for his evangelistic purposes; but the discourses are for the most part more like something a theologian—let us say Paul Tillich—might write for the purposes of communicating an understanding of the faith to other believers.

Third, even if "you may come to believe" is what the author originally wrote, the words could very well have been part of that tradition the Evangelist was using. It is proposed, and I agree, that 20:30–31 once constituted the conclusion of the collection of signs material that the Evangelist used. That source, let us suppose, was a missionary document recounting seven of Jesus' marvelous works. Verses 20:30–31 stood at the conclusion of the little book as a clear and accurate statement of its purpose. The Fourth Evangelist, having used the signs from this source, now appends its own conclusion to the end of her or his work in faithful recognition of a dependence upon the source. But it really is less appropriate for the Gospel than it was in its original setting. (Robert T. Fortna in *The Gospel of Signs* defends this view.)

The second place we look for the purpose of the Gospel is in the implications of the whole document. If you will grant me for the moment that the missionary goal is not entirely adequate as a purpose of the Gospel, we will see what other suggestions we can find in the rest of the Gospel. There is one that is implied at a number of points but most clearly in the story of the healing of the blind man in chapter 9. What is suggestive about this story is not the healing itself, but what follows. Jesus' healing of the man seems to fit that evangelistic purpose we have been considering. The account of the reaction of the authorities to the witness of the man who has just been healed is fascinating. After he has testified a second time to the fact that Jesus has healed him and that Jesus must be from God, the authorities "drove him out" (9:34). Then he encounters Jesus again and makes a full confession of faith (vs. 35–38). In the midst of this narrative we are told that the man's parents are fearful "for the Jews had already agreed that anyone who confessed Jesus to be the Messiah would be put out of the synagogue" (v. 22).

This account might suggest the kind of situation the Evangelist and the Johannine community experienced and one of the reasons for the writing of the Gospel. We know that the Jews who were converted to Christianity gradually separated themselves from the synagogue. Most likely they sometimes did so of their own volition and sometimes the separation occurred as a result of pressure from their sisters and brothers in the synagogue. Acts hints at this several times (see Acts 9:1–2; 14:1–7; 17:1–9; 18:4–7; 19:8–10), and the Gospel of Matthew suggests the First Evangelist knew about the dispute between Jews and Christians (see 10:17; 23:34–36). What the story in John 9 seems to imply is that there was indeed a struggle going on between the Jews who believed Jesus was the Messiah and those who did not. Some Jewish Christians were continuing to worship in the synagogue in the conviction that their new faith was not incompatible with their Jewish life and practice. Members of synagogues in some locales, however, were not willing to accept that position and were expelling from the Jewish worshiping community anyone who adhered to the Christian faith. In other words, there was a tension between the Christians and the Jews in *the city where the Fourth Evangelist wrote*. That tension was mounting. Moreover, it was causing a good many persons a great deal of agony. Jewish Christians felt trapped between their allegiance to their Jewish roots and their new conviction that

Jesus was the long-awaited Messiah. Hence, Christians were caught up in a dispute with their former Jewish colleagues of the synagogue. We shall return to this discussion later in the chapter in order to offer some reasons for the escalating conflict between the Johannine Christians and the members of the synagogue. (It has been proposed that this situation was due to a formal decree issued by a council of rabbis toward the end of the first century. However, that proposal can no longer be sustained, thanks to historical research that shows no evidence of such a decree.)

I propose that this background gives us a good insight into the situation and purpose of the Evangelist. If this is the case, then a lot of things about the Gospel of John begin to make more sense. Let me only suggest a few. It is for this reason that the Gospel speaks as it does of "the Jews." That term is not an ethnic reference in the Fourth Gospel, but it is an allusion to the primary opponents of the Johannine church at the time. For this reason to some degree the Gospel seems to play Jesus and Moses off against one another, or at least seems concerned to show that Jesus is superior to Moses (e.g., 1:16–17; 6:32). The constant effort to describe Jesus as one sent from God and one who has divine status but is still subordinate to the Father is also elucidated. Could this not be the Evangelist's response to charges from the Jewish leaders that Christians believe in two gods—Jesus and the Father? Perhaps, too, the dominance of the death plot against Jesus in the Fourth Gospel is explained. (That plot appears early in the Fourth Gospel, you will recall—5:18 and by implication back in 2:23–25—as opposed to the Synoptic Gospels.) Perhaps the actual physical persecution of Christians by the Jews was giving new meaning to the suffering of Jesus several decades earlier. Finally, Nicodemus (chapter 3) might be an example of what some Jews were doing in the Evangelist's own day. They were secretly Christian or were secretly exploring the possibilities of Christian belief. But they did it under the cover of darkness, lest their colleagues discover their intent. (This proposal is founded upon the study of J. Louis Martyn, *History and Theology in the Fourth Gospel*.)

I think that, as we explore the thought and symbolism of the Gospel of John further, it will become more and more obvious that this proposed situation for the writing of the Gospel makes a good deal of sense. The Evangelist served a community locked in a crucial dispute with the local Jewish synagogue. The Jewish opposition was threatening the Christian community, just as the Christian evangelistic efforts among the Jews were threatening the stability of the Jewish synagogue. The result was that both communities were defending themselves. The Evangelist contributed to the defense of the Christian community by addressing her or his writing primarily to members of that community. By using the traditions at hand and adapting them, the Evangelist offered a relevant message to the first readers. The author showed them how they might argue with their Jewish neighbors in response to the charges posed against Christianity. She or he dramatically portrayed Jesus as engaged in a struggle with his fellow Jews who would not accept him and would eventually put him to death. She or he showed them how Jesus was the completion of the Mosaic tradition, not its contradiction. This was particularly relevant because some readers (although not all) were of Jewish heritage.

The primary purpose of the Gospel, then, was not evangelical, not missionary. It was addressed to the Christian community by one of their esteemed leaders. It was designed to strengthen them in their struggle in that local situation. It was, if you will, an intrachurch document. It was a Gospel intended for the family. To be sure, the Evangelist may have had hopes that some of the Jews who had some interest in the Christian faith would be persuaded by this writing. For that reason the missionary intent of 20:30–31 is not inappropriate. But the Evangelist wanted less to convert than to nurture, less to evangelize than to encourage those already in the faith.

It may be a slight digression to do so, but it is important that we raise a question at this point in our discussion: Why did the Evangelist choose to write a *gospel*? That is, in order to accomplish the Gospel's purpose, why did the author select from among the many possible literary genres this rather uniquely Christian form of literature we have come to call gospel? Of course, the author nowhere in the work calls it a gospel (unlike Mark 1:1). Still, the Evangelist elects to give expression to the document's purpose by describing the figure of Jesus in a narrative, which at least appears to have a historical sequence. As Paul and perhaps others had done, a pastoral letter might have been chosen. Or the apocalyptic form, like the one used by John of Patmos some years later, might have been given the honor of encouraging Christians in crisis.

This question is complicated, I believe, if the Fourth Evangelist did not know the other Gospels in their literary form. Perhaps she or he knew traditions (oral and written) which were ingredients for the gospel form, but had never seen an entire Christian gospel. We believe that it was the Evangelist we call Mark who invented the gospel form in Christian tradition (perhaps with a knowledge of certain Hellenistic literature that may have been similar to the Gospels). But if the Fourth Evangelist had never seen the Gospel of Mark or the other Gospels, why was the gospel genre chosen? Some would say that this question puts the lie to our contention that the Fourth Evangelist was not dependent upon the literary form of at least one of the Synoptic Gospels. But I think there are other possibilities.

First, it has been proposed by some that the signs source that we believe the Fourth Evangelist used in writing this document was itself an early form of gospel genre. That is, it recounted the wondrous works of Jesus along with some other narrative materials in a historical sequence. It did so with the purpose of proclaiming the "good news" of the faith, which is, of course, the literal meaning of "gospel." The author of the Fourth Gospel simply adopted that literary form from the source and filled it out with discourses and additional narratives (including perhaps the passion story). (See the works of Robert T. Fortna listed in the bibliography.)

A second possibility, which strikes me as a bit more likely, is that the oral tradition that the Evangelist knew and used was already shaped in what we would call gospel form. Hence, in the attempt to re-present that tradition as faithfully as possible, the Evangelist fell into the literary form of the gospel. This is to suggest that the creation of the literary gospel form was not so much the genius of the author of the written material (the Gospels of Mark and John), but the gradual and less than deliberate effort of the early Christian community to preserve the materials it had at its disposal. The oral tradition, then, based upon a historical recollection of Jesus of Nazareth, shaped itself into gospel. By filling out the historical material with legend, myth, and new teachings from what they believed to be the living Christ, the early Christians gradually shaped the gospel form in the preliterary tradition.

To return from our digression; this discussion has thus far laid out my point of view with regard to the purpose of the Gospel and the concrete situation that caused it to be written. Likewise, we have made clear that the Gospel is directed toward a community of Christians to which the Evangelist probably belonged. It is a community comprised, I think, of Christians of a mixed background. Some are Jews, as we have already seen. Others are doubtless of Gentile origin. It is for that reason that the Evangelist cannot assume that the reader understands Hebrew. Consequently, care is taken to translate certain Hebrew words, for example, 1:38 and 42. We are left now with one additional consideration—the intellectual environment of the Evangelist.

If you want to understand a person, it is necessary to know a little about his or her background. If you want to understand your friend's strange reaction, say, to persons of the opposite sex, you may want to learn something about his or her parents and siblings. Only then can you understand why the person behaves as she or he does.

The same is true of a piece of literature. It helps to know a little bit about Shakespeare when you read his plays. The life of Albert Camus and the influence of French existentialism make reading his novels significantly more enlightening.

We have tried to fill in some of that essential background for the Gospel of John, but we are left with the question of the intellectual influence on the thought of the document. With what kinds of ideas had the Evangelist come in contact? What writings had shaped the thought of this author? Are there ideas and expressions in the Gospel on loan from elsewhere? All these are ways of asking about the intellectual atmosphere in which the Fourth Evangelist worked—the conceptual air that she or he breathed.

The situation in which the Evangelist wrote already suggests the essential thing that we need to know for our purposes. First of all, it is obvious from what has been said above that I believe the Evangelist was significantly influenced by Jewish thought. This means that the Jewish scriptures and extrabiblical writings were part of the author's intellectual diet. There is evidence, however, that the Judaism the Fourth Evangelist knew, and may have embraced at one time, was not simply the rabbinic Judaism that became the mainstream tradition after the first century. The parallels between Johannine thought and the literature discovered in the so-called Dead Sea Scrolls are enough to convince us that the Evangelist was acquainted with a broad type of Judaism that embraced a great variety of forms and expressions. We may find strikingly rabbinic-like features in the Gospel. For instance, the discourse in chapter 6 reads much like a rabbinic interpretation of a scripture passage. But we also find many less than mainline rabbinic characteristics— the dualistic thought of the Gospel, for instance (see chapter 2).

I cannot argue this position at length here. I only ask that you accept this as a tentative hypothesis on which we can continue: The Evangelist was primarily under the influence of a mixed Judaism. It was a Judaism that could tolerate a strict Pharisee on the one hand and an apocalyptic fanatic (like some of those responsible for the Dead Sea Scrolls) on the other. It was a Judaism that even tolerated for a time the Christian movement (as a sect) within its midst.

Such a Judaism as is described here, however, would not be free from influences coming upon it from the Hellenistic world: revived Greek philosophies, imported mystery religions (some from the East), speculative philosophies, and maybe even the Roman emperor cult. All these forms of religious and quasi-religious beliefs touched Judaism in the first century C.E. as they had in the two previous centuries. The result was that the Judaism that influenced the Fourth Evangelist was no more free of Hellenistic thought than a Democrat today is free of all Republicanism!

The consequence of this mixture of ideas and influences is that the Fourth Evangelist's conceptual storehouse was full to overflowing. This author had at her or his disposal ideas fairly glistening with implications from different traditions. A ready example is the rich concept employed to introduce the Gospel, namely, the Word or (to use the Greek) *Logos*. Logos was a term that had deep roots in Greek philosophy—Stoicism, to be specific. But it was also founded on the concept of the Word of God in the Hebrew Bible and was fleshed out with the Jewish speculation concerning wisdom. We can imagine, then, that our Evangelist often employed symbolism and ideas that were the product of the influence of numerous religious and philosophical heritages. Our author may have been conscious of the richness of many of these. We can also imagine that some of the ideas and expressions of the Gospel may have been so commonplace that their richness was taken for granted by both author and readers. However that may be, the result was an Evangelist peculiarly equipped to write a gospel of exciting concepts and puzzling breadth. It is just this, in part, which contributed to the formation of this maverick piece of early Christian literature.

There you have it: An author richly endowed with conceptuality and symbolism, the benefactor of a valuable and stimulating tradition, placed in a situation of crisis proportions for the Christian community. When is it most likely that this took place? It is difficult to say with any certainty, and in a sense it is not necessary to decide a date for the Gospel with any precision. We know that the Fourth Gospel was circulating in Egypt before the middle of the second century, for the oldest fragment of New Testament material we have is a little chunk of the Gospel of John. That means, the scholars claim, that the Gospel had to have been written before the turn of the century.

We may assume, too, that it was not written before 70 C.E. when the Jerusalem Temple was destroyed in the war between the Jews and the Romans. The manner in which the Temple is alluded to in the Gospel has convinced most scholars of that (see 2:13–22).

I propose then a date of 75–85. But the decision for a precise dating hinges on a difficult question: When might the situation that occasioned the writing have occurred? My proposed dating rests on another proposal. Picture this: In a synagogue of a certain city the messianic believers (whom we call Christians) were tolerated for a considerable time. In this heterodox synagogue it was easy to have still another group of believers who held strange views! Two things may have occurred to cause the dominant body of believers to begin to question their tolerance. The first was perhaps the fault of the Christian Jews. They were becoming more and more evangelistic in their posture toward the other Jews. Possibly, too, the use of the source eventually incorporated into the Gospel stirred discontent. It is one thing in a religious community to tolerate different views when there is full and mutual respect. But what happens when one of the constituent groups begins to say something like this: "Our view is more truthful than yours and you are religiously inferior to us because you do not hold our views"? Tolerance begins to fade. Understandably, the Jews of the synagogue grew discontented with harboring these Christians in their midst.

Second, the destruction of the Jerusalem Temple in 70 C.E. sent shock waves through the Jewish community. What was Judaism to be without a Temple? What did it mean to be Jewish? The Jewish Christians might well have been making matters worse by claiming that the Roman destruction of the Temple was God's judgment on Judaism (see John 2:13–22). The self-questioning of the synagogue members and perhaps the view of the Christian members of that community aroused a natural impulse: "Let's clean house. Those who hold views other than the self-understanding that we are trying to develop here in this synagogue should go elsewhere." Ironically the expulsion of the Christians from the synagogue arose from the new questions of Jewish self-identity caused by the destruction of the Temple. Then it thrust the Christians into their own identity problem—Who are we if not Jews who believe Jesus to be the long-awaited Messiah?

All this would likely have occurred within a decade of the destruction of the Temple. Therefore, I think it reasonable to imagine the Gospel to have been written between 75 and 85.

Perhaps you have wondered why we have come this far without any mention of the identity of the Fourth Evangelist who has come to be known as John. The reason for the delay is that I believe we can say almost nothing about the author other than what has already been suggested in this Introduction. This figure stands too far back in the shadows of history for us to make out anything more than a vague outline. Hence, the author of our Gospel will probably remain forever anonymous. Critical scholarship has correctly called into question the traditional association of the Fourth Evangelist with John, the son of Zebedee, known from the Synoptic Gospels. I doubt, too, that we can identify the Evangelist with the mysterious "disciple whom Jesus loved" (although many do not share my skepticism on this matter). All we have to go on is the document itself, and only so much can legitimately be read between its lines. We have tried to describe the background of the author that so well suited him or her for the task of writing this Gospel. Moreover, we have claimed that the tradition available to the Fourth Evangelist was rich and full. To claim more than this about the writer would be to venture unnecessarily far out on the limb of speculation. To deny the possibility that this author was a woman is unfair and betrays the prejudice of previous centuries. (See Appendix B, "The Women of the Gospel of John," for a brief defense of the possibility that the Fourth Evangelist was indeed a woman.)

What we have attempted to do in this Introduction is suggest the manner in which the Fourth Gospel is the maverick of the canonical Gospels—that it "walks on its hands" compared to the Synoptics. It presents us with a unique literary structure and evokes a reading experience distinct from that of the Synoptic Gospels. Moreover, it has been proposed that there are reasons for this Gospel's maverick nature. It was written on the basis of a tradition that was distinct from that embodied in the Synoptics. It was written by an Evangelist who was uniquely equipped with a vast array of concepts and symbolism arising out of a mixed Judaism and influenced by Hellenistic thought as well. It was addressed to the Christian church amid a vital dispute with the Jewish synagogue—a situation that called for new and radical ideas. All of these contributed to the final product: A gospel that did not easily conform to the developing standard brand of Christianity. We can be grateful to the early church for not excluding the Fourth Gospel from its canon. Had it done so, we would be far poorer.

It is now time to turn to the exposition of the religious thought and symbolism of this Gospel. That exposition will further demonstrate the point made in this Introduction, I think, namely, that the Fourth Gospel is a different sort of early Christian thought. At the same time, we will begin to see how universal the Fourth Gospel is in its thinking and how it supplies us with a prime example of the way religious persons wrestle with a series of vital questions.

1. THE FATHER'S SON—
JOHANNINE CHRISTOLOGY

The history of religions is filled with accounts of extraordinary founders of religious movements. Most (but not all) of the major religious traditions of the world are rooted in one originator. These traditions look back to that founder and recognize his or her role in uncovering the gem of truth that has become the touchstone of that religion. These founding figures are claimed to have had some sort of special revelation or inspiration. That insight has been preserved for later generations through the institutional structures of the religion. At a minimum the founder of the tradition is viewed as the historical origin of the faith.

Likewise, every religious tradition rooted in a historical figure develops claims for the uniqueness of the founder's person as well as his or her revelation. This development is elaborate and varied. In some cases, the experience of the founder is the type of religious experience available to all of the devout followers of the faith. Such would appear to be the case in some forms of Buddhism, for instance, where the enlightenment of Gautama is the goal of all those who adhere to the religion. In other cases, the uniqueness of the founder is so stressed that it is not the founder's experience that can be repeated, but *the believers' own experience of the person of the founder*. Traditional Christianity would seem to be an example of this latter view. But in either case, the uniqueness of the founder and his or her revelation is vital to the development of the religion and tends to be viewed as a self-evident fact about the historical figure of the founder. So Mohammed, Moses, Zoroaster, and Gautama are believed by their respective religions to have been certain and conspicuous in their extraordinary qualities.

The claim for the uniqueness of the founder is, however, a development in these traditions. That is, the religion elaborates on the nature of its founder until eventually something like a final and "orthodox" view emerges. The final view may range all the way from a simple claim for peculiar piety (Mohammed), to extraordinary birth (Gautama), to divine nature (Christ). What is obviously similar among the world religions is that nearly all have a founder for whom radical claims are made, and those claims are developed within the history of the religion. The truth of the claim is usually hidden in the obscurity of history, but it is clearly witnessed to by the adherents of the faith.

It is the struggle of a religious tradition to define the nature of its founder that interests us at this point. The explication of the nature of the founder is one of the early and vitally important stages in the emergence of a major religious tradition. Take up the study of almost any religion, and you will find a fascinating history of the evolution of views of its founder. In the Jewish tradition, for instance, one finds already in the Hebrew Bible itself an honorific attitude toward Moses (e.g., in Deuteronomy 34:10). Then in Jewish thought following the close of the period of the Hebrew Bible there is elaborate speculation about Moses. Legends abound. It is asserted, for instance, that Moses never really died but was taken up into heaven (*The Assumption of Moses*). A religious tradition does not easily come up with a definition of its founder. That is the result of a long process of thought and discussion, of formulation and reformulation.

The truth of these remarks for early Christianity is clear. The struggle of Christians to settle upon some common view of the nature of Jesus of Nazareth begins in the earliest years of the movement. It climaxes (but does not end) in the Nicene Council and its creedal statement (325). The New Testament presents us with ample evidence of the efforts of the early Christians to formulate what they wanted to say about Jesus, his person, and his work. If one tries to abstract from the New Testament a single, consistent view of Christ, trouble arises. It seems to say a number of different things about the person of Jesus. The picture one gets, I think, is of early Christian thinkers struggling to find words adequate to express their faith about Christ.

The Fourth Gospel represents an important contribution to that emerging view of Christ among the first-century Christians. It takes up the Christ figure from a different point of view and makes some radical statements about him. It is fair to say that with the Fourth Gospel the view of Christ in early Christian thinking made a giant leap forward in one direction. As it happened, that direction proved eventually to be the way the later church would go in its statements of faith about the person of Christ. Still, we should not approach the Fourth Gospel with the impression that it has only one consistent view of Christ it intends to propagate. The Gospel presents not one but a number of assertions about the religion's founder. Those statements are not always fully consistent with one another in the way that a modern theologian would like them to be. But they tend to move in a particular direction. The importance of those assertions for later Christian thought is hard to overemphasize.

This chapter will look at a number of aspects of the Fourth Gospel in terms of what is claimed for the person and work of Christ. Five topics will occupy us: (1) the Logos or Word Christology of the Prologue to John; (2) the variety of titles for Christ employed in 1:19–51; (3) the Son of Man and the relationship of the Father and Son in the Gospel; (4) the importance of the "I am" sayings for Christology; (5) the work of Christ accomplished in his death.

28

THE LOGOS CHRISTOLOGY

Reader's Preparation: Read again the Prologue to the Gospel (1:1–18). Pay special attention to what it affirms concerning the nature and work of the Word.

The first eighteen verses of the Fourth Gospel are among the most significant of the entire New Testament. They are also among the most puzzling. It is accurate to say that this passage is one of the most frequently studied portions of early Christian literature. There are a number of concerns about this passage that we are going to ignore, and I think the reader ought to be alerted to them. The first is the hymnic quality of these verses. Many students of the Fourth Gospel sense that the bulk of the passage reads like a piece of poetry, and they speculate that it was used in Christian worship in some way or another. This presents a further question: Did the Fourth Evangelist write these words or incorporate a popular Christian hymn at the first of the Gospel? (The latter might have been a good attention grabber with which to begin the work.) Or, is it possible that these verses were attached to the Gospel some time after it had been written? The proposal that they are a later addition has one strong piece of evidence in its favor: Nowhere else in the Gospel is the Word referred to in any way similar to its use in these verses. The Evangelist may have composed this passage or may have used a Christian hymn as the introduction to the Gospel. In either case, would it not be likely that the author would have explicitly tied the rest of the Gospel in with the affirmations of this introduction?

I believe that the affirmations of this passage contain a good number of themes consistent with the rest of the Gospel. Not least among them are the rejection of Christ (e.g., vs. 10–11) and the superiority of the revelation of God in Christ to the revelation on which Judaism is based (e.g., vs. 17–18). Because of the abundance of these themes, I am convinced that the prologue is closely linked with the rest of the Gospel—just as overture to an opera captures the mood of the entire work. Thanks to this feature, I am inclined to think that the Fourth Evangelist or the Johannine community is responsible for its content. If it were a later addition to the Gospel, it was surely added by someone who fully and correctly understood the ambience of the entire work. Whatever its origin, it constitutes an important part of the whole Gospel. Therefore, we must study it for what it says about the view of Christ held by the Evangelist and/or the Johannine community.

The Introduction has already alluded to the richness of the idea of the Word or the Logos. Much time has been spent seeking out the historical precedents of this concept. Our concern is only to expand the point we have already made that the Logos was an idea rooted in several different religious and philosophical settings. First, in Stoicism current in Hellenistic philosophies, the Logos was conceived as a sort of cosmic reason. It was the mind at the center of the universe. It gave order and structure to the whole sense of the operation of the universe. A bit of that universal Logos resides in every person, this view affirmed, and hence related every person to the heart of the cosmos.

Of course, the Hebrews had an equally ancient tradition of the Word of God—the *dabar Yahweh*. It was the Word of God that brought all existence into being, according to the tradition embedded in Genesis 1. It was the Word of God that addressed the prophets and filled them with their message for the Hebrew people. It is as if the Word of God was the bridge between the transcendent God of Hebraic thought and the human world.

Later Jewish thought made much of the concept of wisdom. Wisdom resided with God and informed the devout person. Wisdom was made into a divine being, in a sense, in some Jewish literature such as Proverbs 8:22–31. Late in the period of the Hebrew Bible and beyond that period through the first century of the common era, Jewish speculation about wisdom related it to the Torah, the written word of God. Likewise, it became identified with the Word of God (*memra*, the Aramaic for "word"). In an oversimplified way of summarizing a long history, wisdom was personified, then tied in and harmonized with the earlier tradition of the Word of God.

Out of this rich heritage the author of the Prologue to the Gospel drew meaning. One can see how the meaning of the Prologue could be similar to the significance of the Logos in Stoic thought, how it relates to the concept of Word of God in the Hebrew scriptures, and how "word" might be a translation of "wisdom" as it was conceived in Jewish thought. Whatever its specific roots, the author intends Logos to have a rich and varied meaning. He or she may have wanted its specific precedents to be elusive so that both Jewish and Gentile readers could resonate with its implied meanings.

Even so, our author intends to say something specific about Jesus with these concepts. She or he intends to apply this broad religious-philosophical category of Logos to Jesus in order to say that Jesus fulfilled the whole vast tradition of many different religions and philosophical views of the universe. The author is saying, in effect: Yes, Christ is all of this—Stoic Logos, Hebrew Bible Word, and Jewish Wisdom—rolled into one person. That is the thrust of the Prologue, I believe: Logos for the Christian is a *person.* The Logos is not an abstract philosophical concept. It is not a category of religious experience. Nor is it speculative religious mythology. It is person, enfleshed, living, historical person. Therein lies the genius of the Prologue. It claims that the abstract, the subjectively experienced, the myth has become and is person, That is quite a claim. Whether you believe it is true or not, you must recognize its importance as a Christian claim for Christ.

But let us get into the Prologue itself. What does the passage affirm about this Logos? The following is said about the Word:

Existed from the beginning
  Existed with God
    Was God
      Was the agent of creation
        Was life that was light to persons
          (Was not John the Baptist)
            Was in, but not recognized by, the world
              Was rejected by his own
                Was source of power to become children of God
              Became flesh and dwelt in the world
            Revealed Glory
          Was God's Son
        (John the Baptist witnessed to him)
      Was the means of grace and truth
    Was superior to Moses
Made God known as never before

A number of these affirmations demand our examination, not least of which is the very first. This constitutes one of the highest claims the Christian has made for Christ: He existed from the beginning. (I will refer to the Logos with masculine pronouns only because of the assertions that the Logos is person and that the preexistent Christ became incarnate as a man. Actually, I would prefer to suggest that the Logos, like God, is both male and female and that only in the incarnation does the Word take masculine form.) The preexistence of the Logos affirms not only that he existed before creation itself, but that he existed before "all things began." His existence goes back into that mysterious time before time—into the realm of temporality that eludes human conceptuality. While we cannot fathom what it would mean to exist before all else, we can try to fathom what the author is trying to affirm by saying this. Christ is so important that he could not simply have come into being like any other person or object. Christ is made to transcend beings and things by the assertion of his pretemporal existence. The evangelists responsible for the Gospels of Matthew and Luke said something like this when they incorporated the stories of the virgin birth and/or conception by the Holy Spirit. They were affirming that Christ's significance in the lives of persons precludes his having come into being in an ordinary way. His origin is by extraordinary divine initiative. The Fourth Evangelist (or the author of the Prologue) has gone one step further to say the same thing. Christ is no created being. He is before creation. The point I want to stress is that this affirmation is an expression of the sense of the absolute significance of Christ.

Another affirmation that leaps out from among those in the Prologue is that the Logos was the agent of creation. "All things came into being through him, and without him not one thing came into being" (v. 3). Here is a fascinating expansion of Christian thought about Christ. The earliest Christians surely affirmed the redeeming quality of the life and death of Jesus of Nazareth. He is the source of a new kind of life—one attuned to the divine purpose for human existence. But somewhere in the growth of early Christian thought came a further step—a leap, I would say. This redeeming, saving person is also the agent of divine creation. Our Prologue may or may not have been the first known literary expression of that idea. It vies for the honor with the christological hymn in Colossians 1:15–20 (see especially v. 16). What an overwhelming idea it is! Again one is driven to ask what the early Christians meant to say with this concept of Christ as the creative agent. They might well have neatly kept the function of Christ confined to divine redemption. But, no, they had to go further and complicated matters by assigning him a function in creation. Surely the affirmation again arises from roots in the existential meaning of Christ for human life. So fundamental to the sense and purpose of existence is the revelation in Christ that he must be conceived as the shaping force in the very beginnings of existence!

What then is the relationship of this preexistent, creative Logos to God? The prologue is tantalizing at this point. It is almost as if the author is teasing the reader with the language of the very first verse. The Greek reads something like this: "The Logos was with the God." The preposition "with" suggests relationship. "And the Word was God." God and the Word are identified. The definite article before "God" in the first clause of the sentence is missing in the second. That little grammatical detail has suggested to some that the identity of the Logos and God is not intended to be complete. It means something like, "The Logos was divine." I think, however, that such an interpretation is pressing the significance of the absence of the definite article too far.

This sentence of the Prologue introduces the reader immediately to a basic view of Christ in the Fourth Gospel: The Logos is a distinct being, yet identical with God. That is, there is both *individuality* and *identification* in the relationship between God and Logos (or Christ). "With God"—"Was God"! We do not want to make the Prologue read like a later church christological confession. It was written at a time long before the church wrestled with Trinitarian concepts. Still, honest interpretation of the passage necessitates our understanding that the author is introducing us here to a paradox at the heart of the relationship of Christ and God. How can there be individuality (distinctiveness, separateness, twoness) and identity (oneness, sameness) at the same time? The author does not tell us. One can almost hear Johannine laughter in the wings as we try to stretch our minds to get them around the meaning of these words.

At the very least, the author means that Christ is the expressive dimension of divine being. The Logos-Christ is God's revealing, outward-directed activity. Let me invoke a simplistic analogy: A person may be said to have two sides or dimensions. There is that side of a person's being that expresses who she or he is. In actions and words to friends and intimates, one reveals who he or she is. But there is another side to personal being. It is the inner, unexpressed (or seldom expressed) dimension. Depending on the quality of intimacy one has with others, this side of personal being may be sizable or nearly negligible. Forgive the application, but the Logos is that expressed, outward side of God. That does not mean that God is exhausted in the Logos, but (Christians would affirm) the significance of divine existence for humans is manifested in that expressive being of God. If this is what the author of the prologue has in mind, she or he is saying that Logos is that dimension of God which has come to expression for the comprehension of humans.

This leads us to the heart of the prologue as it now stands in the Gospel—the famous verse 14, "And the Word became flesh and lived among us." The expression of divine being takes up abode in a single human creature and lives among other humans for a time. The expressive side of God's being is *physically* present. It is made sensual so that it can be touched, seen, heard, and felt. This "sensual Logos" is, of course, for the Fourth Evangelist the man, Jesus of Nazareth. This statement constitutes the normative affirmation of incarnational Christology for Christianity. It has been claimed that the Logos is God and now Logos has become human person.

One cannot grasp the full significance of this effort to articulate the identity of the founder of the Christian movement without briefly comparing it to other such statements in the New Testament. It could be argued that there are three fundamental concepts of Christ in the New Testament. We will label them "adoptionistic," "agency," and "incarnational."

The adoptionistic Christology suggests that Jesus was a man who because of his obedience to God was adopted as God's Messiah. This adoption may have taken place sometime in the ministry of Jesus, but more often it is declared to have been the meaning of the resurrection. By this view there is no preexistence of Christ or even divine initiative in his birth. He lives an obedient life and is then made God's special person, the Messiah. This kind of christological thought, I believe, was the earliest way by which Christians conceived of their founder. But it is only faintly present in the literature of the New Testament, for Christians very soon began thinking of Christ in (shall we say) more noble terms. The presence of an early adoptionistic Christology, however, lurks behind these passages in the New Testament: Acts 2:36; 3:13; Romans 1:3–4. (For further defense of this position, see J. A. T. Robinson, *Twelve New Testament Studies*, pp. 139–153.)

Agency Christology is more common in the New Testament. In some form it declares that God took the initiative to send a personal agent to perform a revelatory and saving function. This kind of thinking is present in all those passages in the New Testament which are satisfied simply to say that Jesus was "sent" by God. Interestingly enough, one of the favorite expressions of the Fourth Gospel is something like this (e.g., 3:34). It is also represented in other New Testament literature such as Matthew 10:40 and Romans 8:3. Jesus is thus sometimes conceived as a prophet of God sent out with a message and mission. But I take it that the birth narratives in the Gospels of Matthew and Luke are essentially expressions of a form of agency Christology. In this case, the agent is more than just a man. His being is shaped by God's special action in one way or another. Still, whether the nature of the agent is that of a specially chosen person or an extrahuman being, his function is to be an agent, a representative, or, if you will, an ambassador.

The boldest of the claims for Christ is embodied in incarnational Christology. In this way of conceiving of Christ, some form of his prior existence is asserted. He is thought to have existed before his appearance as a man in this world. This is equal in importance to and logically necessitated by the central theme of incarnational Christology: The divine being has become a human person. The contribution of incarnational Christology then is to claim the divine nature of Christ and at the same time to claim that this divine Christ has taken a human form. The Prologue to the Fourth Gospel is the fullest and clearest statement of incarnational Christology in the New Testament. Yet Colossians 1:15–20 nearly rivals the Prologue for its incarnational affirmation. The Philippian hymn (2:6–11) is often debated, but it may express a similar view.

If I might, I would like to adapt Reginald H. Fuller's diagrammatic summaries of these three views, shown in figure 1–1 (see *The Foundations of New Testament Christology*, pp. 243–246).

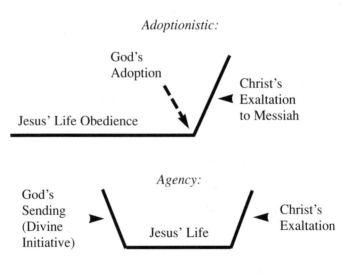

Fig. 1–1

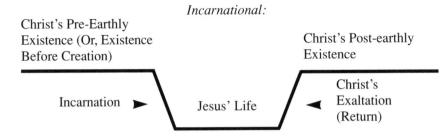

Incarnational:

Christ's Pre-Earthly
Existence (Or, Existence
Before Creation)

Christ's Post-earthly
Existence

Incarnation ▶   Jesus' Life   ◀ Christ's
Exaltation
(Return)

The Prologue to the Fourth Gospel, then, presents us with the finest specimen of early Christian incarnational thought. Here the divine nature of the preexistent Logos is most clearly affirmed and here the humanization or enfleshment of that Logos is flatly declared. Not only does 1:14 declare that humanization, but it suggests more. The verb translated "lived" literally means something like "put up camp for a while." The implication is that the Logos is on a journey, and he camped out in this world for a time as a part of his itinerary. Here the heart of Christian gospel is articulated. It is not our task to argue for or against that gospel, but only to point out and to marvel at the religious mind (or community of minds) responsible for it.

I would call the content of the prologue prime Christ myth. I mean by that not that the claims for Christ made here are necessarily untrue (surely, that misuse of the word "myth" should be put to rest once and for all). I mean that these claims for the cosmic, extraworldly existence and behavior of the Logos are poetic and imaginative in the most profound sense. They are means of expressing the significance and status of Christ in the personal lives of the Christian community. The prologue bursts out of mundane, historical, and "factual" description to tell us something about the early Christians and their perception of reality. The myth is that perspective on human life and the world that informed and structured existence for them. Whenever one declares what it is that gives life meaning and purpose, one speaks mythologically. To do so is to put forth a model of understanding the world that accurately fits the experience and stance of the believer. This is the function the Christ myth of the prologue played in the community out of which it arose. It articulated that model of meaning and purpose. It presented a cosmic perspective that encompassed all of the experience of the worshiping community. It articulated a perspective within which life could be lived without deadly fear and/or utter despair. So it is that every religious community articulates itself in a myth that gives meaning to life. Our prologue is a supreme example of such myth in the origins of Christianity.

THE CHRISTOLOGICAL TITLES IN 1:19–51

Reader's Preparation: Read 1:19–51. List all of the titles used in reference to Christ in the passage. Also note any other claims made for him there.

Chapter 1 of the Gospel is packed to the brim with christological affirmations. The prologue has confronted us with the claims associated with the Logos and his incarnation. In the verses following the conclusion of the prologue a whole series of titles are applied to Christ. Actually a survey of these titles is in effect a summary of many of the major labels by which the Fourth Gospel explicates its understanding of Christ.

The first title for Christ to confront the reader in this passage is found on the lips of John the Baptist: "Lamb of God" (vs. 29, 36). This title evokes a whole series of possible meanings, which we will only sketch. Like most of the titles used of Christ here and elsewhere in the New Testament, this one could have a number of meanings. The most obvious we have already mentioned in the Introduction, namely, the Paschal Lamb. The lamb had special affiliations with the Passover celebration and would evoke images of the liberation of people from bondage. The Baptist further qualifies the sense of the expression "Lamb of God" by saying it is he "who takes away the sin of the world." This suggests that the meaning of the expression is not the Passover lamb, but a sacrificial lamb (or the Passover lamb understood sacrificially— see 1 Corinthians 5:17). It is one whose death is symbolic of the remorse of the worshipers. Its death is expiatory in some way; it is offered to God and its offering removes sin. The Passover lamb and the sacrificial lamb may have been associated, although whether or not the Passover lamb's death was thought of as a form of sacrifice is debatable.

The third association of the title Lamb of God appears in Jewish apocalyptic literature. Much of this literature has a lamb in the drama of the end times. This lamb is a central figure in the destruction of evil in the world. (An example of this sort of lamb imagery appears in Revelation 5.) Finally, the Suffering Servant of 2 Isaiah (42:1–4; 49:1–6; 50:4–9; 52:13–53:12) is described as a lamb in one of the passages (53:7). Since many believe that the early Christians interpreted Christ out of the context of this Suffering Servant imagery, some naturally find servant allusions in this use of the title Lamb of God. (I am indebted to Raymond Brown's *The Gospel According to John* for some of this summary of possible meanings in the title.)

What do we have then? By using the title Lamb of God, the Evangelist may mean to say about Christ any or all of the following: (1) He is the symbol of the new Passover, the new liberation from bondage, offered by God. (2) He is the innocent victim whose suffering and death gain the removal of human sin. (3) He is the figure who appears at the end of time to destroy all evil in the world. (4) He is the servant of God whose suffering atones for the sin of others. The apocalyptic notion of Christ as one who destroys evil is mentioned in the Gospel (e.g., 12:31), but this is not a prominent theme. The Passover reference is appealing, since according to the Evangelist's scheme of things Jesus is crucified precisely at the time the Passover lambs are being slain in preparation for the meal. That idea of liberation is surely associated with the sacrificial lamb—the victim whose death effects the release from sin. That idea, in turn, has clear roots in the concept of the Suffering Servant in 2 Isaiah.

What the Evangelist wants us to understand, then, by the claim that Jesus is the Lamb of God is, I believe, that this is the agent of God whose life and death result in liberation. In the Fourth Gospel a minimum of language and thought suggests that Jesus is conceived as an expiation for sin. For our Evangelist the death of Jesus is not so much a sacrifice as an ironic means of exaltation of Jesus. Therefore, it is likely that the Fourth Evangelist wanted the liberating qualities of Christ to be understood in broader terms than that of an expiatory death. "You will know the truth, and the truth will make you free" (8:32), and of course, it is Christ himself who is the truth, according to the Fourth Gospel (14:6). The Lamb of God is the liberating revealer of God. His freeing function occurs not strictly through his suffering and death but through his very person. To know him is to be freed. In this way, the Fourth Evangelist has employed the title Lamb of God but has given it a new and fresh meaning that is nonetheless not discontinuous with its previous meanings.

Next we meet in this passage the first of several titles that all have the same essential meaning, namely, Jesus' messiahship: "God's chosen one" (1:34, margin), "Messiah" (v. 41), "him about whom Moses in the law and also the prophets wrote" (v. 45), and "King of Israel" (v. 49). They all are ways of referring to the special agent of God who is to come and are packed with Jewish expectation of an ideal king who will rule justly. But by the first century of the common era all the messianic titles were suggestive of more than a political ruler. They connoted one who would rescue the people from economic as well as political oppression; who would correct religious injustices and falsehoods; who would destroy the forces of evil in the world; who was variously thought of as a man, a superman, and an angelic type of divine creature.

In these titles the Evangelist emphasizes the conviction that this Jesus was indeed the fulfillment of the whole body of messianic expectation. Faced with opposition from the Jewish leaders of the city, the Fourth Evangelist wants to make one fact clear at the very beginning of this Gospel: Jesus is the Messiah. The whole range of titles used for the Messiah are grouped here to make that point. The passage asks loud and clear, "Is there anyone who is still unsure about whether or not we Christians believe Jesus is the Messiah?"

That leads us to the title "Son of God," used in verse 49. Here we have to ask again what historical precedents have converged to produce the meaning the Evangelist intends. Son of God may mean from its background in the Hebrew Bible simply the anointed king of Israel—the one especially chosen by God (e.g., 2 Samuel 7:14). The people of Israel themselves are sometimes called sons of God (Hosea 1:10, RSV). The concept of the Son of God as a divine being emerges out of the Hellenistic world. The divine man is one especially gifted with powers that have their source in deity. That title was adopted by the Christians very early as a title for Christ and was intended to convey his special status in relation to God (e.g., Romans 8:3).

In applying this title to Christ, to what extent does the Evangelist intend to say that Christ is divine? We will explore the use of the general title "Son" below. The author means it to carry the special weight of divinity. But here the title "Son of God" appears in close association with the messianic title. Nathanael is made to use the title "Son of God" as an apparent synonym for "King of Israel." Hence, here it has a traditional messianic sense. The Evangelist wants to explode this meaning into greater significance. The intent is to show that Jesus is indeed the Messiah, the Son of God, the King of Israel, but he is much more than that.

Before we go to the climax of this series of christological titles in the second part of the first chapter, we must note another issue present in this passage. Along with these titles there is a persistent theme of the relationship between Jesus and John the Baptist. In the course of the narrative describing the witness of the Baptist to Christ, three points are made with regard to the relationship:

1. Christ is greater than the Baptist. We are told this not once but twice. The Baptist is not good enough even to bend down and loosen Jesus' shoes (John 1: 27), for Christ ranks far ahead of the Baptist (v. 30).

2. The Baptist claims, "he was before me" (v. 30). This might mean simply that Jesus is older than John. But given the theme of the preexistence of Christ in the Gospel (8:58, as well as the prologue), it is pretty clear that the Evangelist here has the Baptist witnessing to the preexistence of Christ.

3. The Baptism of John is with water. Christ baptizes with the Holy Spirit (v. 33). Clearly the assertion is made that Christ is superior to the Baptist by virtue of Christ's bestowing the gift of the Spirit itself. John's gift is a water baptism, symbolic of repentance.

We should add to this list the assertion of the prologue that John was not the light but only a witness to the light (v. 8).

Why all this concern to show that Jesus is superior to John the Baptist? Some argue that the Fourth Evangelist knew a group of persons who believed that the Baptist was the Messiah. Hence, the argument here is a polemic against those persons. This is possible, for it does seem that the Baptist attracted a group of followers (see v. 35). They could very well have claimed that their leader was the Messiah, especially after his death. More likely, I believe, is that here again the Evangelist is answering a charge leveled against Christians by Jewish leaders. Those leaders were saying, "Your Jesus was just another prophetic voice similar to that of the Baptist. He was nothing more!" The Evangelist is answering that charge with the claim that Jesus is in an entirely different category from the Baptist. To make this reply carry the greatest possible weight, the author has put it on the lips of John the Baptist himself.

So, Jesus is all of these: Lamb of God, God's Chosen One, Messiah, the man spoken of by Moses in the Law and by the prophets, King of Israel, and far greater than John the Baptist. Now we reach the climax of this little treatise on the identity of Jesus. The last title used of Christ in this series is "Son of Man." It is important that the Evangelist has Jesus receive all of the previous titles. The Johannine Jesus never objects to or corrects the various confessions directed toward him. But after Nathanael's strong confession in verse 49, Jesus replies, "You will see heaven opened and the angels of God ascending and descending upon the Son of Man" (v. 51). Surely Jesus is the Messiah in the sense that all of these titles suggest. Surely he is greater than John the Baptist. But his real identity is tucked away in the meaning of this expression, Son of Man.

Much has been written in quest of the meaning of this title. It is enough for us to say simply that this title denoted a special divine agent of God. Jewish mythology had given birth to a heavenly man figure who resided with God from creation. He would come among humans at a time of God's choosing, at the end of the present age to overcome evil and establish the reign of God upon the earth. He represented the messianic figure but also a figure whose nature was extrahuman. He was at once the prototype of human beings and the eschatological restorer of humanity. His being is mysterious and hidden until that time when he is destined to enter history and bring it to its grand climax. (See Daniel 7:13–14. Here the Hebrew expression "son of man" appears, which the NRSV translates "a human being.")

I think the Evangelist is saying, If you want to use a title for Christ, Son of Man best suits him. Our author seems clearly to prefer this title from among the various ones employed for Jesus in this passage. This is so for a number of reasons: First, the Son of Man title had a prominent place in the tradition the Evangelist received. Of course, the Fourth Gospel shares this title and its prominence with the Synoptic Gospels. This is one of the points held in common by the traditions. Second, the Evangelist may have preferred this title to the others because it provided some elbow room. It designated a mysterious being. Our Evangelist liked that, for he or she could use that ambiguity to advantage. The author shaped the meaning of Son of Man out of the convictions about Christ found in the Johannine community's traditions and its own interpretation of those traditions. The title permitted the creative development of the peculiar claims for Christ we find in the Gospel—claims that burst the preconceived notions of the Messiah.

Out of this title, Son of Man, I think the Evangelist used the Gospel's favorite title, simply Son. It is this designation for Jesus that dominates the names for Christ in the Fourth Gospel, and we have only scratched the surface of Johannine Christology until we have looked deeper into the affirmations of the Fourth Gospel about the Son and his relationship with the Father. Because of the prominence of the Son of Man title in John 1:19–51 (as well as its use twelve additional times, e.g., in 6:53; 9:35; and 13:32), I am inclined to think that the Son title functions throughout the Gospel as an abbreviation for the Son of Man title. However, Son of God also appears, but in only seven passages (e.g., 3:18, 11:27, and the potent 20:31). The unembellished Son title may well be a Johannine synthesis of the content and associations of both the longer Son designations. The Son title scarcely appears in the Synoptics. It occurs in Matthew 11:27 and Luke 10:22 (a Q passage), Matthew 24:36 and Mark 13:32 (where the First Evangelist seems dependent on the Gospel of Mark), and Matthew 28:19 (a passage peculiar to the Gospel of Matthew). Paul occasionally employs it (e.g., Romans 1:3, 9; 8:3, 29, 32; 1 Corinthians 1:9; 15:28; Galatians 1:16; 4:4, 6; 1 Thessalonians 1:10). This may suggest that it was widely known in early Christian tradition but not favored to the degree it was in the Johannine tradition.

THE SON OF MAN AND THE FATHER-SON RELATIONSHIP

> *Reader's Preparation*: In order to understand the heart of Johannine Christology, you should read the following scattered passages for what they say about the Son of Man and the relationship between the Father and Son:
> 1. The Son of Man passages: 1:51; 3:13–15; 5:27; 6:27, 53, 62; 8:28; 9:35–38; 12:23, 34–36; 13:31.
> 2. The Father-Son relationship: 3:16–17, 31–35; 4:34; 5:19–23, 37; 6:29, 38, 40–46; 7:16, 28–29; 8:16, 36–38, 42, 54; 10:17, 30–38; 12:45–49; 14:9–11, 20, 28; 16:5, 28; 17:8, 11–24.

The Son of Man and Son titles constitute the heart of Johannine Christology. Our task now is to try to understand what the Fourth Evangelist says about Christ as Son and as the Son of Man, and his relationship with the Father. We will do so by summarizing in nine statements what the relevant passages seem to say. You are invited to test these assertions against the evidence you have been asked to examine in the Gospel.

First, Jesus is the Son of Man (9:35–38). This is an obvious point, perhaps, but it needs to be asserted in the beginning. The Evangelist wants readers to understand that the man Jesus of Nazareth was indeed this mysterious Son of Man.

Second, his home is in the heavenly realm with God. John 3:13–15 is the simplest statement of this idea. The Son of Man originates in that heavenly home, descends into the human world, and will once again ascend after the completion of his task (3:13; 6:62; 16:28). He does not belong to this world. His origin is elsewhere—it is divine. He appears mysteriously from nowhere, lingers among persons for a time, and then departs. Hence, there is a great deal of discussion in the Fourth Gospel about where Jesus is from. When he claims to be the bread that has come down from heaven, his opponents are puzzled. They say they know his father and mother. They know where he is from, and it is not heaven (6:42–43)! Similarly, they cannot believe that the Messiah would be from Galilee (7:41). When Jesus speaks of his ascent once again to heaven in terms of "going away," his hearers are further confused. Maybe he means he is going to kill himself (8:22)! The descent and ascent themes are good examples of the way in which the Evangelist represents the crowd as totally misunderstanding the words of Jesus. The origin of the Messiah was an important credential for Jewish thought in the first century, and our Evangelist uses that concern to make the point repeatedly that the Son of Man has no worldly origin.

Third, the idea that the Son has been *sent* by the Father is associated with his heavenly origin and destination. The passages that express this idea are too numerous to examine, but suffice it for now to mention 3:34; 4:34; 8:26; 9:4; 17:3. Like a kind of cosmic prophet, the Son is sent forth into the world of humans. As one sent by God, he represents the Father and speaks for God. Typical of the emissary thought of the time, the one sent carries the authority of the sender. (We will note the authority of the Son of Man in our sixth point.) Like a diplomatic envoy, the Son is commissioned by the Father, carries the authority of the Father, and acts in God's behalf. Much of what we have to say below about the authority of the Son of Man and his assumption of the Father's functions is rooted here in the concept of his being sent. What we have called the agency Christology figures very prominently in the Christology of the Fourth Gospel. But this agent is no mere prophet (like John the Baptist?). He is none other than the Son of Man.

The fourth assertion about the Son of Man is related to his ascent into heaven. The sayings relevant to this ascent are of two kinds. The first are those in which Jesus is made to speak of his "glorification." He claims that his death is his glorification (12:23) and that honoring him is the honoring of the Father (13:31). The irony is already obvious. He will die and his death will be in actual fact his glorification. The second kind of passages intensify that irony. Three times Jesus speaks of his being "lifted up" (3:13–15; 8:28; 12:32). The Greek word is an ambiguous one. It can mean the act of crucifying—lifting the victim up onto the cross. But it can also mean exaltation— the honoring of a person. In having Jesus speak of his death as being lifted up, the Fourth Gospel is suggesting that in the very act of the crucifixion with all of its humiliation, Jesus is honored. It is his elevation. When he is lifted up, Jesus says, his true identity will become clear (8:28), and his departure to his heavenly home will be accomplished (12:34–36).

There are two observations about this theme of being lifted up that merit a slight pause in our hurried pace. First, it is a good example of Johannine irony and double meaning. The Fourth Evangelist likes to make little wordplays with terms that have double meanings. I call them wordplays to suggest that the Evangelist is toying with language, but this technique always makes a serious and important point. You can almost feel the resolute paradox in the passage, "When you have lifted up the Son of Man, then you will realize that I am he" (8:28). "When you execute me as a common criminal in the most demeaning way, you will bring about my exaltation, the revelation of my true identity." Another example of the use of words with double meaning is in the Greek word *pneuma* in 3:8. It means both "wind" and "spirit." In 3:8 with the use of this one word with two meanings, the Evangelist has spun a little metaphor. As the wind moves about freely and uncontrolled by human effort, so does the spirit of God!

Second, the theme of the Son of Man's being lifted up is the Johannine theology of the cross in a nutshell! John emphasizes throughout the Gospel—and specifically in the account of the passion story—that Jesus' death is the revelation of Jesus' identity. Hence, it means that the crucifixion is the honoring of the Son of Man for who he really is. It has been observed many times that Jesus does not act like a victim in the Johannine passion story. He does not appear as the one who is suffering disgrace and humilia-tion. Rather, he behaves as the sovereign lord of the proceedings. And from the Johannine point of view, rightly so, for the passion story in John is the story of the king going to his coronation. It is the account of the anonymous monarch revealing his identity for all his subjects to behold. The conse-quence is that the humiliation theme is hardly present in the Gospel. If it is there—if Jesus seems humiliated—it is a humiliation that is part of the process of exaltation. The Son of Man, the Johannine Christ, cannot be humiliated. He is not subject to human influence, except as he permits it as a means toward his glorification.

This aspect of Johannine theology becomes evident when we compare the Fourth Gospel with the point of view of the Gospel of Luke and Acts. The latter clearly distinguishes the crucifixion and resurrection from the ascension. For a period of forty days the resurrected Christ appears to his disciples (Acts 1:3). Then, as they look on, Christ "was lifted up, and a cloud took him out of their sight" (Acts 1:9). The suggestion of most of the Gospel of John, on the other hand, is that the crucifixion is that "lifting up." The res-urrected Christ is not to be distinguished from the exalted Christ. Crucifixion means exaltation of which resurrection is the expression. Hence, crucifixion and resurrection are bound together in the Gospel of John. The resurrection is in itself the meaning of the crucifixion. Resurrection is the exaltation that crucifixion brings. Consequently, the Fourth Evangelist has no use for an ascension scene similar to that found in the Acts of the Apostles.

We must confess, however, that the evidence is not quite this neat. There is one passage that seems to speak of an ascension beyond resurrection. The resurrected Christ says to Mary, "Do not hold on to me, because I have not yet ascended to the Father" (20:17). That allusion to a future ascension does not fit neatly into the scheme of Johannine thought elsewhere. One is led to suspect that in 20:17 the Evangelist is repeating an older tradition. The allu-sion to the future ascension of the resurrected Christ is repeated, even though the Evangelist's own view is that the ascension has in effect taken place in the crucifixion-resurrection. If this is the case, it may explain some of the contradictions we find in the Fourth Gospel. They may be the result of the author's dual efforts to preserve the community's tradition, on the one hand, and to articulate new interpretations of that tradition, on the other hand.

The fifth assertion made about the Son of Man and the Father-Son relationship is this: The functions of the Son are the functions of God. The Father has given over to the Son those tasks which are usually thought to be preserved for divine prerogative. The Son does then what one would usually expect God to do. An example is the matter of judgment. The Son judges on behalf of the Father (3:18; 5:22, 27). Likewise, the Son of Man (or Son) is the giver of life (or eternal life) (3:13–15; 6:27, 53). Briefly, it is the gift of authentic existence, the true quality of human existence, or human existence as it was created to be. In John, Jesus is the one who bestows that kind of life. Likewise, the Son reveals the glory of God. In the Hebrew Bible, glory denotes the very presence of God. In saying that the Son reveals the glory of God (13:31) the Evangelist is asserting that the presence of God is in the presence of Jesus. God's self-revelation has been delegated to the Son. The Father's work is the work of the Son, which leads us to a sixth point.

The Son carries the full authority of the Father. The Father has placed the divine "seal" upon the Son (6:27). The authority of the Son is asserted, too, in Jesus' insistence that his glorification is that of the Father (13:31). This matter of divine authority residing in the Son is probably the meaning of the enigmatic statement at 1:51. What does it mean to claim that the disciple will "see heaven opened and the angels of God ascending and descending upon the Son of Man"? It is a difficult concept, but it surely means this much: The authority of the divine realm resides in the Son. The Son has clear channels of communication with the Father. If you will, the messengers of God are constantly coming and going in the relationship between the Son and the Father. The Son is then the bearer of divine authority. His words, his acts, and his very person have the force of God's own self.

The Father and Son are represented as one, yet with distinct individuality. This is our seventh point. We have asserted in the discussion of the prologue that it is characteristic Johannine Christology to say that there is identity between the Father and Christ, yet there is also individuality. That point is borne out by the examination of the passages that speak of the relationship between the Father and Son. On the one hand, there is a series of passages that speak of an identity between the two (10:30 and 38; 17:1 and 22). It is pointedly stated that they are one, and it is further stressed that their works are one (5:19). They form, as it were, a community of single action. What the Son does is what the Father does. The Son works as the Father directs. So we may conclude that, at least at face value, the Fourth Gospel claims that the Father and Son are one in *being* and in *action*.

On the other hand, there are passages that clearly suggest that there is a distinction between the Father and Son. The Son is said to be obedient to the

Father (4:34). Such a statement would suggest that the Son is a separate and free agent who chooses to obey the Father. Obedience implies individuality. Similarly, love implies individuality. The Father loves the Son (3:35). Can there be love unless one supposes a relationship, which in turn implies individuality? Finally, the Father is greater than the Son (14:28). Surely this again suggests individuality. It also articulates an apparent subordination of the Son to the Father that contradicts any conclusion that the Father and Son in the Fourth Gospel are fully one and equal.

I want to avoid saying either that the Evangelist was muddleheaded in this description of the Father-Son relationship or that it is the first self-conscious statement of Trinitarian theology. Neither is true. I think the Evangelist must have known what she or he was doing in presenting the sayings we have just surveyed. The paradoxical relationship suggested by these passages was far from lost on the Fourth Evangelist. Yet this is no modern theologian concerned with articulating a consistent and logical relationship between the Father and Son. It might well be the case that the author was trying to reconcile divergent factors in the community's tradition or in her or his own thought.

It is the case, at any rate, that the Gospel leaves the reader with a profound paradox. This Son is one with the Father but not identical. He is divine, yet he is in a sense subordinate to God. The Evangelist is struggling to define the relationship of the founder of his faith to God, but has no pat solutions to offer. We must admire the author for that. What is clear is that the Son is the divine agent who participates in the being of the Father, yet has a distinct individuality of his own.

Our eighth point is simpler. The Evangelist calls Jesus the "only Son" (3:16, 18, and possibly 1:18). The Greek word *monogenēs* (translated "only" in the NRSV) means "one of its kind." While the Evangelist does not make extensive use of this adjective, it seems important that the meaning of Son is qualified with it on these two or three occasions. Possibly the qualification means to suggest the absolute distinction between the sonship of Jesus and any ideas of humans as sons of God (since they may be "children of God," 1:12). The sonship of the Son of Man, Christ, is absolutely unique. There is none other of comparable nature. Hence, it may also mean that whatever other divine beings there may be, Jesus is superior to them in his unique sonship. The author of Hebrews was concerned about combating some sort of argument that Jesus was just one of the host of angels (chapter 1). Our Evangelist again might be responding to Jewish charges that the Jesus whom Christians call Messiah is at best an angel. Not so, responds the Evangelist. He is God's unique, one-of-a-kind Son.

Finally, it is obvious that the Fourth Evangelist wants the reader to get one message loud and clear: To respond to Jesus, the Son, is to respond to God, the Father (5:23). The point of the discussions of the identity of the Johannine Jesus is not a purely theological one when it comes right down to it. The point the Evangelist is making is a practical one. However you define the specific relationship between the Son and the Father, how you respond to the Son constitutes your response to God. Accept him and you have accepted God. Reject him and you have rejected God. It is as if the Evangelist is saying, "Well, I am not enough of a theologian to say any more than what I have about the relationship between the Son and the Father. But of this much we Christians are sure: Your relationship with Christ comprises your relationship with God." Coming out of this christological discussion then is a pragmatic point.

Therefore, Christ's sonship in the Fourth Gospel means a unique relationship with God by one who himself participates in God's very being (and hence is divine). I might add by way of conclusion to this section that again Johannine Christology is a creative wedding of two different themes. In Jewish thought to be a son of God was primarily a matter of obedience. To be obedient to God made one a son of God. Even today the expression *bar* or *bat mitzvah* means that one is a son or daughter of the commandment when one takes up those commandments in obedience. But sonship of the deity in Hellenistic thought was a cosmic or ontological matter. To be the Son of God was to have the nature of deity in one's person. The sons of God were mythologically begotten by the gods. Hence, Hellenistic divine sonship was a matter of the essence of the person, while Jewish divine sonship was a matter of the function or behavior of the person. The Evangelist has portrayed Jesus as the Father's Son in a way that bridges the difference. Jesus is the Father's Son most certainly by virtue of his obedience to the Father (4:34). But he is more. His very essence is the essence of the Father (10:30). We do not want to impose later essentialistic language upon our Evangelist. But we may credit the author with perceiving the difference between the meanings of sonship in Hellenistic and in Jewish thought and then proceeding to make Jesus' sonship the fulfillment of both.

THE CHRISTOLOGICAL MEANING OF THE "I AM" SAYINGS

Reader's Preparation: Here are the most significant passages in which the "I am" expression appears in the Greek.
 1. Without a predicate: 8:24, 28, 58; 13:19.
 2. With an implied predicate: 6:20; 18:5.
 3. With an explicit predicate: 6:35, 51; 8:12, 18, 23; 9:5; 10:7, 9, 11, 14; 11:25; 14:6; 15:1, 5; possibly 4:26.
It may help you to read the following alterations of some of the New Revised Standard Version translations. I have translated more literally or emphasized the Greek "I am" construction more literally and italicized it to help you spot it.
6:20—"But he said to them, '*I am*; do not be afraid.'"
8:18—"*I am* the one who testifies concerning myself."
8:23—"*I am* from above. You are of this world; *I am* not of this world."
8:24—"You will die in your sins unless you believe that *I am*."

45

8:28—"When you have lifted up the Son of Man, then you will realize that
   I am."

13:19—"I tell you this now, before it occurs, so that when it does occur,
   you may believe that *I am.*"

18:5—"Jesus replied, '*I am.*'"

The Johannine Christ is the eternal Word of God who has become incarnate. He is all that the Jewish Messiah is but more, namely, the Son of the Father and the Son of Man. As such he is one who fully participates in the being of God and yet has individuality from the Father. To this picture of Christ in the Fourth Gospel we must add still another element, the christological meaning of the enigmatic "I am" sayings. These sayings should be investigated from several different angles, but this brief introductory glimpse will be concerned only with what they suggest about the view of Christ in the Fourth Gospel.

First of all, what is an "I am" saying? It is a purported word of Jesus in which an emphatic construction (*egō eimi*) appears in the Greek. The normal way in which one would write "I am" in koine Greek (the form of Greek in which the New Testament was written) is *eimi*. For emphasis one might add the first person pronoun, *egō*. The result is literally something like, "I, myself am!" But we will see that the peculiar construction seems to have meaning beyond a simple emphasis upon the pronoun.

This emphatic construction appears on the lips of Jesus in three ways in the Fourth Gospel. First is "I am" with an explicit predicate. An example is 6:35, "I am the bread of life." Another form is the "I am" with what appears to be an implied predicate. An example of this form is 6:20. The translation in the New Revised Standard Version quite correctly supplies the predicate in its rendering, "It is I." The Greek however reads simply, *egō eimi*, "I am." The sense of these formulations with an implied predicate may very well be something like, "I am he," but the emphatic form suggests the Evangelist has something special in mind. That special meaning is obviously intended in the so-called absolute "I am" sayings, those without any predicate either implicit or explicit. John 8:24 will serve as our example here: Jesus says, "For you will die in your sin unless you believe that I am he." Again the New Revised Standard Version has helped the reader by supplying a predicate ("I am he"). That hypothetical predicate may be quite appropriate. But the Greek reads, "If you do not believe that I am, you will die in your sins." (Examples from the Synoptic Gospels include Mark 14:62 and Luke 22:70.)

Most interpreters of the Fourth Gospel agree that the "I am" sayings are more than simple emphatic statements. They believe that the Fourth Gospel uses this formulation in a profound christological way. The heart of the problem is the absolute "I am" sayings (those without predicates). The meaning of the absolute form may suggest the deeper meaning of those with both explicit and implicit predicates.

46

The meaning of the "I am" sayings may be hinted at in the affinity they have with similar kinds of sayings in other religious traditions. Among certain of the religions of the Hellenistic world of the first century the revealer gods spoke with the emphatic *egō eimi*. The god Isis is quoted in inscriptions using the "I am" saying with predicates. (See Howard Clark Kee's *The Origins of Christianity: Sources and Documents*, pp. 83–84.) Similarly, parallels can be found in that body of literature called the Hermetic Corpus, particularly where Poimandres reveals himself to Hermes. Others have claimed that the Mandean literature is relevant. Although that literature actually dates much later than the first century of the common era, it is argued that the religious movement dated from a time contemporaneous with the origin of Christianity. The Mandean literature contains passages that seem to have parallel "I am" constructions. Most of these parallels in Hellenistic religions are comparable to the Johannine sayings in which a predicate follows the "I am." For instance, in the Hermetical literature the following can be found: "The messenger of light am I" and "the treasure am I, the treasure of life"; or, in the Mandean literature: "A shepherd am I, who loves his sheep" and "a fisherman am I who. . . . " (These examples are drawn for the most part from Rudolf Bultmann's *The Gospel of John*.)

It appears then that there was a precedent in Hellenistic religious thought and practice for attributing to the god such emphatic "I am" sayings—at least in their form with a predicate. Some believe that the "I am" sayings in the Fourth Gospel are intentionally modeled after these uses in Hellenistic religions. Further, they suggest that the Fourth Evangelist is asserting the identity of Christ in contrast to some of the claims of Hellenistic gods. Hence, when Jesus says emphatically, "I am the good shepherd" (10:14), a contrast with other claims for divine status in the Hellenistic world is deliberately intended. Whether or not this is the case, it is clear that Hellenistic religions offer a precedent for the revealer god using the emphatic "I am." Such a statement on the lips of the god signaled the utterance of a revelation of the truth that the god had to offer.

When we turn in the direction of the Hebrew Bible and Jewish religion for a precedent for the "I am" saying, we find there something like the absolute "I am." The Hellenistic literature seems to offer parallels only for the "I am" speeches with predicates. Not so the Hebrew Bible. Recall the meaning of the sacred name for God revealed to Moses in Exodus 3:14. It is difficult to say how the Hebrew there should be translated. One of the most likely translations reads, "I AM: that is who I am. Tell them that I AM has sent you to them." Could it be that the Fourth Evangelist intends to stir in the reader a recognition that the sacred name for God, YHWH, was rooted in God's self-naming, "I am"?

The pursuit of Jewish parallels gets hotter when we turn to the Greek translation of the Hebrew Bible. This translation (called the Septuagint or LXX) was commonly used among Greek-speaking Jews and Christians in the first century. In many passages we find that the translators have used the emphatic *egō eimi* to render the original Hebrew. In a number of places the Hebrew, which reads something like "I, Yahweh," is translated by the LXX, "I am" (*egō eimi*, Isaiah 41:4; 45:18, Hosea 13:4, Joel 2:27). In some passages in Isaiah in which the Hebrew reads "I, I am He," the Greek translation is "I am I am." These passages all have to do with the direct speaking of God. They all emphasize the oneness of God's existence. (Thanks to Raymond Brown for his excellent appendix on the "I am" sayings in *The Gospel According to John*, Anchor Bible, vol. 29.)

Out of these sketchy allusions to the possible precedents for the use of the "I am" formulation in religious literature of the first century, we can begin to construct the meaning intended by the Fourth Evangelist. First, we can claim with some degree of safety that the Evangelist means the "I am" formulation to signal the speaking of God. Out of both the Hellenistic and Jewish backgrounds our author drew the idea of the use of this construction in connection with the divine revelation. The occurrence of this construction marks a theophany—the appearance and revelation (speaking) of God. The Fourth Evangelist intends to use a formula that sets off sirens in the minds of both Hellenistic and Jewish Christian readers. When either read that stately "I am," they thought of the revelation of the divine to humans.

Second, we can conclude that the Evangelist was making an exclusive claim for Christ with the use of the "I am" sayings. Maybe the contrast with other religious claims is implicit in some of the "I am" sayings with predicates like "the good shepherd" and "the bread of life." The Fourth Evangelist is saying that whatever other claims you have heard, Jesus is the true divine revealer. Hence, there is in the Fourth Gospel an awareness of the use of the *egō eimi* in Hellenistic religions. However, that claim for the exclusive truth of Christ is also rooted in the Jewish tradition. Our writer is saying that just as Yahweh is the one true God, so Christ is the one true divine revealer. None other is comparable.

Finally, it is likely that the sound of those words "I am" in the locale of the Evangelist meant the very name of God. That name could not be uttered. Jewish piety had long forbidden the pronouncing of the sacred name, YHWH. So, when Jesus is made to say "I am," it is the very name of God he is uttering. The implication is that he himself *is* God. He may allow that sacred name to pass from his lips, because he is the one whom the name designates. As Yahweh in the Hebrew Bible speaks the divine name, so Christ may speak that name. If this is so, then we have here one of the highest claims for Christ's divinity in the entire New Testament. If this is so, we have an unequivocal indication that the Fourth Evangelist held Christ to be God, at least as far as practical human matters were concerned.

In summary, the Fourth Evangelist employs this tantalizing Greek construction in full knowledge of its religious significance, both Hellenistic and Jewish. He or she uses it to assert the divinity of the founder of the Christian faith and to claim that that founder is the only source of truth and full human existence. When Christ speaks, it is God who speaks. All of this seems quite consistent with the view of Jesus we have seen emerging in the other parts of the Gospel. It is consistent with the Prologue to the Fourth Gospel, with the insistence of the Evangelist that Christ is more than the Jewish Messiah, and with the Son of Man and Father-Son relationship passages. What it does is to underline the *functional equivalency* of God and Christ. That is, it says in effect that so far as human concerns go, Christ and God are one and the same. The words of Christ are God's words. The actions of Christ are God's actions. The human response to Christ is the response to God. For all human purposes, then, the Christ figure is God. The Fourth Evangelist does this consistently, and the mysterious "I am" formula furthers that point.

THE WORK OF CHRIST ACCOMPLISHED IN HIS DEATH

> *Reader's Preparation*: Read again chapters 18 through 20 and take note of how the Gospel interprets the trial, death, and resurrection of Jesus.

Our peek into the Gospel's understanding of Jesus is not quite complete. There is another subject beckoning for our attention. Theologians sometimes divide the issue of Christology into two subtopics. They call the first the "person" of Jesus and the second his "work." They mean by this distinction that who Jesus is (his nature and identity) can be divided for purposes of discussion from what he accomplished (especially in his death). Of course, the distinction is not sharp, since the accomplishment of Christ and his person are interrelated. Consequently, we cannot expect that the Fourth Evangelist would have thought of these two as separable issues.

Still, the Johannine view of Christ cannot be understood apart from what the Gospel seems to teach he accomplished. As a matter of fact, this issue has already intruded into our discussion. To summarize those intrusions: We have suggested that there is little talk of Jesus' death as expiation and many more indications that his death was liberation. Jesus' death is viewed as a glorification. The ironic character of his death is epitomized in the expression "lifted up." The passion story in John reads more like a coronation than a humiliation and is claimed to be a revelation of Jesus' identity. Even with all of this already said, we must still try to pull together the bits and pieces into a more systematic statement of the view of the cross in the Gospel.

We preface our efforts with the observation that the New Testament presents a variety of ways of understanding the cross. Like the view of Jesus' person, the earliest Christians had not yet settled on one single view of the cross. Actually, early on, the cross was doubtless somewhat of an embarrassment to the Christians. They had to understand why it was that the promised Messiah suffered the humiliation of execution as a common criminal at the hands of the Roman Empire. Paul calls the cross "a stumbling block to Jews and foolishness to Gentiles," even while it is the "power of God and wisdom of God" for the Christian (1 Corinthians 1:23–24).

The "foolishness" of God in allowing the Messiah to suffer death puzzled the Christians, even though they experienced their Lord's suffering as a divine act for human salvation. How should the cross be understood? What language could express its meaning? The New Testament witnesses to diverse efforts to answer these questions. The Gospel of Luke, for instance, employs a relatively simple imagery. Jesus dies a martyr's death as an innocent victim of social brutality (see Luke 23:47; cf. Mark 15:39). Paul, however, speaks at times of the cross with language borrowed from Jewish sacrificial worship, calling it an "expiation" (Romans 3:25). The letter to the Hebrews carries that comparison to the extreme, presenting Jesus as both the high priest and the sacrifice the high priest offers (Hebrews 9:12). The use of images drawn from Jewish sacrificial worship to understand the cross seems to be winning a prominent place for itself as the New Testament era comes to a close (see further 1 John 4:10).

Leave it to the Gospel of John to give us a different view of the matter! If we were to reduce the Johannine ideas about the cross into molten ore and pour it into one of the molds extracted from other New Testament writings, it would refuse to adhere to the confines of the mold. Walking on its hands, the Johannine view of the cross tickles our imaginations and evades our grasp. Can we get a firmer grasp of the maverick at this point?

Let us begin with a brief review of the story of Jesus' passion in the Gospel of John. The story follows the basic structure of the passion narratives we know from the other three Gospels. Yet it has its own peculiarities. As we have observed, there is no agony in the garden of Gethsemane (or Mount of Olives—but see 12:27). The arrest is accomplished without an emphasis on the fleeing disciples found in the Synoptics, but it is followed by a religious hearing and political trial, even as in the other Gospels. But two major differences stand out. The first is that the religious hearing is conducted by Annas, the father-in-law of the high priest, Caiaphas (18:13ff.). Jesus defends himself, however briefly, before the religious leader. Peter's denial is told in two scenes interspersed during the narration of the religious hearing (18:15–18, 25–27). As a result, his cowardice is posed over against Jesus' unswerving defense. When we are told that Annas sent Jesus to Caiaphas the high priest (18:24), the scene flashes back to Peter in the court-yard (vs. 25–27), only to return to Jesus being led from the house of Caiaphas to the headquarters of Pilate (v. 28). We are never given an account of the hearing before Caiaphas.

The second major difference in the trial episodes is the prominence given the inquisition of Jesus before Pilate. While the religious hearing is recounted in six verses, the political trial occupies twenty-nine verses (18:28–19:16). The trial before Pilate is skillfully presented as a dramatic mini-tragedy, told in eight scenes. Pilate's fatal flaw is his reluctance to endanger his popularity with the people, and he finally hands Jesus over to be crucified. The Roman's one remaining shred of integrity is his insistence on the sign to be placed on the cross: "Jesus of Nazareth, the King of the Jews." In spite of the protests, he will not have it removed or revised (19:17–22).

The crucifixion scene is told with economy. The soldiers cast lots for Jesus' robe to fulfill prophecy (19:23–24). Jesus speaks to his mother and the beloved disciple from the cross (vs. 25–27). Jesus thirsts and is given vinegar (vs. 28–30a). He then says, "It is finished" and he "bowed his head and gave up his spirit" (or, more literally, "gave up the spirit"). To fulfill prophecy, Jesus' legs are not broken, but his side is pierced to assure his executioners that they have done their job and Jesus is actually dead. From the wound come blood and water (vs. 31–37). The body is claimed by Joseph of Arimathea and the elusive Nicodemus and is laid in a new tomb (vs. 38–42). There follow the discovery of the empty tomb and three appearances of the risen Christ (20:1–29), with still another appearance recounted in chapter 21.

Lots of issues in the Johannine passion narrative might detain us, but we must be content with a few generalizations about the unique emphases of this story. (See my commentary, *John*, for some further discussion of the details.)

The first emphasis of the Johannine passion story is the remarkable attention given to Pilate. Interestingly, the Roman procurator is the one supporting actor in the whole drama of the Gospel whose character is explored most fully. It appears that the Evangelist did not want us to slip through the Gospel without becoming aware of how dangerous it is to try to remain neutral to this Jesus figure. The second emphasis is the certain responsibility of the Jewish leaders for the death of Jesus, even to the ridiculous extreme of making it sound as if the chief priests do the crucifying (notice the antecedent of the pronoun "they" in 19:17)! This can only be due to the Evangelist's concern to attack the community's opponents in the synagogue. One should not, therefore, conclude from this strange statement a historical proof that the Jews in general were responsible for Christ's death. (For a discussion of the Jews in the Gospel of John, see Chapter 2.)

The third emphasis of John's passion narrative is the centrality of Jesus himself. The camera never fails to keep Jesus in focus, even when it turns briefly to view Peter in his denials or when Pilate stands on stage with the accused. Only a careful eye might pick up the fourth emphasis. The story never really states that Jesus died! Surely, the story of the crucifixion means to affirm the reality of his death. But Jesus says, "It is finished." The assignment has been completed. Then he "gives up the spirit." The author teases us with the question of whose spirit it is that is given up. Does it mean that Jesus voluntarily allows his own spirit to depart? Does it mean that Jesus, having completed his mission, releases the Spirit of God? Or, are we to suppose that the poet-Evangelist again intentionally uses an expression with a surplus of meaning—in voluntarily surrendering his life, Jesus hands over God's Spirit to believers? This writer is not going to do the readers' work for them. Let them puzzle over that for themselves. Finally, then, we could hardly characterize the leading actor of this passion narrative as humiliated or victimized. Yes, he is beaten and mocked (18:22; 19:1–5). But this Johannine Jesus deports himself with dignity and composure. Indeed, he is a king on the way to his enthronement.

The passion story gives us the clues to the meaning of the accomplishment of Jesus as the Fourth Evangelist understands it. But those clues only send us scurrying to the context of the whole Gospel for the solution to the puzzle. Maybe it would help to pull the meaning of the death of Jesus in the Gospel of John together around a series of themes, most of which are familiar to us by this time.

Obviously the first theme must be this: *The cross is the enthronement of Jesus as king.* This theme is suggested by the "lifted up" sayings (3:14; 8:28; 12:32–34). The crucifixion is both the scandalous death of Jesus and his enthronement. The enthronement is further suggested by the emphasis in the passion narrative on the sign Pilate has placed on the cross. His persistence that it be there, hanging above the head of the crucified, is an ironic statement of the truth. Pilate means the sign as a taunt of the Jewish leaders and a mockery of Jesus. But it is true! Jesus is the king! And not the king of the Jewish people alone. So, the words are written in Hebrew, Latin, and Greek. This one is the universal king.

Add to these bits of evidence the kingly posture of Jesus throughout the passion narrative, and you have the picture. Jesus is never really a victim but is always in control of his own destiny (e.g., 19:11). He allows his arrest (18:6–8). He never really dies (19:30). Furthermore, the whole trial with Pilate is really a discussion of who is the real king, Caesar or Christ? (See 19:14–15.) The Gospel claims that the cross is the means by which Christ takes his rightful place on the throne to rule as king of humanity and the whole of creation.

The cross is the ascension and glorification of Jesus. This second theme points to part of the process by which Jesus "goes away" (16:7; 20:17). Coupled with the resurrection, the crucifixion is the departure of the revealer from this world and his ascension, after he has completed his role here. The One who has descended must once again ascend to his heavenly home (3:13), and the crucifixion-resurrection is the imagery of that ascension. It is not an easy concept to grasp, especially for those of us brought up on the Lukan distinction between the crucifixion, resurrection, and ascension. But it is clearly a Johannine concept.

The ascension is accomplished through glorification. To glorify means basically to honor a person. In the Fourth Gospel the expression has to do with the appearance of the divine presence with power and clarity. The cross for this Evangelist is the event at which the divine presence is poured out on

Jesus for all to see (12:28; 17:1). The cross glorifies Jesus in the sense that it projects the divine presence with unmistakable lucidity. It glorifies God in that it makes God's presence known in the world. In these themes our author says that in the cross God honors Jesus and sanctions the works and words of the revealer by the evidence of the Creator's presence.

The cross is the new Passover. That is our third theme. Much has already been said about this, but let us review the evidence. The first is the Passover framework of the entire Gospel, which stands out like a sore thumb (2:13; 6:4; 11:55). The whole picture of the ministry of Jesus is framed in Passovers. Jesus' death corresponds to the time of the death of the Passover lambs in preparation for the commemorative meal that evening (19:14; see the Introduction). Christ is the new Passover lamb by which God once again and decisively liberates people from oppression. Consequently, the cross is presented as a new exodus, a new act of God to free humanity from all the oppressive forces that prevent their being God's own children (see 1:12). How is that liberation effected? By the revelation of the true nature of God. When humans know who God really is, they are freed of the oppression of false understandings. That leads us to the fourth and final theme.

The cross is God's supreme act of love. This theme is anticipated in 3:16 and scattered throughout the Gospel in many different forms. The motivation for God's sending the Son is divine love for the world, evil though the world may be. This love is also found in 15:13. Jesus obeys the will of his heavenly Parent and gives his life for his "friends," the believers. Thus the death of Jesus changes the relationship of humans to God. They are no longer servants but beloved friends. (The Greek word for friends is *philoi* and is rooted in *philia*, one of the words for love.) The cross then becomes the model for what it means to "love one another" (v. 12). The cross is the paradigm of love.

In the context of this emphasis on love and its expression in the self-giving death of Jesus, a number of other passages in the Gospel begin to make more sense. Jesus claims that his crucifixion will result in the "drawing" of all persons to himself (12:32). If the cross is the supreme expression of God's love, it is the power of that love that draws humans to Christ, attracting them like a magnet pulls bits of metal to itself.

Divine love also casts the little parable of the seed in 12:24 in a new light. Love of the Father and humanity leads Jesus to his death. But like a seed in the ground, something new sprouts up because of that death. Jesus' death is the sprouting of divine love in the world. Consider also 11:50 in which Caiaphas unwittingly suggests that Jesus' death is for the whole nation. The self-giving love of the crucified Jesus is for the whole people. Love, too, explains how Jesus' death is a cleansing. We might want to explain the washing of the cross in terms of images borrowed from sacrificial worship (such as the popular expression, "washed in the blood"). It might also be explained in terms of the kind of cleansing one experiences in the love of another. Jesus' act of washing the feet of his disciples cleanses them (13:8ff.), because it is an act of love in anticipation of the supreme act of love in the cross.

Finally, the cross creates a new family of God. The prologue announces to us that those who dare to receive and believe in the Word are given power (or authority) to become children of God (1:12). In the cross that announcement is realized. Hanging on the cross Jesus creates the new family of God. He names his mother the mother of the beloved disciple, and the beloved disciple the child of his mother. The death of Jesus facilitates the new creation of a family of God centered in the divine love expressed in the cross. Like a pair of bookends, the claim of the gift of the power to become children of God in the prologue and the scene at the cross encompass the whole Gospel. (My thanks to Alan Culpepper for this insight. See his *Anatomy of the Fourth Gospel*.)

These are the four themes around which the Johannine understanding of the cross pivots: The cross is the enthronement of Jesus as king, his ascension and glorification, the liberating new Passover, and the supreme expression of God's love.

Now, perhaps, we are in a position to summarize in a more concise and systematic way all the discussion of the accomplishments of Christ in the cross. We may say, first of all, *The meaning of the cross in the Fourth Gospel is the completion of revelation and revelation is atoning* (that is, it brings humans into a friendly relationship with God). The revelation of God's true self has within it power to overcome the alienation of humans from God. The brokenness of humanity is rooted in an absence of the truth. The manifestation of that truth (God's identity) occasions the reestablishment of relationship with God. Hence, "knowing the truth" (8:32) is synonymous with entering the right relationship with God.

Then we may say, *The revelation of the cross and of Jesus' entire ministry is an expression of love, and love liberates.* The revelation of God's true self is the articulation of the love that God has for humans. Knowing that love is the power that breaks the bonds of sin and alienation, so that one can relate to God as "friend." Implicit in this view of the cross is an understanding of the power of divine love.

Finally, all of this is shot through with irony. So, we must say, *The cross is God's irony, and the revelation itself is ironic.* The revelation is ironic, for it conveys the opposite of what humanity takes to be the divine. The means of that revelation is the cross. Ironically the execution of God's Son is the very opposite of what we humans would suppose a revelation of the Ultimate Reality might be. But that cross is the demonstration of God's very self. Irony is more than a literary technique in the Fourth Gospel. It is a theological category, for the revealing act of God is—from the human perspective—ironic. (See Gail O'Day's provocative book, *Revelation in the Fourth Gospel*.)

CONCLUSION

The Fourth Evangelist has expressed a clear view of the founder of the Christian movement. The Christian experience of the founder is the primary evidence for the formulation of the view put forward in the Gospel. That is, what is said about the Christ figure is an effort to say what it is Christians experience in their community of faith. We might confront the Evangelist with the charge that she or he is dealing in speculation. A simple historical figure, the man Jesus of Nazareth, has been made into something that he was not. But with a little imagination we can construct the Evangelist's response. The Johannine community of faith knows this man Jesus in a different way. They know him as one who has brought a totally new orientation to life. Their faith in him has brought them what they consider to be the true essence of human life—eternal life, if you will. They know their founder not as one buried in history but as a living presence communicated to them through the activity of the Spirit (see Chapter 4). Hence, the author of our Gospel would disclaim any charge of speculation or distortion of history. Rather, our Evangelist would understand the Fourth Gospel as an articulation of reality as experienced by the Johannine community of faith.

The founder of that faith was none other than the Father's Son, claims the Fourth Gospel. This means that the Evangelist and the Johannine community have concluded that one who could communicate truth in the way that Christ has brought them to truth could be none other than God's own self. It is a quality of truth that cannot be communicated secondhand. It was not a truth that has been filtered through a human prophet. Divine truth had been communicated to Israel and to persons of the Hellenistic world through human prophets and revealers. But the reality that the Johannine community has found in the revelation attributed to this man Jesus is of another quality. It is the "real thing," encountered in Christ. No intermediary can be responsible for this truth. Otherwise, how could it so radically turn the believers around, so radically alter their lives?

The Evangelist states flatly and unashamedly that it is only in this Christ figure that one finds the divine reality. He is the true bread, the light, the life, the resurrection, and the way of authentic human existence. The Johannine Jesus epitomizes this exclusivism in the assertion, "No one comes to the Father except through me" (14:6). Such a claim for exclusive access to the Ultimate Reality startles the modern mind. It sounds dogmatic and narrow. It can only be understood in the context of a community of faith for whom the founder has been the avenue of a new relationship with that Ultimate Reality.

The Evangelist recognizes that the founder is the Father's Son. All the statements that assert the divinity of Christ are qualified by the fact that he is the Father's Son, not the Father's own self. The Fourth Evangelist is no systematic theologian, but she or he is theologically sophisticated enough to make clear that Christ is not to be confused with God. Christ is divine and participates in the very being of God, but is distinct and subordinate to the Father. He is the expressive dimension of God's being, or the Son who is fully obedient to and sent by the Father. Our Evangelist recognizes that whatever the incarnation of the Logos means it cannot mean that a human being is in every way fully the being of God. Had the Johannine community known the concept of the self-emptying (*kenōsis*) of Christ found in the Philippian christological hymn (2:7), they might well have employed it. As it is, their faith is expressed in paradoxical claims both that Christ is God and that Christ possesses individuality and distinctiveness and is subordinate to God. In other words, Christ is the Father's Son.

To say it another way, the Fourth Evangelist claims that Christ is the functional equivalent of God. In being, the two may be distinct. But in practice they are one. As far as human beings are concerned, Christ is God in their midst. We are thus led to acknowledge that the Evangelist's main concern is not the construction of a theological doctrine but rather the support of practical faith. The Gospel's function is to articulate a point of view that is pragmatic, useful. In practice Christians may think of Christ as God in their midst. The reason for this claim is that it reflects the real and undeniable experience of the Evangelist's own Christian community.

The religious experience of the Christian community is thus the first basis on which the Evangelist formulated the thought of the Gospel. The second is the opposition the church faced from the synagogue. This unusual Gospel is in part a reaction to the allegations brought against the Christians. They are charged with worshiping two Gods. Their Christ is declared to be less than divine by their opponents. He is cast as an angel, a prophet, or maybe even a pretender to the messianic throne. But he is certainly not the Messiah or divine. The author of the Fourth Gospel responds to these charges. That response formulates a view of Christ that claims he is the Messiah, is divine, and yet does not represent a second God. How well the response succeeds at this task I leave to your judgment. But it is important to see the Christology of the Fourth Gospel in the context of this controversy between the church and its opponents.

It is fair, then, to say that the Christology of the Gospel is reactionary. It is the reaction—the response—to the assault of the opponents. In realizing this, we are helped to understand the exclusivism of the Johannine community. That exclusive claim for Christ that we witnessed in the section on the "I am" sayings is due to the church's situation at the time. The church is playing defense, battling to defend its own goal line. It is struggling for its survival against a formidable foe. Religious communities in this kind of situation state their cases in the most radical form. Also in this kind of situation religious communities are likely to do the most creative and formative thinking about their faith. A faith under fire is forced to think carefully and definitively.

Consequently, the Christology of the Fourth Gospel is a concept fashioned out of a real, lived situation. These two aspects of that situation are vital for our understanding of the Evangelist: The church's profound faith experience of Christ and its intense struggle with local opposition. The Christology of the Gospel is then an admirable example of a faith community's effort to think amid a concrete situation in a new way about its founder. We may feel that the view of Christ represented in the Fourth Gospel needs to be balanced by the perspectives of the other Gospels as well as by the later thought of the church. We may even want to question the Johannine understanding of the early Christian experience itself. Nevertheless, we can still understand the concerns of this Gospel and appreciate the way it states its central theme. We can empathize with the situation of the Johannine community and appreciate its response to the issues it faced. In a faithful and creative way, the author of this document rethought the answers to fundamental questions that had been raised regarding the nature and function of the founder of the Christian movement and did so in the light of believers' real experience. In this way, the Fourth Evangelist did what each constructive religious thinker must do in every period of history and what we too must often do ourselves.

2. TWO DIFFERENT WORLDS— JOHANNINE DUALISM

Why is there evil? Why do humans continually encounter that which is senseless and wasteful of human life? Why do good people suffer for no apparent reason? Why are there earthquakes, storms, and other forms of natural destruction? If many of the undesirable aspects of life can be blamed upon human ignorance and immaturity, what about that dimension of nature which strikes us as senseless? How can one account for that? What explanation can be offered for the whole reality of evil?

Of course, all persons throughout history have encountered these questions. It can even be said that one of the most important dimensions of religious thought has been the attempt either to understand or to come to terms with the problem of evil. The simplest religious explanation was to attribute evil to the actions of the gods. It was the manifestation of their wrath, and if humans were to escape destruction they must somehow appease the divine beings. From the simplest of religious explanations of evil to the more complex, religious systems have offered their adherents ways of dealing with this puzzling dimension of human existence. The various ways of handling evil within religious systems are numerous. In some religions (Hinduism, for example) evil is simply illusion. It is only the appearance of reality, and salvation is insight that reveals apparent evil for what it really is. For others (such as Zoroastrianism) evil is very real. It is the result of some suprahuman will that opposes the divine will. That opposition wreaks disaster and distress throughout the course of world history, but will finally be overcome at the conclusion of history. Even in those systems of human thought and action that are only quasi-religious, there is an effort to deal with the reality of evil. It is a part of the rhythm of nature (Confucianism), or it is entirely the result of human decisions (humanism).

Hence, the question of evil is no simple intellectual puzzle for idle speculators. It is a basic human problem encountered by every person sooner or later. Its difficulty is not simply an academic matter, but one that is rooted at the core of the human personality. It is, if you will, a *lived* problem. That is, it is one we experience directly and forcefully. The reality of evil rocks us and shakes the foundations of our confidence in the meaningfulness of existence. It touches all of our lives. One need not be a Christian to wrestle with the radically undesirable experiences of life and still go on affirming that life is worthwhile.

Early Christianity inherited a modified dualism from its parent body, Judaism. In the five centuries before the birth of Christianity, Judaism had developed an understanding of evil that was essentially a qualified dualism, which held that there was an opposing suprahuman force that thwarted the divine will. That opposition, however, was understood to be short-lived. Its days were numbered, for in a climactic event in which the long-awaited Messiah would appear, all opposition to the sovereign Lord of creation would be overcome. God would again reign supreme in the world. In the meantime, the force of evil was not only very real but prominent.

The early Christians apparently believed that in the events of the life of Jesus of Nazareth the powerful rule of Satan was decisively defeated. The second appearance of Christ from the heavens would bring the annihilation of all semblance of evil. Hence, these early Christians conceived of themselves as living in the interim period between the first appearance of Christ and the defeat of evil, on the one side, and his second appearance, which would actualize the elimination of all traces of evil, on the other. Their belief was then a limited dualism in the sense that the forces of evil were real, but were not ultimately as powerful as God, and would eventually cease to exist.

Theirs was also a dualism of time. History was divided into two basic periods—the present era still dominated by the power of Satan, and the age to come in which Satan and his force would be destroyed and God's reign actualized. We might like to think of this double dualism in the way shown in figure 2–1. The vertical dimension represents a cosmic dualism and the horizontal dimension a temporal (or historical) dualism. (The term "cosmic" is used here to mean that which is built into reality in any time or place.)

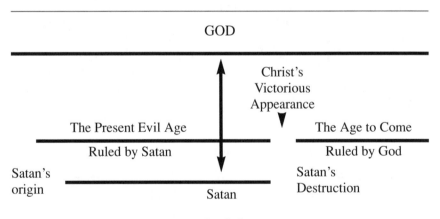

Fig. 2–1

Our Fourth Gospel characteristically does not accept this view in total. It presents a revision of the dualistic thought of the New Testament in general. It is among the most dualistic of the New Testament literature; yet, it is not a simple continuation of this early Christian view. We need to discuss the revisions of early Christian thought at the hand of the Fourth Evangelist under two general headings. In this chapter we will discuss Johannine dualism in general. In Chapter 4 we will return to this theme when we attempt to understand Johannine eschatology.

For now, we will have our work cut out for us as we try to grasp how the Fourth Evangelist uses dualistic symbols. Therefore, we will divide our discussion into three sections:

1. The dualistic symbols of the Fourth Gospel
2. The peculiar attitude of the Gospel toward "the Jews"
3. The question of determinism in the Gospel

THE DUALISTIC SYMBOLS OF THE FOURTH GOSPEL

Reader's Preparation: Skim through the Gospel again. This time try to find and list all the pairs of opposites that appear. Sometimes you may sense that a word or phrase is used to mean either the negative or positive side of a pair, but you may not find the explicit use of the opposite member. List these as well. An example of what you are looking for is the "light-darkness" opposites.

You should not have to read far into the Gospel before you are struck with the writer's use of dualistic symbols. The prologue presents us with the dualism of the light and the darkness; "The light shines in the darkness, and the darkness did not overcome it" (1:5). Of course, such pairs of opposites are not unusual in the New Testament or in the Hebrew Bible. What is unusual in our Gospel is their prominence. It would appear that the whole system of religious thought presented in the Fourth Gospel hangs within a dualistic framework that contains two anchoring points between which the writer has woven the thought of the Gospel. Figure 2–2 shows only a partial list of some of the most obvious pairs of opposite symbols employed by the Evangelist. Your list will likely include several that this abbreviated chart omits. Write in your additions.

POSITIVE POLE	EXAMPLE	NEGATIVE POLE
light	1:5	darkness
above	8:23	below
spirit	3:6	flesh
life (eternal)	3:36	death
truth	8:44f.	falsehood (lie)
heaven	3:31	earth
God	13:27	Satan
Israel	1:19 and 47	"The Jews" (sometimes)
	17:14	the world (sometimes)

Fig. 2–2

60

Let us now try to explore the meaning of this dualism. We will attempt to do so through the investigation of one of the very important Johannine symbols, "world" (*kosmos*). First, we will try to ascertain what the Evangelist means by this term and characterize its role in the dualistic system. Second, we will employ the meaning we find in the uses of world to make some general assertions about Johannine dualism. We choose this concept of the world because it is so crucial to the thought of the Gospel and because it exemplifies the complex use of symbols throughout the document.

Reader's Preparation: You should try to catch the flavor of the way in which the Fourth Evangelist uses the term, "world." The following are some of the passages you might read and ponder. Ask yourself, What does "world" mean in each of these cases? 1:10; 3:16; 8:12, 23; 9:32, 39; 11:9–10; 12:25, 31–33, 46; 13:1; 14:17, 31; 16:7–11; 18:36.

[handwritten margin note: this world, the world]

First, we must note that the Gospel's use of the term *kosmos* is not consistent. We have listed it above as one of the symbols used for the negative pole of the Johannine dualism. And that it is, *sometimes*. However, the reader of the Gospel must watch the context in which this word (and other key terms) is used, for it can have a variety of meanings.

In a number of passages this term is employed in a neutral or even positive and affirming sense. In these cases world means the creation itself—the physical reality of the earth. Some possible examples include 1:9; 3:16; 16:21; 17:24. These instances should help us better understand what is meant by the negative uses of the term. The writer of the Gospel does not have a gloomy view of the physical world itself. When the Gospel uses *kosmos* in a negative, dualistic sense, it does not refer to the physical world in which we live. Although the *kosmos* may be distorted into the realm of unbelief, this created earth is the object of God's love (3:16) and the realm in which the light enlightens persons (1:9). Some Christian interpretations in past years have seriously misunderstood the Gospel at this point. They have taken the Fourth Evangelist to be depreciating the physical world. Hence they understand that the Gospel calls on Christians to be only remotely in contact with the materiality of this earth (e.g., 17:18).

So, what does the writer mean when she or he uses this term in a negative way? The world, in these cases, seems to be a symbol representing the realm of unbelief, the area in which there is total rejection of the truth of God revealed in Christ. It is used in conjunction with judgment and with Satan in 9:39; 12:31; and 16:11. It symbolizes that way of being—that way of living—which is opposed to God and the divine plan of salvation for humans. It is a stance in life that finds relationship with God unnecessary and undesirable. It is what Bultmann has called "the perversion of creation." "The delusion that arises from the will to exist of and by one's self perverts the truth into a lie, perverts the creation into the 'world'" (*The Theology of the New Testament*, vol. 2, p. 29). Creation necessitates human dependence upon God. The world symbolizes the pretense that human existence can be independent of God. It is a way of living in which humans try to be something they are not, namely, independent beings, having no need of the One responsible for existence.

If this is a correct interpretation of the Johannine meaning, then it implies that creation is a correct, authentic way of being human. However, creation may be and, indeed, has been distorted. The result is an inauthentic, phony way of conceiving of oneself. In the negative and dualistic use of world, the Evangelist has in mind this distortion. The distinction is not basically a moral one between those who live "good lives" and those who live "bad lives." The distinction is between two ways of understanding oneself in relationship to the whole of reality—between two ways in which a person might answer the question, Who am I? When the world is tied to the negative pole of the Gospel's dualism, it refers to a misunderstanding of who we humans are. Then (and only then) is the world shrouded in darkness (8:12) and ruled by Satan (12:31).

We have yet to wrestle with the fully dualistic uses of the term. In 8:23 and 13:1 this world is set over against another realm. In both cases the point is that Jesus' home is not this world but another. "You are of this world, I am not of this world" (8:23). "Jesus knew that his hour had come to depart from this world and go to the Father" (13:1). Here the world is a sphere of being distinct from the sphere of the divine, and it would seem that this distinction is synonymous with several others in the Fourth Gospel: for instance, earth and heaven, below and above. The domain of the divine is other than this world; it is elsewhere. Jesus' home is in that other place, and he comes into the worldly sphere only temporarily. The distinction is between the world as the human-natural region over against the uncreated, divine realm. The first is dependent and created, while the second is independent and uncreated.

This use of the world as a sphere distinct from the heavenly realm along with the use of other polarities like above and below or heaven and earth suggests an important point. It would seem that the Fourth Evangelist embraced a cosmic dualism of two worlds. Much of the New Testament literature implies a kind of three-story universe: God and the angels in the highest level, Satan and the demons in the lowest, with human beings and nature stuck between the two. But nowhere else is the cosmic dualism so evident as in the Fourth Gospel. Some scholars have suggested that here the historical dualism of early Christian thought (the horizontal dimension of figure 2–1) has been entirely transposed into a cosmic dualism (the vertical dimension of figure 2–1). Part of the reason for saying this is the impression that many references to the historical eschatology are absent from John's Gospel. That is, allusions to the end of the present age and the commencement of the age to come (the eternal age) are conspicuously missing in the Fourth Gospel. In their place stands the radical cosmic dualism. If this is so, then the Fourth Evangelist has detemporalized the historical dualism of early Christianity and produced a cosmic dualism. (See Chapter 4 for further discussion of this possibility.)

We are still faced with some difficulties, however. Let us grant that there is some truth to the suggestion that the temporal dualism has been transposed into a cosmic one in the Fourth Gospel. (Remnants of the temporal division can be found in the Fourth Gospel, however.) What then is the relationship of this cosmic dualism to the dualism of human self-understanding that we mentioned earlier? We have the division of persons between those who live authentically as creatures of God and those who live inauthentically as if they were independent of God. Is that dualism different from the cosmic dualism of the world above and the world below that we have just encountered? Or, to pose the question differently, how literally did the Fourth Evangelist and the Johannine church embrace this cosmic dualism? Did they really believe in two different worlds?

There are two possibilities. One is that we have in the Fourth Gospel two kinds of dualism, both represented in the use of the word "world": a human dualism—two ways of self-understanding—and a cosmic dualism—two realms of being. In this case we would want to read the cosmic dualism rather literally. We might suggest that, for this way of understanding the Gospel of John, the cosmic dualism would be almost a kind of Platonic division of reality. The other possibility is that the cosmic dualism represents another way of stating the human dualism. That is, the two different worlds—the world of the human and the world of the divine—are picture language to say that persons may (and must) choose to understand themselves either as independent of God or as dependent creatures. In this case, the Fourth Evangelist would not mean that there are literally two different realms within this cosmos. Rather, those two realms are a poetic way of expressing the conviction that humans must choose either to live under the rule of God or try to escape that rule. The two-story cosmos of the Gospel of John would then be a metaphor for human life-styles.

Here we are up against a very difficult matter. It is difficult, because our choice between these two interpretations of the cosmic dualism calls for a basic understanding of how the Evangelist used symbols. We are wedded to a distinction between literal and poetic description. Modern science in all disciplines (history as well as biology, for instance) has helped us to try to keep separate the times when we want to describe objective and subjective reality. We talk about "facts," on the one hand, and the poetic and imaginative (subjective experience or understanding), on the other. We keep these separate. We do not want the biologist telling us how she or he *feels* about the little living creatures being studied; we want her or him to describe that form of life to us as exactly as possible. But when we read poetry or a novel we have no expectation that its assertions are "scientific."

Now this distinction is a modern one. It is one that our Evangelist did not know. The first-century Christians did not carefully divide historical description from the interpretation of the meaning of historical events. The writers of the New Testament could flow from fact to subjective meaning and back again without any break and without any concern to delineate the difference. Therefore, myth and objective truth are mixed in early Christian literature. Picture language and descriptive language are found within the same sentence.

All this means that our Evangelist might not have made the distinctions we are trying to make in the interpretation of the dualistic symbols of the Gospel. Do they describe the cosmos? Or, do they describe the way persons must decide how to understand themselves? The Johannine Christians probably did not think this way. If the cosmic dualism is really picture language about human self-understanding, the first readers of the Gospel probably did not consciously think of it this way. This is not to say that they or the Gospel are any less sophisticated than we, but only that they lived in a prescientific age and were not restricted by the distinctions forced upon us. We must not expect the Gospel to nuance the different kinds of language the way we do.

I am inclined to think that the Johannine human dualism is continuous with its cosmic dualism. The Gospel makes the point primarily that humans are faced with two inescapable possibilities, and that cosmic dualism enters into its language for two reasons. First, it reinforces the importance of the human dualism. I maintain again that the reference to the divine, other realm (as in Christology) is a signal of the existential importance the matter carried for the Evangelist and Johannine Christians in general. Second, the Gospel introduces the cosmic dualism to tie the bipolarity of life to Christology. Christ is from the realm of self-understanding that is divinely oriented. This world (*kosmos*) continues to represent the other, phony kind of human self-understanding. Having said that, I would not want to deny that the Johannine Christians believed in a kind of two-story cosmos. They very well might have. What I think they would say, however, is that belief in the structure of the cosmos is not the important thing. The vital issue is whether you will accept yourself as God's creature and all that that implies, or whether you will try to pretend that you can live independently from God as if your life were your own doing.

The Gospel of John, therefore, tells a story in which the historical, temporal realm is wedded to the cosmic, other, transhistorical, and transtemporal realm. The mystery of transcendence is mixed in with the worldly. The hero of the story is both a historic person and a being from the transcendent realm. The human response to him is both a historical event and an event that has transcendent value. It is not unlike the way a simple physical gesture (an embrace or a kiss) is both a historical and temporal event and at the same time an expression of the reality of love—a reality that transcends the single event. Consequently, one of the additional features of the Gospel of John and its story is that time is both historical and beyond history. So, for instance, the temporal sequence of crucifixion, resurrection, and ascension that we know so well from other Gospels (especially Luke) is blurred in the Fourth Gospel. Jesus speaks of his ascending (20:17), but the reader is never quite sure when that event occurs. Time is penetrated by and permeated with the divine realm, beyond time. The result is that temporal sequence is obscured. In much the same way, the human and the cosmic dualisms are meshed.

Reader's Preparation: Now read some passages where other pairs of opposites are used or implied and see what meaning they seem to have: 1:4–5; 3:1–21, 31–36; 8:21–26; 9:5; 13:27–30.

We now have the key to unlock the mysteries of other Johannine dualistic symbols. There is a negative pole that describes the state of misdirected and confused human life. That state is described variously as darkness, falsehood, flesh, death, Satan's realm, and the below. Even the Evangelist's use of "night" may suggest the darkness that characterizes erroneous human self-understanding (13:30; 3:2). The positive pole is symbolized as light, truth, spirit, life and eternal life, God's rule, and the above. Again we have a double dualism—a cosmic division of all reality into two realms, the created and the divine (especially 8:23), and a division between ways of being human, best expressed, perhaps, in the truth-falsehood dualism. The various symbols all mean the same thing. There is no essential difference between the dualism of light and darkness and the split of the above and the below. The positive pole of the split represents one point: God's revelation in Christ enables persons to become who they really are. "Truth" means the truth that saves humans from a misguided, contorted existence. God's love motivates the revelation of the true human identity. If a child for some reason thinks of her or himself as a dog, the concerned parents do all they can to correct the child's misunderstood and warped identity. God is doing nothing else in the effort to demonstrate to humans that they are creatures and dependent on their Creator for existence.

The Johannine dualism of two different worlds is then the Evangelist's understanding of the human need for salvation and the nature of that salvation. It is a way of saying that all the evil of the world is rooted in a misconstrued self-understanding. The darkness and falsehood of this world result because persons try to be other than what they are. That sounds amazingly simple, but it seems to be the Johannine view of the matter. Why is there evil? Because humans are confused as to their identity. How is evil overcome? By the correction of human misunderstanding. The two different worlds of John are two different identities!

We may summarize this view of Johannine dualism by means of a simple diagram (figure 2–3). The form of the diagram is intended to suggest that the Evangelist's human dualism flows into a cosmic dualism and that the latter is really in final analysis an expression of the former.

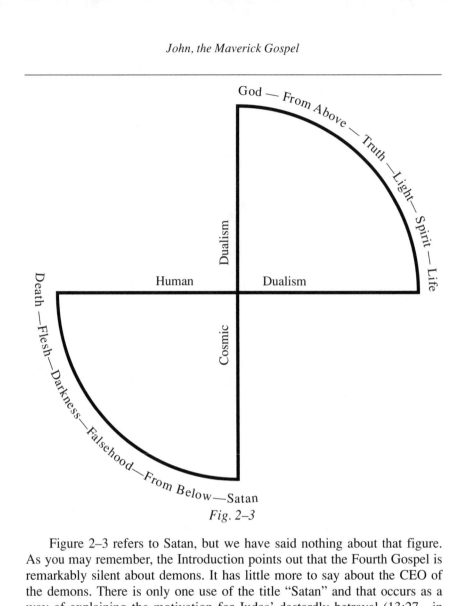

Fig. 2–3

Figure 2–3 refers to Satan, but we have said nothing about that figure. As you may remember, the Introduction points out that the Fourth Gospel is remarkably silent about demons. It has little more to say about the CEO of the demons. There is only one use of the title "Satan" and that occurs as a way of explaining the motivation for Judas' dastardly betrayal (13:27—in much the same way the Gospel of Luke does in 22:3). More common in the Gospel of John is the title "ruler of this world" (12:31; 14:30; 16:11). In keeping with the Johannine understanding of the world (*kosmos*) as the realm of evil and unbelief, the personification of evil is characterized as the one who exercises authority over the world. This evil figure is associated exclusively with the crucifixion of Jesus. The Gospel has little interest in the image of a cosmic figure who is responsible for evil, and in that lack of interest departs significantly from much other New Testament literature. The Gospel is more concerned with the way in which human existence is deformed by misunderstanding and seems almost intent on avoiding the temptation to abdicate responsibility for that deformity by thrusting culpability on to some cosmic embodiment of evil.

The dualism of the Fourth Gospel is complicated by two other matters that lie at the heart of this question of human self-understanding. One is its strange (and dangerous) use of the expression "the Jews." The other is the thorny question of whether or not persons are determined by God to hold one or the other self-understanding.

"THE JEWS" IN THE FOURTH GOSPEL

Reader's Preparation: Skim through the Gospel and mark all the uses of the expression "the Jews." Try to decide in which cases it is used in a neutral way to designate an ethnic group of people and where it is used in a pejorative manner. You might compare the way the term is used in chapters 11 and 12 with its use in chapter 8.

One of the strange facts about this Gospel is that, while the Synoptic Gospels each refer to the Jews five or six times, the Fourth Evangelist has over seventy such occurrences. Yet the common Synoptic distinctions among Scribes, Pharisees, and Sadducees are found less frequently in the Gospel of John. The manner in which the Fourth Gospel refers to the Jews has had some tragic consequences. It has been used again and again as a basis for a Christian anti-Semitism. No other Gospel appears to set the Jews so radically over against the Christians as their enemies. Hence, those in need of scapegoats for their hostility have seized upon the apparent anti-Jewishness of the Gospel and have used it as a rationale for a belief in divine wrath against the Jews. Christians concerned with wiping out all traces of anti-Semitism are embarrassed by the Fourth Gospel. The use of the term "the Jews" has not only had important social ramifications, but it is important for the general understanding of the religious thought of this Gospel. These are two important reasons for trying to get behind the Evangelist's use of this expression.

First, we must note again that John's use of the term is not consistent. I hope that in your reading you found that the term is ambiguous, that it seems to be used one way here and another there. Let us deal with the easy one first. Sometimes it is used simply to identify a group of persons—nationally, ethnically, and religiously. In 11:45, for instance, the term appears simply to identify a group from which some believers in Christ emerged. In 4:22 Jesus says (speaking as a Jew himself) that it is from the Jews that salvation comes. This is supplemented by the fact that the mighty figures of Judaism's past are recognized to be important forerunners of the revealer (5:46; 8:39). With this we have no problem. It represents the Jews as the preparation for the appearance of the Johannine Christ and suggests the continuity of early Christianity and Judaism.

Second, the knotty problem arises when we encounter the polemic-sounding uses of the expression. The Jews are most often the villains in the Gospel. They persecute Jesus (5:16); they misunderstand him (8:22); they attempt to stone him (8:59); they are responsible for his arrest and crucifixion (18:12; 19:12). Most characteristically, they are the ones who refuse to believe in him (10:31–39).

Raymond E. Brown presents a cogent argument for why we cannot read these polemical passages as referring in general to the Jewish people. First, the term "the Jews" often has nothing to do with religious, national, or ethnic considerations. The parents of the blind man in chapter 9 are afraid of "the Jews," but they themselves are surely Jews! Second, the expression is often used interchangeably with the religious leaders of the people (compare 18:3 with 18:12, and 8:13 with 8:22). Third, when we compare the Fourth Gospel with the Synoptics, "the Jews" perform those functions that in the Synoptics are assigned to the Sanhedrin (18:28–31, cf. Mark 15:1). It is Brown's contention then that "the Jews" is an expression used to designate only the religious authorities of Judaism who are opposed to Christ (see Brown, *The Gospel According to John*, Anchor Bible, vol. 29, p. lxxi).

I suggest a somewhat broader meaning for the expression in the Fourth Gospel. "The Jews" often refers to the religious authorities, to be sure, but the term also includes a wider class of opponents. The Jews are *stylized types* of those who reject Christ, and that usage illuminates this strange category. The specific ethnic characteristic is lost in the Fourth Gospel. The term no longer designates a religious body of persons, because the Fourth Evangelist has used it to make them simply a type, not specific persons.

Let me suggest an analogy. In the sundry adventure and mystery stories involving private investigators, the official police play a consistent role. They are always rather dull, slow, bogged down in red tape, and easily thrown off the scent. They are a foil with which the writer demonstrates the skill and brilliance of the private detective, the writer's hero. We can say that in these stories the police have become stylized types, who have no distinctive personalities. The author is interested in them for one reason, namely, as a contrast to the hero. Hence, there is in this literary and media genre a massive generalization.

The analogy helps us understand what the Fourth Evangelist has done with the Jews. There is no interest in them as a people. There are often no significant distinctions drawn among them (except occasionally when some seem to believe in Jesus). The interest in them is restricted to the role they play as *types of unbelief.*

It may help us to understand this strange characterization of the Jews if we propose two complementary reasons for their being cast as they are in the Fourth Gospel. The first reason is literary. The Jews are the literary foil over against the hero of the story, the divine revealer. Every story needs an antagonist against whom to portray the narrative's hero. In our Gospel the Jews function only to give the Evangelist a chance to say certain things about Christ. Hence, we must not conclude that she or he had an anti-Semitic motive in mind. We do not say that the author of the private detective story is an anti-establishment, anti-police revolutionary. Neither can we accuse our author of being anti-Semitic. The casting of characters is a strategy for telling the story.

But why have the Jews specifically been chosen for this unseemly role? Why has the author not used some group among the Jews, such as the Pharisees (as is the case in the Synoptic Gospels)? Our second reason, then, is a historical one. We must recall some suggestions made in the Introduction. Remember that the Evangelist is writing amid a ferocious dispute with the synagogue—one that may even have erupted into violence from time to time. The immediate problem for the Johannine community is the charges leveled against them by their former brothers and sisters in the synagogue. For this reason, the Fourth Evangelist selects the story's antagonist from the original readers' environment and portrays the Jews as a type of unbelief. It was the pressure of the concrete situation that caused this selection. We may even assume that the writer of the Gospel is of Jewish ancestry, or at least that a large number (even a majority) of those in the local Christian community were Jewish. Hence, the Gospel is not issuing a judgment on the Jewish people as a group. It implies, however, that the Jewish opponents of the church at that time and place are typical of the human failure to accept Christ. The Gospel represents that kind of rejection with the symbol of "the Jews," as unfortunate as that may be for future generations of readers of the Gospel. The casting of the Jews as the *symbol of unbelief*, we may conclude, was an accident of history, and a most tragic one at that!

Hence, we have the religious significance of the expression, "the Jews." The symbol is a part of the broader Johannine dualism. Those human beings who fail to see that in Christ there is a fulfillment of the heritage of the Hebrew Bible, those humans who cling to their pride in themselves, those humans who cannot accept that self-understanding presented in the revelation of God in Christ—these are the persons represented in the symbol "the Jews." They stand on the negative pole of the dualistic scheme as examples of unbelief. They are not an ethnic, geographical, national, or even religious group as much as a stereotype of rejection. *Any person who refuses to accept the human identity proposed by Christ in the Gospel is for the Evangelist a "Jew."* It may be that the positive pole of the dualistic pair in this case is "Israelite." The Israelite is the one who accepts the revelation (1:31).

But why is it that the Gospel is not consistent in its use of the term, "the Jews"? If it is a stylized type that is being used when reference is made to the Jews, how can we account for the passages cited early in this section in which the term is not used in that pejorative manner? The question may be unanswerable in the final analysis, but there are some possibilities. One is that the Evangelist was simply not as consistent a writer as we would like.

There are lapses in the stylistic use of the expression, due perhaps to the author's own carelessness. In these cases he or she uses the expression in its simple descriptive meaning.

A better (but complementary) explanation is that this inconsistency is a result of the Evangelist's use of traditional materials. The Johannine church had at its disposal stories and sayings that were nurtured in the community before the split from the synagogue. Back in the days when the Christians were still welcome participants in the synagogue, narratives and sayings were preserved and developed that used the word "Jews" in its ordinary and positive meaning (e.g., 4:22). Only when the Evangelist drew together the traditional materials and wrote the first draft of the Gospel did the stylistic symbol "the Jews" come into use. This was done after the Christians had been expelled from the synagogue and when the Jews and Christians were engaged in a lively dispute. As we have suggested above, the Evangelist's manner was to preserve traditional materials, perhaps often in their original form. The older narratives and sayings were not always revised to make them consistent with the general perspective of the Gospel, specifically its use of "the Jews." Rather, an older sense of the expression was left at some points in the Gospel and allowed to carry its original meaning; hence, the phrase was used inconsistently. From the modern point of view, our Evangelist's editorial work left something to be desired. But as a preserver of the tradition of the community, there was none better.

Let it be said, finally, that all of this does not ultimately defuse the dangerously anti-Semitic quality of the Gospel. We can understand the portrayal of the Jews from both literary and historical perspectives, but that does not alleviate the tone of the Gospel when it is read today. Christians concerned for the improvement of relationships with their Jewish sisters and brothers in faith must finally denounce the Gospel of John at this specific point. They must confess that this feature of the Gospel does not represent a normative and divinely inspired attitude. Our maverick Gospel has its weaknesses alongside its many strengths. (See further Robert Kysar, "Anti-Semitism in the Gospel of John" in *Faith and Polemic,* ed. Craig Evans and Donald Hagner.)

JOHANNINE DETERMINISM

Reader's Preparation: The following passages are among those in which something is said concerning the transition from unbelief to belief. Read them carefully and decide for yourself whether or not the Gospel teaches a determinism. Do these passages suggest that the Evangelist thought only those chosen by God could move from the inauthentic life to authentic existence? Make a list of those features you find in these passages which seem to stress a determinism and those which seem to suggest human freedom. 3:18, 21, 33–36; 5:24; 6:35–40, 44–47, 65; 8:47; 10:3–5, 14, 25–26; 11:25–26; 12:39–48; 17:2, 9, 12, 24; 18:37.

[handwritten marginal annotations:] D. D. D→H. - reciprocal - God calls

H. talk about "coming" to believe — drawn by the Father to come to God — we recognize His voice

D. no movement towards

How does one make the transition from the realm of darkness, the world, and the Jews, to the realm of truth, the light, the above? How does one move from an inauthentic existence, posited upon the assumption that persons are independent, to an authentic existence that acknowledges creaturehood and dependence upon God? Or, to pose the question in the context of this chapter, how is evil overcome? If it is rooted in false human identity, how can that identity be altered? What controls the transition between the two different worlds of John's thought?

These questions lead us into the concept of faith in the Fourth Gospel, and that issue must occupy us fully in Chapter 3. For now we must examine whether or not it is primarily God's predetermining that affects the destiny of persons or the free will of individuals. Is it free will alone that produces evil, or is it in part the work of God? Again, the Fourth Gospel does not give us a clear answer. There are passages that seem to favor human freedom and those that suggest the dominating will of God. Our task will be to lay out the evidence and then explore some possible conclusions.

In the Gospel there are frequent occurrences of what sounds like a determinism. Jesus in the Fourth Gospel is made often to speak as if the will of God has determined those who would respond to the divine revelation in Christ. God *gives* Christ those who are to believe (6:39; 17:2, 6, 9, 12, 24). This suggests that the first step in the movement from the negative to the positive side of Johannine dualism is the work of God. God gives over to Christ those who are chosen to believe. Jesus sometimes claims that one must be "drawn" by God in order to believe (6:44). Does God draw some but not others? According to 6:65, belief is not possible unless it is *granted*. Believing in Christ and appropriating true human identity are not simply the work of the individual will. They are the result of an act of God within an individual's life. Some people are children of God and others are not. Those who listen to the truth and embrace it are those who are "from God" (8:47). The same point is made in a metaphor: Some are sheep of the Good Shepherd and know his voice; others are not (10:3, 26). God even seems to make belief impossible for some persons (12:37–40). Certain people are made deaf to the truth and blind to the falsehood of their way of life (8:37).

This kind of language is set beside a clearly implied freedom to believe or not. We need not belabor this theme of the Gospel, for it seems obvious. In many passages believing appears to be up to the will of the individual. There are, for instance, cases of the use of "all," "everyone," or "whoever" in connection with belief, suggesting an invitation to believe (3:16, 20–21, 33, 36; 4:13; 6:45, 47, 67–69; 12:32; and possibly 3:8). Belief is commanded in some passages (12:36; 14:11). The comments of the narrator of the story, as well as certain sayings of Jesus, seem to suggest the freedom to believe or not (19:35; 20:31). The invitation to believe, the command to believe, and the testimony of others designed to evoke belief—all these imply that the individual is responsible for his or her own faith or unbelief. How can one *accept*, how can one *obey*, or how can one *put faith* in the revelation unless a person by nature has the capacity to choose freely? A teacher does not offer a class the choice between writing a research paper or a series of book reports if she or he has already decided that every female student shall be required to write a research paper and every male student a book report. The reality of human freedom seems clearly to underlie much of the Gospel.

Here is one of the most puzzling of the contradictions in this enigmatic Gospel. How shall we resolve it? Again, let us explore the possibilities.

First, it could be claimed that one set of passages must be read in the light of the other. Either the freedom passages are to be taken as the predominant teaching of the Gospel and only qualified by the deterministic ones, or the reverse. So, the point of the Gospel may be that *all* persons are selected by God for belief. All are given to the Son; all are drawn by God; all are granted the capacity for faith. It then becomes a matter of individual freedom whether one chooses to accept or reject the God-given capacity to believe. This is a popular and viable way of understanding the Gospel. The opposite approach assumes that the deterministic passages are the controlling motif of the Evangelist's mind. Only those who are selected by God are given the capacity for faith. Others are ruled out by divine decision. Although this position is less popular, it is supportable. The flavor of Johannine thought sometimes seems to suggest that all people are divided into two groups—some of whom have a heavenly origin and destiny and some of whom do not (e.g., the expression that some are not "from God" as in 8:47). Building on this suggestion, second-century Gnostic Christians used the Fourth Gospel to construct their view that only a select few have the gift to hear and respond to the revelation of truth.

Second, perhaps the Gospel deliberately presents a contradiction on this issue. Perhaps it intends to say that there is a paradoxical dimension to religious belief. While human choice seems to enter into the acceptance of the truth, the matter is not as simple as that. God has a hand in the origin of religious faith. One does not believe unless it is divinely granted her or him to do so. The Fourth Evangelist—if indeed this was his or her position—does not attempt to work out the relationship between these two facts. The author is not like a modern theologian who might attempt a logical exposition of how divine determination and human freedom are woven together to produce belief. Both kinds of assertions are left side by side in the Gospel with no explanation (much to the frustration of later interpreters like us). The Evangelist may be asserting that there is a mystery about the origin of faith. The reason why some persons are capable of believing and some are not is elusive.

Psychologists of religion probe this puzzle and offer their theories, but the mystery remains. Perhaps you have known a family in which several of the children have developed a genuine religious faith, following the example of their parents, but another child has refused to believe. He or she is the religious outsider of the family. Why? Maybe psychological and sociological—even physiological—data help to understand such a situation. But no explanation seems convincing or certain. The Fourth Evangelist may have known just such situations in the Johannine church. What the Gospel intends to say through its contradictory deterministic and decisional languages is that there is a mystery involved in the human capacity to believe. If this is indeed the explanation of the puzzling presence of these opposite motifs in the document, then we must credit the Evangelist with being sensitive to a peculiarly religious mystery and with being honest enough not to claim a pat answer to the question.

This ambiguity forces us to face a third possibility—an unpopular and unattractive one for most readers of the Gospel. It is that the document is the product of one who was simply not theologically astute enough to see the contradictions of the work. There was no awareness that the two sets of passages posed a logical problem, only a naive insensitivity to their implications. If this is the case, the author has produced something like the research paper in which the professor spots a glaring contradiction that had entirely evaded the beginning student. Between this option for understanding the Gospel and possibility number two, we are back to the fork in the road: The Fourth Evangelist was either a very profound theologian or else a very naive one!

Finally, we invoke one of our favorite themes in this volume: The suggestion that the Gospel records, side by side, both the author's own convictions and those of the tradition of the Johannine community. Once again the author's views and the traditional materials have not been reconciled. The traditions have been honored for their point of view, but so too have the views of the Evangelist who preserved them. Now there is a danger that this kind of distinction between the tradition and the Evangelist's own thought could become an easy solution to every contradiction we find in the Gospel. We must beware of using it at every turn of the road. Yet if the orientation of our survey of Johannine thought is correct, such an answer remains a possibility. I want to leave it at that—just a possibility. I do this because I am not prepared to argue at length that one of the sets of passages we have found is the result of traditional material and that another is the Evangelist's point of view.

I will, however, pose a question for your consideration. Could it be that the traditional material the Evangelist used originated in a day when the Christians were very optimistic about converting persons to their faith? If so, might not that material have stressed the point that all one must do is decide for the faith? By the time the Evangelist wrote, the missionary work of the church had come upon hard days. There were fewer and fewer who were willing to accept the teachings of the church. Especially among the Jews—where the missionary efforts of the Christians had flourished when the traditional material originated—there were drastically fewer converts. So, the Johannine Christians have grown a bit hesitant. Their experience has led them to think that it took more than an act of will for a person to believe; it took a particular divine gift, God's "drawing" of the person to Christ. Our Evangelist is not so bold as to attempt an explanation of the relationship of that divine drawing to human freedom. She or he is simply asserting that there seems to be more involved than our fathers and mothers thought back in the "good old days" of the rapid expansion of the church. It is not as simple as, "Believe if you will!" There is a sense in which some will never believe, and God must have something to do with that fact.

If this latter option is indeed the case (and we see that it has affinities with elements of some of the other alternatives), the Evangelist is quite understandable. We can imagine that this kind of change in the church's situation could have come about. Furthermore, it is easy for us to understand how the Christians of the Johannine community could have responded to it the way they did. Back in the 1960s amid the protests against the war in Vietnam, a similar thing happened in America among the antiwar protesters. There was at first a feeling that any sane person, if he or she gave it a moment's thought, would see the senselessness and immorality of the war. Then as the years wore on and the leaders of the protest movement became more seasoned, they lost their optimism. They realized that there was far more at stake for many people in their decision on the war. Economic factors, psychological characteristics, and social affiliations affected the decision whether one would support or oppose the military involvement of the United States in Vietnam. They grew less optimistic about the number of converts their cause would win, but at the same time they grew more realistic and more astute in their analysis of human beings. Such may have been the case in the Johannine community. They too became less optimistic about the freedom of persons to believe the revelation they had found in Christ, but they also became more profound in their understanding of the psychology of religious belief. And, of course, their only explanation was to speak of the hesitancy to believe in terms of God's actions among persons.

Whatever the origin of the Gospel's teaching, it leaves us with a paradoxical view of the genesis of faith. On the one hand, it insists that no one can take credit for belief. One cannot boast, "I have decided to have faith," for faith is always at least in large part a gift from God. On the other hand, the Gospel persists in holding humans responsible for *unbelief*. One cannot boast of one's faith, but neither can one excuse one's lack of faith. We are left to ponder the paradox!

CONCLUSION

It may appear that we have strayed afield from our original concern for the explanation of evil and from Johannine dualism. But not so. We have moved from the initial question of the cause of evil to its Johannine resolution in a human dualism and then on to the question of freedom versus determinism. But such a range of issues is necessary in order to trace the outline of the thought of the Fourth Gospel. From the community's insistence on two different worlds of human self-understanding, they must have been led, as we have been, to the question of how one is brought to abandon the way of life that produces evil and take up its opposite. They could not long embrace their dualism without asking whether or not it was bridgeable. And if it is possible to move from the negative to the positive pole, how? By human decision alone or by God's powerful persuasion?

I have argued that for the Fourth Evangelist evil has its roots in humans. More specifically it is rooted in a particular aspect of human life, namely, identity. When persons conceive of themselves as beings who are not dependent upon a creator for their existence, the whole character of existence is thrown out of balance. Because of such a misconstruing of self, the whole of creation is distorted, with the result that evil is rampant. Hence, there are two ways of existence open to persons—the way of evil with its pretense of independence, or the way of truth with its acknowledgment of dependence upon God. These are poles apart and constitute two entirely different worlds. Those two worlds are described in the Gospel in terms of both a human dualism and a cosmic dualism, but the latter is probably simply a way of asserting the enormous importance of the former. The Fourth Evangelist utilizes a wide spectrum of symbols to describe these two worlds. Moreover, he or she proposes that the transition from one world to the other is not a simple process dependent entirely upon human choice.

An observation of a sociological nature is appropriate here. The dualistic response to the reality of evil taught by the Fourth Gospel has roots in the social situation of the Johannine community. The church has undergone social dislocation. These Christians have been expelled from their original home in the synagogue alongside their Jewish colleagues, resulting in a kind of social trauma. Their roots are torn up. They are tossed out into the world, stripped of their social alignment with the Jews. Suddenly they have no home and no identity. Suddenly they are aliens in the city in which they had become accustomed to living as members of the synagogue. They experience a trauma similar to that known to the modern-day refugees who come to America to escape unbearable conditions in their former land. Their whole social orientation is disrupted. The result in the Johannine community is perhaps a natural tendency to draw into themselves. They nurture their own community and group identity. They develop, as it were, an in-group that looks upon others with suspicion as an out-group. They do this both as an effort to reconstruct a social identity—to make a new home for themselves in their city—and to defend themselves against the onslaught of their opponents. Attacked from without, a group always tends to draw in and solidify its unity and to find its identity there. (See the provocative article by Wayne Meeks, "The Man from Heaven in Johannine Sectarianism," in *The Interpretation of John*, ed. John Ashton, pp. 141–173.)

One of the results of this social reorientation is that a dualistic view of the world developed. The split between the "us" and "them" is natural. Along with it comes a tendency to think of themselves as those born from above, as the truth, as the light in a dark world, and in similar ways. Likewise, they think of others who oppose them and their religious faith as born from below, as the world, as darkness, as "the Jews." Dualistic thought satisfies both a theological necessity and a sociological one. Those who are not among us are not only confused about life, they are blind to the truth. They will not believe as we do partly because they have not experienced the divine drawing with which we have been gifted.

Now there is an immediate tendency to judge such a course of thought as self-righteous. Nothing is more maddening than a group of persons who believe that they have the truth, and that those outside the group are hopelessly lost. However, with a bit of empathy we can understand why the Johannine community thinks the way it does. We can imagine that we ourselves might do the same thing if we were in their shoes. Threatened by opponents, socially disrupted, and still in the process of maturing theologically, they understandably find a dualistic distinction between "us" and "them" appealing. The Fourth Gospel offers the community a way of understanding what is happening to them. Its symbols offer solace and reorientation. Its teaching provides the framework for a new and clearer identity. Its view of evil strengthens the Christians by offering them a way of interpreting their situation. What more does religious belief ever do?

A final point with regard to this sociological discussion of the thought of the Fourth Evangelist: Theology (or religious thought) is never purely a mental exercise. It is always rooted in the social situation of the believers. We are social animals. When our social situation shifts radically, we usually shift our religious perspective accordingly. The Fourth Evangelist and the Johannine community are no exception to this rule. The dualism of the Gospel is a result of theological minds coming to grips with a social as well as a religious crisis.

The explanation for the reality of evil accepted by the Fourth Evangelist may or may not be adequate. It may strike you as eminently useful in dealing with the undesirable aspects of life, or it may appear to you as an interesting thesis of a former age that is no longer relevant. It should be obvious to all, however, that our Evangelist has taken on a mighty issue and that the thesis concerning evil is only a part of the author's larger understanding of the meaning of Christ. It is helpful to remember that however he or she deals with that issue, it may represent for us the context of life's tragedy and perplexity in which we hear the Bible's witness to Christ. The two different worlds of the Gospel of John are a gallant effort to understand an age-old problem that continues to trouble us.

What we have found is that the Johannine dualism trails off into another subject equally important—the nature and origin of religious faith. It is to that subject we must turn. This is properly so, because the religious response to the reality of evil always hinges upon the matter of faith. Whatever a religion teaches with regard to how one deals with evil, it always counsels that its teaching depends upon a faith perspective. You are asked to believe that evil is an illusion, or to believe that it is rooted in a cosmic being opposed to God, or to believe that it is simply the rhythm of nature. But always you are asked to *believe*. How does one believe? What originates faith? And what after all is meant by faith?

3. SEEING IS BELIEVING—
JOHANNINE CONCEPTS OF FAITH

That old slogan "Seeing is believing" contains a realistic idea: Our belief in anything must have some basis in experience. We ordinarily believe on the basis of the kind of experience that gives reason and motivation for the belief. If someone asserts a point of view that seems to be questionable, we naturally ask for some reason to believe that it is true rather than false.

It sometimes seems that those assertions susceptible to scientific inquiry are most easily tested. When individuals in the sciences claim their ideas are true, they will offer us the results of experiments that supposedly demonstrate that the claim is accurate. Similarly, in dealing with everyday needs, we often want some sensory experience before we believe: "The chair will hold you up. Watch me. I'll sit on it." Our experience either enables us to believe or prohibits belief. I watch the television commercial claiming excellent miles per gallon performance by some new automobile, but the new automobile I just bought does not produce such performance. My own experience makes it impossible for me to accept the claims made by the commercial.

Likewise, religious affirmations require a basis in experience. Religions traditionally make their appeals for belief with the claim that experience offers supportive evidence of one kind or another. This experience is, of course, regarded as much different from that which is usually observed or measured in scientific procedures. Religion claims that internal, subjective kinds of experience lend validity to its ideas and insights. You have heard the testimonies of religious proponents. Peace of mind, satisfaction, serenity, and enrichment are often claimed as the bases for faith. The Zen Buddhist speaks of the great peace and the penetrating insight into experience that result from enlightenment (*satori*). The Christian Scientists testify to a joyful serenity and the release from physical as well as mental pain as a result of their adherence to the teachings of Mary Baker Eddy. Confucians make their case on the basis of the way in which the totality of life makes supreme sense as a result of the practice of their ethic. More primitive forms of religion spoke of the successful experiences in farming, the absence of storms, and the blessed presence of children in their families as evidence that the religious ceremonies were effective. In previous centuries the Calvinists, it is sometimes said, claimed that the truth of their doctrines could be confirmed by the fact that the so-called elect were prosperous and wealthy. What more persuasive experience need one have to embrace the faith? Recently claims of Christianity, in some circles, have been given supposed validation in the experience of success. We hear how Christianity brings peace of mind and success in business, social, and family relationships.

Conversions are often the result of deeply emotional experiences of some sort. John Wesley, the eighteenth-century originator of the Methodist denomination, spoke of the experience of having his heart "strangely warmed." Today we hear claims made for the experiential "proof" of prayer and faith healing. Even the most sophisticated and intellectual advocates for certain forms of Christianity sometimes say that their adherents' faith is based on experience. As a result of their beliefs, they claim, their lives are richer and more meaningful, and their relationships deeper.

In general, then, religions assert that there is a positive relationship between faith and experience. Believing originates from an experience or a search for an experience. And continuing belief is founded on the actual experience of living life from a certain faith perspective. Hermann Hesse's famous and intriguing novel, *Siddhartha*, is the story of one man's search for a faith that was supported by his actual experience. While a religion cannot usually make any claim that its position is proven or scientifically verified, it can nonetheless suggest that experience points in the direction of the validity of its claims.

The relationship of faith and experience in religion, however, is often rather intricate. Frequently it is observed that a degree of faith is required *before* we find in our experience the elements that are supportive of belief. In other words, faith is made credible by experience, but before we can understand our experience in a way that supports faith, we must have faith. One might say that the very nature of faith is a willingness to trust some claim to truth in expectation that experience will verify that truth. To put it this way, persons must have enough faith to pray at least once before they have the experience that assures them that their faith is well-founded. We might say, then, that there is in religion often a pre-experiential faith and an experiential faith—one that precedes the supportive experience and one that results from the experience. The relationship of faith and experience in any religion—especially Christianity— is a subtle one.

That subtlety is not lost in the New Testament. Everywhere in its pages we find the exploration of the relationship of faith and experience. Paul's letters reflect his personal experiences and their relationship to his growing faith. But nowhere else in the New Testament do we find, I think, the careful and complex treatment of faith and experience that is contained in the Fourth Gospel. This document seems especially concerned with the question of how one is able to affirm Christ without experience and what kind of experience is appropriate to the faithful acceptance of the revelation. In Chapter 2 we saw that the Evangelist undertook the complexity of the relationship of free choice and divine activity in the origin of faith. That boldness in attacking formidable questions continues in the Fourth Gospel as we witness the Evangelist engage the issue of faith and experience. The task is made difficult by a situation shared with most of the other New Testament writers. The first generation of Christians apparently had some immediate or very close experience of Jesus of Nazareth. The earliest Christians are convinced by the experience represented in the Gospels as the resurrection appearances of Christ. Well and good. But what of later generations? What experience leads them to faith? Is it the case that the first generation of Christians stand in a privileged position and none of their descendants had hope of such an experientially based faith? Are Christians after that first group doomed to a secondhand experience upon which to build their faith? In the context of these questions the Evangelist approaches this theme. Writing probably some fifty years after the conclusion of the earthly ministry of Jesus, the author of John must try to understand how experience and faith are related.

Our discussion will deal with a number of interrelated themes:

1. The "signs" as provocators of faith
2. Seeing and hearing as faith perception
3. Knowing and believing
4. A summary view of faith in the Fourth Gospel

THE "SIGNS" AS PROVOCATORS OF FAITH IN THE FOURTH GOSPEL

Reader's Preparation: Study the passages listed below and try to answer two questions: (1) What does the Fourth Gospel mean by the word "sign"? (2) What is the role of the signs in initiating and nurturing faith in Christ? 2:1–11, 18–25; 4:46–54; 5:1–9; 6:1–28; 9:1–12; 11:1–46; 12:37–41; 20:30–31; 21:1–14. Also read the narrative concerning Thomas in 20:24–29.

"Sign" (*sēmeion*) is the term the Fourth Gospel uses to designate Jesus' wondrous deeds (see the Introduction). For one acquainted with the Synoptic Gospels, it is a startling use of the term. When those Gospels employ the term in relationship to Jesus' marvelous acts, it is most often given a negative connotation. Jesus is asked to perform a sign to convince doubters of his identity, and he reprimands them for the request (Matthew 16:1–4; Mark 8:11–13; 12:38–42; Luke 11:16–17, 29–32). The interest in seeing a sign as a basis for faith is condemned as an expression of distrust and suspicion. Strange, then, that our Gospel uses it in a positive way. The Acts of the Apostles, however, does provide a New Testament parallel to the Johannine use of the word. Acts reports that Peter spoke of Jesus' "deeds of power, wonders, and signs" (Acts 2:22) and that the apostles did "great wonders and signs" that provoked the awe of others (6:8). Sign in the Gospel of John, however, has a more specific sense. We might tentatively define the Johannine meaning of sign as *an act of Jesus that provides the witness an opportunity for insight into Jesus' true identity.* Actually, that definition is an oversimplification of the meaning of the word in this Gospel and its relationship to faith.

What the Fourth Gospel calls the signs performed by Jesus seem to have an ambiguous role in relation to believing in the revelation offered by the

Christ. As we find in our explorations of nearly every theme, this Gospel does not give an easy answer. It is no different in the case of the relation of the experience of signs and faith in Christ.

The signs are works of God, wonders, or expressions of the power of God that produce faith. This is true of each of the seven or eight major signs performed by Christ in the Gospel:

1. Changing the water into wine (2:1–11)
2. Healing the nobleman's son (4:46–54)
3. Healing the man who had been crippled for thirty-eight years (5:1–9)
4. Feeding the multitude (6:1–14)
5. Walking on the water and the miraculous landing (6:15–25)
6. Healing of the man born blind (9:1–8)
7. Raising of Lazarus (11:1–46)
8. Catching a miraculous number of fish (21:1–14)

These incidents are told in such a way as to suggest that they lead to faith. Of the transformation of water into wine it is said, "Jesus did this, the first of his signs, in Cana of Galilee, and revealed his glory; and his disciples believed in him" (2:11). The signs produce a widespread faith in Christ, we are told in 2:23. Moreover, the Evangelist confesses in 20:30–31 that he has reported a few of the many signs Jesus performed in order to provoke faith on the part of the reader.

The implication is that these signs are offered as evidence that Jesus really is the Messiah (e.g., 2:18). They are his credentials, as it were, and legitimate his claims to that office. Much as one who holds a Ph.D. is expected to legitimate her or his status with learned discussions, so the Messiah is expected to show his identity by performing wonderful deeds. That was, of course, a common Jewish expectation during the first century.

However, the Evangelist seems to draw a line between believing in Jesus for the sake of his wondrous acts and "seeing signs." What do you make of 6:26? After the feeding of the multitude Jesus again encounters the crowd and says to them, "You are looking for me, *not because you saw signs*, but because you ate your fill of the loaves" (emphasis added). It appears that what the Evangelist means here is that attraction to Jesus in the hope of getting something to eat or of profiting physically or materially in other ways is not the same as following him as a result of seeing the signs he has done. To follow Jesus simply for the sake of his gifts or benefits is not enough. (This would be like following a millionaire and waiting for him to give away five-dollar bills.) To do so is not an indication that one really perceives the identity of Christ given expression in the sign. To "see the sign" involves something more than benefiting from this person who can supply your needs.

What then is meant by "seeing signs"? This question gets us ahead of our story. But for now it seems that seeing the wonderful act of Jesus is more than a visual perception of what Jesus does or the experience of benefiting from those acts. It is an insight into the identity of the performer of the sign, grasping that this person is more than a wonder-worker. He is the Christ, the heavenly revealer, the Father's unique Son. Hence, the Evangelist has proposed two levels of experiencing the signs of Jesus—a perception of Jesus as a filler of human physical needs and a perception of Jesus as the divine revealer.

In all these cases, the signs are treated in the Fourth Gospel in a very positive way. Even in the last instance cited, in which there is reservation about following Jesus merely for the sake of the benefits of his wondrous works, the signs are still regarded as a positive means of provoking faith in people. Elsewhere the Fourth Gospel has much more serious reservations about the effectiveness of signs in producing genuine faith. It presents them in a positive way in what we have just surveyed, but in a negative way in other passages. First, the Gospel recognizes that the signs do not always produce faith; they seem powerless to arouse faith in some who experience them (12:37).

This is not a major reservation. But the Gospel goes on. It pictures Jesus speaking in such a way as to cast doubt on all faith grounded in the experience of the signs. Read once again the healing of the son of the officer in the royal service (4:46–53). Jesus did the healing but only after complaining about belief based on signs and wonderful acts. Is verse 48 of this story a mild rebuke of an excessive dependence upon signs as the basis of faith? Or is it a repudiation of all signs-based faith? Is Jesus saying that faith founded upon wondrous acts has no value at all? Or (a third alternative) are we to infer from these words that faith based upon signs is inferior to a faith that does not require signs? This is a key verse in our examination of the relationship of faith and experience as it pertains to the signs. Much of what can be said on this subject will depend on our understanding of the words in verse 48.

There are a number of views that can and have been taken. The first is that the faith founded on signs is a legitimate, mature faith, so long as it is not self-seeking (as mentioned in 6:26). Verse 4:48 is nothing more than a test of the faith of the nobleman. The officer expressed his continuing confidence in Jesus in verse 49. This is similar to the story of the healing of the daughter of the Canaanite woman in Matthew 15:21–28. There Jesus rebukes the woman in response to her request for healing. Her reply to Jesus suggests such profound faith that he immediately effects the healing. The rebuke is not a depreciation of the request for a wondrous deed, but a probing of the degree of faith with which it is made.

The other alternatives are of a different kind. They suggest that this first option does not take account of the fact that a more serious reservation about the role of signs is hinted at in the Gospel. The following three ways of reading the Gospel all propose that the Fourth Evangelist wanted to revise an improper view of the signs.

82

1. Some say that the Fourth Evangelist wanted to repudiate signs-faith altogether. The signs source that the Evangelist may have used in the composition of the Gospel (see the Introduction), it is proposed, contained a very simple theology of the relationship of signs and faith. According to this source, signs were wondrous acts that provoke a genuine and adequate faith. The Evangelist uses this source, but tries to correct it along the way. Such signs-faith is not faith at all, the Gospel claims. It is self-seeking satisfaction. Hence, 6:26 is the Evangelist's comment on that pseudo faith built on signs, and 4:48 is a full repudiation of such sign-seeking. If this is so, we again have a situation in which the Evangelist utilized the community's tradition (in this case the so-called signs source) but tried to correct it. The Evangelist's point of view would seem to be implied in 20:29, where the text commends the kind of faith that blossoms without dependence on the experience of signs.

2. The position just reviewed is a bit radical. It tries to make too much out of too little in the Gospel. But it does come closer to the truth than the view that sees no reservation in the Gospel about signs-faith. A more moderate position is that the Evangelist recognizes a faith built upon signs as the first level of faith—the initial stage of faith. But the author wants to suggest that such a beginning faith must grow into something more. Faith may begin with a dependence upon signs, but it must grow out of that dependence until it matches the faith mentioned in 20:29. This view holds also that the Fourth Evangelist utilizes a source that holds a more simplistic view of faith. The signs-faith in the source is not repudiated, only qualified. In effect, it is all right to build one's faith upon the experience of wondrous works in the beginning. But faith needs to overcome the need for such experiences. It is like the training wheels parents put on their child's first bicycle. It is all right for the child to depend upon those extra little wheels to hold up the bike for a time, but eventually the child must abandon the helper wheels and learn to balance the bike without dependence upon them. Otherwise, as an adult he or she will be out buying training wheels for a brand new ten-speed! Let faith depend on the wondrous works of Jesus for a time! But let it be nurtured until finally those wondrous works are no longer a requirement for Christian belief.

3. The third position is only slightly different. The Fourth Evangelist does not regard the believing response to the signs as faith, only a preparation for faith. Those who respond affirmatively to the signs of Jesus do not yet believe, but they have an openness to faith that is commendable. Perceiving the wondrous works of Christ, they are ready truly to "see"—that is, to perceive just who this person is and to accept his claims. The reservations about signs-faith in the Fourth Gospel are again the Evangelist's revisions of the signs source. Those reservations are simple: Signs-faith is not faith, rather it is a valuable first step in the process toward faith. Riding a bicycle with training wheels is not "biking," but it is a necessary step for some toward learning that skill.

The Fourth Gospel is trying to say a number of things about signs and their role in provoking faith. First, it is important to note that the Gospel recognizes the ambiguity of the signs. Wondrous works are no surefire way of producing faith. There is no certain, experiential foundation for faith in Christ, the Gospel tells us. No matter what roots religious faith has in experience, that experience is never proof of faith. This is so because, as the Evangelist apparently knew, experience is always ambiguous. It is always susceptible to numerous interpretations. What one person calls a profoundly religious experience of God, another understands to be the result of certain psychological preconditioning. Our Evangelist is no philosopher of religion, but he or she saw this clearly enough. The most marvelous acts of Jesus are not certainty for faith. They can be understood as acts of one other than the revealer. So the Fourth Gospel repeats the Synoptic testimony that some respond to Jesus and his deeds by asserting not that he was the Christ, but that he was possessed by a demon (8:48). The signs of Jesus simply open up the possibilities—either Jesus is one empowered by God in a special way, or else he gains his power from other sources, most likely demonic. In this way, the Fourth Evangelist continues a biblical view of wondrous deeds, namely, that in themselves they are not absolute proof, but always ambiguous.

Second, in order for signs to contribute in a positive way to the birth and growth of religious faith, they must be perceived in a certain way. They must be seen from a perspective that is open to the possibility of God's active involvement in human history. Hence, in order for signs to provoke faith they must be experienced from a perspective that already presupposes faith—at least to a minimal degree. "Seeing signs" then, in the profound sense, is experiencing the acts of Jesus and understanding them correctly. It is seeing through them, as it were, to the true identity of the actor. Insofar as we may call an openness to the possibility of God's reality and activity "faith," the signs *require* faith as well as *provoke* faith. There is an analogy close at hand in the appreciation of art. The viewing of art nurtures one's appreciation of it. Admiring a good painting provokes a new appreciation for artistic expression. But in order to "view" a painting one must already have some subjective standards. Unless the viewer holds some conviction about what constitutes beauty, a Picasso is wasted. That precondition need not be sophisticated or mature. It might only be an inclination, a vague sense that this painting is more pleasant to look at than another, and so on. But there must be some foundational sense of beauty. So, too, the Evangelist seems to be saying that there is a precondition for experiencing a sign in such a way that it provokes faith. Whether we call this faith or only the first ingredient for faith is irrelevant. What is important is that we see what the Evangelist is asserting. Seeing signs before faith is impossible. It is like expecting blossoms from the seed before it is even planted.

Our rough little metaphor about the seed moves us to the third point. Seeing signs in this "faith way" begins a process of believing that evolves until the signs themselves are less and less important and the faith perspec-

84

tive all-important. Just below the surface of the evidence in the Gospel we have surveyed, I think we can ascertain a profound concept of dynamic faith. The experience of grasping the acts of Jesus in a "signful" way requires a kind of embryonic faith. In the Gospel not all who witness Jesus' acts see them as signs (12:37). That embryonic faith is nourished by the experience of the signs. The Evangelist affirms the wondrous acts of Jesus as positive experiences for faith (2:23). But that faith does not finally blossom until it no longer needs continual exposure to signs. It becomes a faith that believes without seeing (20:29). I hesitate to oversimplify a complicated process that the Evangelist is trying to show us. Nevertheless, I venture a diagram (see figure 3–1).

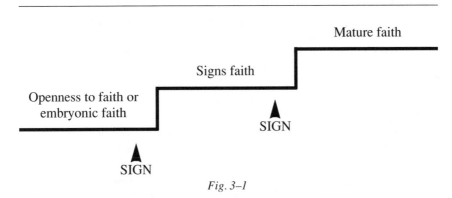

Fig. 3–1

I propose that the Fourth Gospel does not depreciate any of these stages in the maturation of faith, but urges faith to grow beyond its first two stages. Like the developmental psychologist, the Evangelist appreciates each stage in maturation but abhors a fixation at any preliminary stage.

It appears to me likely that the Evangelist uses a signs source that may not understand either the first or third stages of faith. It does not fully appreciate the reasons why some persons do not respond as they should to the wondrous acts of Jesus, nor does it adequately describe how faith must mature beyond its dependence upon signs. The signs source is doubtless a very old collection of narratives having to do with the marvelous works of Jesus, the divine man. The Fourth Evangelist wants to build on that understanding. He or she does so by stressing the ambiguity of the signs and by offering a view of mature faith that needs no signs. The Evangelist does this revision of the signs source because the current generation of Christians have come to know just how unconvincing the recitation of the wondrous works of Jesus can be. Such a recitation is no longer provoking faith as it perhaps once had. Moreover, the glorious deeds among the Christians themselves are not as numerous as once seemed to be the case. Thus, the Fourth Gospel stresses that its generation of believers ought not to have to depend on signs in their midst or on the recitation of signs. They ought to be able to believe without seeing.

One scholar, Robert T. Fortna, proposes that the Evangelist made still another revision in the signs source (see *The Gospel of Signs*). Fortna discerns two levels in the major signs narratives. On one level, it is the physical needs of persons that Jesus fills, such as health or food. On the other level, the physical needs appear as sort of symbols of deeper, spiritual needs. So, while Jesus heals the blind man, the overcoming of blindness is more than a physical healing. In the context of Johannine symbolism, blindness suggests darkness, and the healing of blindness, light. Hence, the physical results of the signs are symbols of the deeper spiritual benefits which Christ offers to believers. Fortna is convinced that the signs source that the Evangelist uses emphasizes that Jesus fulfills these basic physical needs. The Evangelist repeats the narratives from the source but wants readers to appreciate the symbolic meaning they have. So the distinction between following Jesus for the sake of material benefits and seeing his signs (6:26) is the Evangelist's signal that these acts of Jesus have important spiritual meaning. Such a proposal makes a great deal of sense and fits neatly into the way in which the Evangelist seems to have thought. The Johannine community is less interested in the sheer material benefits Jesus may have provided his followers than in more spiritual benefits.

Here is a profound understanding of religious faith and its growth. Faith has no ground of absolute certainty. Even the experience of witnessing the historical Jesus offers no sure proof of faith. Faith is the capacity to view experience from a peculiar perspective. It is to be open to God's revelation in history, even though our experience is always ambiguous. Moreover, faith is a continuous process of reassessment and growth. But we cannot stop here. The Gospel has much more to say on this subject.

SEEING, HEARING, AND BELIEVING IN THE FOURTH GOSPEL

The understanding of faith which we have unearthed in the Gospel in the last section is borne out and further expanded by the Evangelist's use of three other terms: seeing, hearing, and knowing. We will examine the first two in this section and leave the last for the next section.

Reader's Preparation: Take a look at the ways in which the words meaning "to see" are used throughout the Gospel. Try to discern some pattern in the Evangelist's use of these words: 1:14, 50–51; 3:11, 32; 5:19; 6:40; 9:39; 14:7, 9; 17:24; 19:35–37; 20:8, 25, 29.

The Greek words for seeing are used in the Fourth Gospel interchangeably for a sensory perception and a faith perception. Examples of the difference between these two are 1:47 and 14:8. In the first it is stated simply that "Jesus saw Nathanael." Here the verb means the sensual act of perceiving through the eyes. But in 14:8 Philip asks that Jesus show the disciples the Father. Jesus replies, "Whoever has seen me has seen the Father" (v. 9). Here the seeing is obviously something more than the mere act of sensory perception. To see the Father in seeing Jesus surely means some sort of spiritual or faith perception. It is to discern in the person of Jesus the nature of the Ultimate Reality. Such a discernment goes beyond the physical sensations of perception. It may be something like that act by which the browser in the art gallery *sees* the Picasso painting but also sees something more. She sees beauty, form, life given expression. Maybe the distinction between physical perception and appreciative discernment in the art gallery is parallel to the distinction that the Evangelist seems to make between physical sight and faith vision.

The Gospel of John has a profound understanding of the relationship between these two types of perception. This is evident from the manner in which the two types of seeing are connected and even interdependent. Good examples of this interconnection are 6:40; 11:45; and perhaps 12:45. In each of these passages, the act of believing follows closely on the act of perception. Sight seems to be an integral part of the process of faith. More specifically, the point is that faith-seeing is based upon the experience of sensory seeing. Perceiving the truth available to the human is a result of perceiving the sheer material, physical object—in this case, the man Jesus. Hence, faith is rooted in sensory experience, but goes beyond the sensory experience to affirm more than the sheer observable data itself will substantiate.

Faith does not blossom out of the inner self entirely. Here the Fourth Evangelist affirms a basic aspect of the Judeo-Christian tradition. Religious faith is not a result of pure meditation in which one withdraws from the sensory contact with the world into contact alone with one's body. That kind of meditative process may be very good and very helpful. But the Gospel of John, along with the biblical tradition in general, affirms that faith arises from contact with a sensually perceptible object. We might suggest a rough analogy. The young man confidently affirms that the young woman really cares about him because of the way she kissed him. His perception of her care is based upon the physical sensation of the kiss, and we might even say that his understanding of her care *needs* that kiss as a means of communication. But his assertion of her care goes considerably beyond the physical sensation itself. "Ah, it was just a kiss," his friends tease him. But he firmly insists that it meant something more to him. The Christ, John says, affirms the truth of the revelation on the basis of the physical act of seeing Jesus. But that affirmation goes far beyond the physical sensations themselves. The physical or visual observation, with its ordinary interpretations of the data, is needed, but it is only the basis for the further affirmation.

The Evangelist's understanding of how experience lends itself to faith is also reflected in other ways she or he uses the verb "to see." The obviously metaphorical use of it in 9:39 makes sense now. Surely, Jesus' mission is to accomplish some healing—the bestowal of the physical capacities for sight and hearing—but the Evangelist means something more. Jesus grants the gift of perceiving the truth about life and existence. He gives the possibility of seeing and hearing so that one may correct his or her misconstrued self-understanding. The faith perception that is intended with the word "see" is also apparent in the assertion that Jesus sees the Father (5:19). Just as the Son sees the Father, so the believer sees (in the sense of faith perception) the Son.

Now much the same thing is true when we turn to the Evangelist's use of the words meaning "to hear" or "to listen."

> *Reader's Preparation*: Now read some of the passages in which the Greek verb meaning "to hear" or "to listen" is used. What does the Evangelist mean? 3:32; 5:24–26, 30, 37; 6:45, 60; 8:26, 40–43, 45–47; 10:3, 8, 26–27; 12:45–47; 15:15; 18:37.

Hearing may be a purely sensory act, as in 6:60, where the words of Jesus are heard but there is no inner perception of their meaning. It may also be the experience from which faith is born (5:24). In the latter case, a discernment of Jesus' true identity begins with normal "hearing" but goes beyond it. Failure to believe is rooted in the failure to hear fully and discern the voice of God in the Son. "The Jews" cannot believe, for they do not hear properly (8:43).

So faith-hearing, if you will, is the act of discerning the presence of the Ultimate in the voice of this man, Jesus. As with faith-seeing, faith-hearing involves physical perception and the apprehension of its meaning in a believing way. It is finding a dimension of ultimate meaning in an experience of hearing. Likewise, there is the same parallel between the disciples' hearing the Son and the Son's hearing the Father (8:26). Again, we have evidence that, for the Fourth Evangelist, the origin of religious faith is in a peculiar discernment of a physical, sensual experience—seeing and hearing.

Thus, we have in the Gospel of John a two-level experience that is the ground of faith. The base of this experience is the sensual act of seeing the deeds of Jesus and of hearing his words (see figure 3–2).

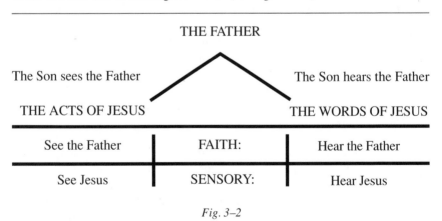

THE FATHER

The Son sees the Father | The Son hears the Father

THE ACTS OF JESUS | THE WORDS OF JESUS

| See the Father | FAITH: | Hear the Father |
| See Jesus | SENSORY: | Hear Jesus |

Fig. 3–2

I hope that you notice the similarity between the distinction between sensory seeing-hearing and faith perception, and the distinction between the perception of Jesus' marvelous acts and "seeing signs." In both cases, the Gospel presents us with a profound relationship between experience and faith. Faith grows out of an experience that is grasped in a particular way. For this Evangelist, then, religious faith is a result—at least in part—of understanding experience. One tries to grasp the meaning of what happens to him or her—what is seen, heard, experienced. Faith is the consequent tendency to understand experience in a certain way—to see and hear the Father in the acts and words of Jesus.

Thus, we are led in a circle back to our previous discussion of determinism and freedom. The author recognizes that the seeing and hearing that produce faith already require a certain kind of faith—a willingness to discern the deeper level of reality presented in our experience. If one does not have that willingness, experience cannot give rise to faith. So, the Evangelist is driven back to the mysterious dimension of this process. Some are "drawn" to discern that deeper reality and others are not. That deeper discernment seems to be a gift from God that precedes any faith. The Evangelist was not willing to eliminate that aspect of mystery or puzzlement from the process of experience that leads to faith. The unwillingness to account for it more fully may seem disappointing to some. Yet it is admirable in some respects, for many of us marvel that some persons understand their experience in such a profound way as to be led to religious faith, while others do not.

We must mention another aspect of Johannine thought in this connection. To do so will again get us far ahead of our story, but it is appropriate here. This understanding of the relationship between experience and faith expressed in the Johannine treatments of the signs and the verbs "to see" and "to hear" is in the profoundest sense *sacramental.* By this I mean that the Fourth Gospel has a deep appreciation for the way sensual experiences lead one to faith. The physical, the sensory, the material is the medium by which faith is born. Christian doctrine through the centuries has claimed that to be the case with regard to particular sensory experiences. The water of baptism, the bread and wine of the Lord's Supper—these are physical elements that nurture faith and through which the divine is opened up. We will argue in Chapter 4 that the Gospel has only limited interest in the Christian sacraments. But I will argue there as well that the Johannine understanding of faith and experience is fundamentally what the Christians mean by sacramentality.

The assertion of the Gospel is a bold one when looked at the way we have in the past few pages. The Ultimate Reality of the universe—God—is to be experienced through the mundane sensory experiences of life! (See 1:14!) That is a startling idea. It is particularly so when it is viewed in the context of other religious traditions of the world. Seeing and hearing are the necessary prerequisites for believing. We must not minimize the Gospel's position on this issue by assuming that it means this portrayal of seeing and hearing only in the context of a particular historical person, Jesus. That is, the Fourth Evangelist does not mean that faith was born among the first disciples through the sensual acts of seeing and hearing Jesus of Nazareth, but that after Jesus' departure this was no longer the same. I think that the Gospel is more concerned with its readers in the 70s and 80s of the first century than that. It is saying that the first disciples saw and heard the historical Jesus and that their faith grew from such physical experiences. The Gospel means too that every Christian's faith is born from the sensual experiences of seeing and hearing. The Christ of faith is still to be seen and heard in the community of believers. From the hearing of Christian preaching and witness and from the seeing of acts done in Christian love, faith is continually born. So, the sensory theology is right for the Gospel's own day, not just for the era of the life of Jesus of Nazareth.

John's solution to the question of experience and faith is an interesting and even daring one. But there is another matter that has attracted our attention—the relationship between knowing and believing.

KNOWING AND BELIEVING IN THE FOURTH GOSPEL

The discussion of the relationship between faith and knowledge is a classic issue in Christian circles. Scholars have fought over the subtleties of the relationship for centuries. Is there a requisite knowledge that one must have before faith? Or, is faith the foundation for knowing? The history of the discussion in Christian circles cannot concern us here, nor do we want to pose the Johannine treatment of these themes necessarily as the answer to the theologians' problems. We want to note, however, that as early as the first century of the Christian movement there were those whose way of thinking encompassed a relationship between faith and knowledge.

> *Reader's Preparation*: The necessary reading for our brief discussion of this subject will be satisfied by the following passages: 6:69; 8:31–32; 17:7–8, 21–23. As you read these three passages, ask yourself, Which comes first in the Johannine scheme—knowing or believing? Is one more important than the other? Are they synonyms?

Do persons know something they did not previously know as a result of belief? More simply, is there knowledge arising from belief? Or, must one first have some knowledge before one believes? Listen to the Fourth Evangelist: In 8:31 it sounds like those who believe in Christ then, as a consequence, know something (10:38 seems to make the same point). But wait; 17:8 suggests the opposite! The disciples know that Christ came from the Father, and therefore (or should we not supply a "therefore" between the sentences?) they believe. (See also 16:30, where the same relationship may be meant).

In the first case,

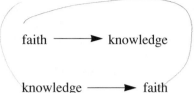

faith ———▶ knowledge

In the second case,

knowledge ———▶ faith

Yet a simple contradiction like this is not enough in our puzzling Gospel. There is a still further confusing factor. In some passages it sounds as if the Greek words for knowing and believing are used synonymously. "We have come to believe and know," confesses Peter (6:69). And in 14:7 and 17:3, it appears we could substitute the word "believe" for the word "know" and have exactly the same meaning. In these cases then,

faith = knowing

There are scholars who would have us make fine distinctions between faith and knowing in the Fourth Gospel. They find a more intellectual sense in those passages where knowing is used and a more volitional one where believing is used. Bultmann wants us to think that knowing in the Fourth Gospel refers to the "structural" quality of believing (*The Theology of the New Testament*, vol. 2). It seems to me, however, that such arguments are straining the evidence. They are trying to get philosophical distinctions out of the text that are not there. The Johannine view is simpler than that!

The reason the Gospel of John can use faith and knowing interchange-ably is that they were really synonymous for the Johannine church. What the Gospel means by "to know" is no different from what is meant by "to believe." So the key to the relationship of these two in the Fourth Gospel is found in those passages in which we sense that we can substitute one word for the other without distorting the meaning. The Fourth Evangelist is not a philosopher and is not concerned with epistemology as such. That does not mean that the equation of these two terms is done thoughtlessly.

The Gospel can use knowing as a synonym for believing, I think, because it uses the former word in something of its Hebraic sense. Even though the Gospel is written in Greek and its original readers understood Greek, it is likely that their backgrounds were, for the most part, Jewish. That led the Johannine Christians to think of knowledge in a Hebraic way. In the Hebrew Bible the word for "knowing" had less of sense of cognitive or intellectual comprehension than did the comparable verb in the Greek lan-guage. Most often in the Hebrew Bible, knowing refers to a personal rela-tionship. It is not detached apprehension of an object. When in English we say that we know something, such as a book, it means that we have exam-ined it, studied it. We can describe it as an object.

We may be confused, then, when the Hebrew Bible says that so and so went in and "knew" his wife and she conceived a son. What does it mean that he knew her? Obviously it means something other than objective, detached observation. The Hebrew word *yada*, which we most readily translate "to know," means to enter into personal, intimate relationship. It pertains to two subjects (or persons) in a relationship of mutual involvement. That which is known is not an object, detached from the knower, but is itself a subject communing with the subject of the knower. It is used of sexual relationship in much the same way that we might say a couple has "intercourse"—two subjects in a relationship of trustful interchange. Similarly when the prophet Hosea says that the people suffer from a lack of knowledge of God (4:6ff.), he is not complaining that their theology is faulty. He is saying rather that their personal relationship with Yahweh is dead.

When the Gospel of John employs the Greek word *gnōskein*, it is used in the Hebraic sense of *yada*. As a subject, one has entered into a personal and trusting relationship with another subject. The Gospel could then use knowing as a synonym for belief, for knowing suggested the same kind of relationship that exists in faith. Thus, there is no intent to suggest some greater degree of intellectual content or exchange when "know" rather than "believe" is used. Both are personal. Both are intimate. Both are subject to subject and not subject to object. In the Johannine sense of knowing there is no detachment but just the opposite—involvement.

If the Fourth Gospel means what we think it means by knowing and if it can use that word as a synonym for faith, then one aspect of what the Gospel means by faith begins to come clear. Faith is the trusting personal relationship between two subjects. It is an interchange on a most intimate level. Belief must not then mean merely the intellectual acceptance of doctrine (although there is some of that in the Fourth Gospel, as we will soon see). It must mean that faith involves the whole person—mind, body, emotions, and all the rest—in a personal relationship.

The story is told of the man who was going to walk a tightrope across Niagara Falls pushing a wheelbarrow in front of him. The crowd gathered on the day for the risky endeavor. The wind was blowing mightily. It whipped the rope back and forth. As the time for the walk grew close, the crowd began calling out advice, "Don't try it! You'll never make it!" Then one man jumped from the crowd and approached the tightrope walker. He said to the adventurer, "Go ahead! Make the walk. You can do it! I have faith in you." To this encouragement the tightrope walker replied with an invitation, "Okay, if you believe in me so strongly, you get in the wheelbarrow and come with me!"

Johannine faith is not a detached intellectual confidence. It is a personal involvement and trust that links the believer and the object of belief together in a kind of unity. That relationship of faith was such that our Evangelist could describe it in the Hebraic sense of knowing. Yet this insight is still something of an overgeneralization. We can further qualify what we have said about the concept of faith in the Fourth Gospel in several very important ways.

SUMMARY VIEW OF FAITH IN THE FOURTH GOSPEL

Reader's Preparation: Skim through the Gospel and make a list of the answers it gives to the following questions: (1) What is the object of belief? (That is, what are the people asked to believe?) (2) What is the nature of belief as it is used in the Gospel?

Ninety-eight times the Gospel uses the verb "to believe" (*pisteuein*). Believe! But what am I asked to believe? There are at least three different objects of faith for the Fourth Gospel. That is, what one is asked to believe or believe in varies.

1. Most often the point seems to be a personal allegiance to Jesus, a personal relationship with him. This occurs for example in 4:39. The most common construction is the use of the verb "believe" with the preposition *eis* (into or in), and the object of the preposition is most often Jesus himself. This construction suggests that our proposals about the nature of faith at the conclusion of the previous section are prominent in the Gospel.

2. Sometimes the object of the belief is not the person but the statements he or she makes. "Believe the words Jesus speaks" (see 2:22). This is not substantially different from the first object of faith, Jesus himself, except here faith is a credence in the statements of the revealer rather than faith in the person of the revealer. One implies the other. If you put your faith in Jesus as the revelation of God, you believe what Jesus says to be true.

3. A different thing is suggested, however, by the third object of faith. Sometimes it is faith in statements *about* Jesus. The reader is not asked to believe in the person of Jesus in the sense of a personal relationship of trust, nor asked to accept as true what Jesus says. The reader is, instead, called to believe that Jesus is the revealer, the Messiah, the Father's Son (e.g., 11:27). This use of the word "believe" has shifted the meaning of faith from a personal relationship to an intellectual acceptance. My faith is a faith in a creed, in this case, not in a person.

The Fourth Evangelist has presented us then with two different kinds of faith in Christ. The first is a personal involvement with and allegiance to Jesus, entailing trust and intimacy. The second is an understanding of faith as acceptance of a creed, or at least of creedal assertions about Christ. The former is the older form of Christian faith; the Pauline concept of faith is essentially of this kind. The second is the kind of faith that we witness emerging only later in the New Testament period and is like the use of the word "faith" in some of the very latest New Testament literature. There faith has been transformed into creed or doctrine. "The faith" is not a dynamic personal relationship between the Christian and Christ, but a set of doctrinal statements about Christ. (See Hebrews 11; James 2:17; 1 John 5:1; 3 John 4–11; Jude 3.) This change is an important one. It utterly transforms the nature of believing. It moves it into an area that can be reduced to mere intellectual matter. The first meaning of faith had a far more personal dimension and demanded the whole being of the believer. It would be like first loving another person, then coming to love the statements you could make about that person. To love the affirmation "She is a really caring individual" is radically different from loving the person herself.

Now, our Evangelist appears to be partly responsible for the beginning of the gradual shift in the early church toward a creedal understanding of faith. The Fourth Gospel is probably among the earliest of the literature in which we can find statements using the word "faith" with a creedal ring. The Fourth Evangelist was probably not aware of the significance of this shift in usage. The author's fundamental sense of faith is the personal relationship. However, the Johannine community is under attack. They are suffering social dislocation and are in the midst of an identity crisis. What clearly separates them from their opponents is that they can make certain affirmations about Christ that structure a sense of identity and group solidarity. "We are the ones who can affirm that Jesus is the Messiah." That confession draws the boundaries between the Johannine community and the world around it. That functional value of the creed seduces the Evangelist into its use. She or he does not see it as a violation of the other fundamental concept of faith—a personal relationship with Christ. Of course, in our Gospel there is as yet no danger of the submersion of the personal, dynamic character of faith beneath creedal formula. The Johannine Christians doubtless believe that a personal relationship with Christ leads naturally and logically to faith statements about who that Christ is. In other words, the motive for the rise of the creedal concept of faith is the desire to speak honestly and clearly about the Christ figure. Regardless of motivation, we must credit (or blame) the Fourth Evangelist for an early reduction of faith to creed. Whether that was a tragic move or only the logical conclusion of the view of faith as personal relationship, I leave to your own judgment.

We must complete this section on a more positive note, having saved the best for last. There is still one other feature of the Johannine concepts of faith that we have not mentioned. It begins with a grammatical observation. The Fourth Evangelist never uses the noun "faith" or "belief," but always and only the verb "to believe." (The Greek has only one word that we must translate either "belief" or "faith.") What does this mean? That the author liked verbs rather than nouns? It means of course that for the Fourth Evangelist belief is always an active matter. Faith is not an inner disposition. Faith is not something one *has*. Faith is something one *does* or what is done for you. Faith is not a state of being but a dynamic becoming. If faith is always a verb, that surely implies that faith is not something one does once and for all time. Rather, faith as a verb means that believing is a decision made once only to have to be made over and over again, or a gift accepted not once but again and again. Faith is a continuing dynamic, not a state of being.

Now this understanding of faith implicit in the use of the verb instead of the noun indicates that the Evangelist's fundamental concept of faith is that of personal relationship. While the Gospel uses the verb "to believe" in conjunction with creedal statements, that is not the primary thrust of its view. It is rather a digression, a lapse—and a very important one at that. Basically, the Fourth Gospel affirms that out of experience comes a trusting relationship with a personal being.

CONCLUSION

The Gospel of John is not a philosophical essay. Its exposition of the relationship of faith and experience is made within the context of a gospel. A gospel is not a philosophical or even a theological treatise. It is rather a document designed to preserve traditional material and address that material in a newly relevant way to the issues confronting a community of faith. The concern of the Fourth Evangelist is to nurture religious faith in the midst of severe trials and difficulties. It is, therefore, unreasonable to expect of this work a logically consistent and complete exposition of the question of the relationship of faith and experience. The philosopher does not read social protest literature for its rational explication of philosophical issues. However, implicit in a social protest are certain views—basic values, understandings of society, of person, and of freedom. So, too, we must not read the Fourth Gospel expecting philosophical dissertations on issues such as faith and experience. The Fourth Gospel articulates a view of the relationship between faith and experience for one reason and one reason alone: that a reader's faith might be nurtured.

What we find then in the Fourth Gospel is a rather profound view of the way in which religious faith is rooted in experience. It is a relatively bold view of the matter, for it affirms the positive role of sensual experience in the origin of faith. It assigns a primary place to the perception of signs and the basic experiences of sensory perception such as seeing and hearing. Yet it claims that beyond the uses of the senses must come a deeper, or extrasensual discernment. If one discerns at this deeper level, then out of experience may be born a personal relationship of trust with the Divine Person. That relationship may be variously described as faith or knowledge (in its Hebraic meaning). From that basic relationship, faith may sometimes be understood as the acceptance of creedal statements.

When we probe beneath what the Gospel means by this kind of faith-perception of the words and deeds of Jesus, we unearth an unsolved mystery. The Gospel leaves us with no clear explanation of the initial openness to the deeper discernment that begins the faith process. A dynamic faith that must grow and mature begins in mystery. Therefore, perhaps we ought to accuse the author of the Gospel of an incomplete argument or, perhaps, of arguing in a circle: Faith is required for experience to give birth to faith! Still, we are left with the sense that the divine participation in one's life begins one's effort to understand and perceive experience from the faith perspective. Could it be, then, that this more adequately explains the paradoxical tension in the Fourth Gospel between the assertions that faith is born by God's action and that faith is generated by human decision? The initial faith is the work of God—the divine drawing, the giving of the individual over to Christ. That initial gift of faith opens the eyes, so that faith-perception might be possible. Beyond that initial sensitizing of one to the experience of divine presence, the human is then responsible for believing and growing in faith. Humans can never boast of their faith, for it originates with God's act in their lives. Nor can humans ever abdicate responsibility for the maturation of faith. Whether or not this is the full meaning of the Gospel's teaching can only be discovered through careful study, but it may offer us a place to begin the quest.

Our Gospel has not settled once and for all the question of experience and faith. Its contribution on this score may seem insignificant in the context of the world's religious traditions, for it is only one among many. But I suggest that the view advocated by this document is at least one of the most creative answers to this question one can find early in a religious tradition. Without benefit of centuries of philosophical discussions and refinements, the Johannine interpretation is both responsible and personal. It most certainly merits our study and criticism in the light of the Christian tradition's ongoing reflection on the meaning of faith.

So the Evangelist explores the meaning of faith and its origin in experience with considerable skill. Faith represents the way the individual passes from one pole of human dualism to the other. It is the means of transition between darkness and light, death and life, and falsehood and truth. But what is the character of this light, this life, and this truth? What is the accomplishment of faith? What has one gained by believing? This leads us to the final major segment of our survey of Johannine thought—the Johannine concept of the life of the believer.

4. ETERNITY IS NOW—
JOHANNINE ESCHATOLOGY

During the presidency of Richard Nixon, a cartoon appeared that suggests the theme of this chapter. The scene is in front of the White House. One bearded and rather weird-looking fellow wearing a long robe is carrying a sign that declares, "The End is Near!" He is looking in surprise at another figure whose back is all we can see. The second person is, however, recognizable as the then-current resident of the White House, who is carrying a sign that reads, "Four More Years!" This blending of religious and political motifs suggests the tension between the present and the future. It epitomizes in the religious figure those who believe that the present is the time of fulfillment and in the political figure those who look expectantly to the future for fulfillment.

This theme of the tension between the future and the present as the time of fulfillment is another classic religious question. All religions teach in one form or another the hope that human fulfillment and satisfaction is available. This teaching is often expressed in the concept of salvation. It declares that human beings may achieve that for which they were intended from their creation. It declares that the deepest longings of the human soul may be fulfilled, that basic needs may be met, and that hopes may be realized. Such a promise of salvation, however, may be in the distant future, or it may come to pass during the believer's lifetime. In some religious traditions, the fullness of salvation is promised only in the future (for instance, in a heavenly home after death). There will come a time, these religions teach, when humanity will be perfected, but that time lies in the future. Christianity and Judaism both seem to fit into this category. In other religious traditions, the fulfillment of the promised salvation is available immediately. The Zen Buddhist master hopes subtly to lead his students to that experience of enlightenment that is the actualization of the serenity for which humans were intended.

Of course, the distinction is never this sharp. Although the Christian tradition generally teaches a future fulfillment, one often finds the declaration of the anticipation of that future realization in the believer's present. The experience of the Holy Spirit is often understood in this way. Indeed, the apostle Paul spoke of the Spirit as a sort of down payment on God's promise. The experience of the Spirit is a guarantee that there shall be a completion of salvation (e.g., Romans 8:23). Among those Christians of a mystical bent, one finds a declaration that the Christian is able in this life to experience nearly the fullness of God's promised salvation. Similarly in the Eastern religions, the promised goal is often unity with God in the state of Brahman or

Nirvana that comes to the most faithful upon their death and ends the cycle of endless life (especially in Hinduism). Still, one experiences something of this final state in this life as a result of meditation. It is obvious that religions blend the ideas of the future and present fulfillment of the promised salvation.

Therein lies the issue at stake in this chapter. Is the salvation promised to the believer a future possibility alone? Or, is it to be found in the believer's present experience? Or, is the present in some way a partial fulfillment that anticipates the completed fulfillment in the future? While generalities break down, there is a degree of truth in the assertion that some religious teaching about salvation is future oriented, some present oriented. In the former case, hope plays a primary role—hope for the future consummation of God's plan. In the case of those who are present oriented, the emphasis shifts. The hope can be realized now. It is being realized. Live for the now! Inherent in this issue is a basic struggle of religions to resolve the present experience of the believer and her or his future hope.

Christianity was probably born amid a belief that the salvation of humanity lay in the future, and that the future was very near. Earliest Christianity was bred amid the fervent hopes of Judaism for the imminent appearance of the Messiah and the age he would inaugurate. Christianity in this regard was not far different from the religious perspective of those Jews responsible for the Dead Sea Scroll literature. In their community at Qumran on the Dead Sea, these Jewish fanatics prepared themselves for the impending appearance of the Messiah and the great battle with evil that would ensue. Nascent Christianity was nurtured on this kind of Jewish apocalypticism. Some of the earliest literature from the Christian movement stresses just this point (e.g., 1 Thessalonians). (Apocalypticism is the name given to a particular way of thinking and writing about the fulfillment of God's promises in the future. It is characterized by at least two peculiar emphases: (1) the radical discontinuity between history and that future fulfillment and (2) the elaborate use of symbols to describe that future.)

Christians quickly came to believe that they could experience divine fulfillment in the present. The believer experienced the presence of the living Christ and was given gifts that were anticipations of the final gift of full salvation. Paul, for instance, speaks of salvation as both a present experience and a future hope. This is clearest in his declaration in Romans 8:24, "For in hope we were saved." Many critics of the New Testament contend that the early Christians had to struggle with the disappointment resulting from the delay of the return of Christ. First, it was believed that Christ would very soon return. (*Parousia* is the term often used in the New Testament for his reappearance.) At that time, he would bring the fullness of God's salvation. But that immediate reappearance did not materialize, at least not in the way it was anticipated. When it did not, and the hope for Christ's appearance in glory was pushed further into the future, more attention was focused upon the sense in which salvation was already present in the believer's life.

Into this drama of the development of early Christian belief comes the Fourth Gospel. Its place in that unfolding struggle between future hope and present realization is significant. In few other pieces of Christian literature is the tension between the present and future dimensions of salvation more evident. Scholarly debate wages over the position of the Fourth Evangelist on this question. But all must agree that there is a remarkably strong emphasis in the Gospel upon the presence of salvation in the believer's life. Perhaps no other New Testament document stresses more strongly than the Fourth Gospel the realized hopes of Christians. That motif of the presence of salvation comes to expression in a number of ways. First, of course, it is present in the way in which the Evangelist deals with eschatological themes. (Eschatology is simply a handy word to summarize those beliefs in what will occur at the "last day"—at the end of time—in Christian thought.) But the presence of salvation is also stressed in the way our Evangelist handles a number of other topics, especially the Spirit, the church, and the sacraments. What ties together the themes that we will be discussing in this chapter is the single idea which the Evangelist held: Salvation is already accessible to the believer in this time. Or, to summarize the idea less prosaically: Eternity is *now*!

The following pages will treat in turn these matters:

1. The Gospel's view of the fulfillment of promises related to the final time (that is, eschatology)
2. Its view of the presence of the Spirit among believers (pneumatology)
3. Its view of the community of Christian believers (the church or ecclesiology)
4. Its view of the sacraments (sacramentality)

Through each of these subjects, the Evangelist says, the promised salvation is already available, fulfilled in the lives of believers. Hence, the views of the Spirit, the church, and the sacraments are intertwined with the understanding of eschatology.

JOHANNINE ESCHATOLOGY

I have already mentioned that critics of the Fourth Gospel are divided on the question of the relationship of the present experience of and the future hope for salvation. This is so because the evidence of the Gospel is not clear. Our first task in this section is to find the relevant passages. In some the Gospel seems to affirm that the full salvation of the individual lies in a future day. In others it seems to declare that those hopes for the future are already realities in the believers' experience.

Reader's Preparation: Below are the most important passages dealing with eschatological hope. Read them carefully and try to determine whether the Evangelist is talking about the fulfillment of these hopes in the future or in the present: 3:18–19, 36; 5:21–29; 6:39–54; 9:39; 11:23–25; 12:25, 31, 48; 14:2–3, 18, 28; 17:1–26. Read chapters 15 and 16 and note what is said there about the tribulations the believers will face or are facing.

By now you have grown accustomed to contradictions in the Gospel. So, you are not surprised to find contradictory statements on this issue. But here the contradictions seem more pronounced. We propose figure 4–1 as a brief summary of the problem of Johannine eschatology. You may want to challenge some of it or add to it in the light of your reading of the evidence.

PRESENT REALITIES	FUTURE REALITIES
Judgment (e.g., 3:18; 9:39)	Judgment (e.g., 12:48)
Eternal Life (e.g., 3:36; 5:24)	Eternal Life (e.g., 12:25)
Resurrection (e.g., 5:21, 24, 26)	Resurrection (e.g., 6:39–40; 54)
	Parousia (e.g., 14:3, 18, 28)
	Tribulations which signal the advent of the Messiah (chapters 15 and 16)
Defeat of the "ruler of this age" (12:31)	

Fig. 4–1

It is understandable if we get frustrated at some point in studying the evidence, for there seem to be no less than three kinds of eschatology in the Fourth Gospel. The first we will call *futuristic eschatology*, because it seems to say that the promised salvation is in the future. Judgment will come at the last day of history (12:48). There will be a resurrection of the dead on that decisive day (6:39–40, 54). The future resurrection and judgment are associated with one another (5:28). To this add the hint of a future coming again of Christ (chapter 14). Further supplement the evidence with the references in chapters 15 and 16 to the tribulations to be experienced by the Christians. A standard idea in the futuristic eschatology of early Christianity and first-century Judaism was that tribulations would occur as the last day approaches. Just before the appearance of the Messiah (in Jewish thought) or the second appearance of Christ (in Christian thought) evil would abound, and believers would be severely persecuted. The references to the suffering in chapters 15 and 16 of the Fourth Gospel sound like those "messianic tribulations." It appears that Johannine Christians accepted the idea that just before things become a whole lot better they are going to get very much worse.

Now these futuristic expectations fit with the traditional early Christian view of eschatology. They express the idea that history would be brought to a grand conclusion. Christ would reappear, this time triumphantly. Evil would be defeated and Satan's rule ended. There would be a mass resurrection of the dead followed by a judgment. Some of those judged would be given eternal life. Nothing in all of this surprises the experienced student of the New Testament who has had an opportunity to explore the culture of the first Christian century. These concepts have roots in the early Christian adaptation of Jewish apocalyptic thought. We find similar ideas not only in other New Testament writings but also in Jewish writings of the two centuries before the common era as well as of the first century itself. These passages affirm a historical dualism. The present age is ruled by Satan, and it will end to be followed by the eternal age ruled by God alone.

There is a second kind of eschatology in the Gospel that we will call *present eschatology*. This is found in those passages in which the Gospel of John seems to say that the future expectations of the Christians are already realized now in their relationship with Christ. One is already judged by his or her response to Christ (e.g., 3:18). Resurrection is the experience of being brought to a new understanding of oneself by belief in Christ. One is brought from death to life in the immediate present by faith (e.g., 5:24). The story of the resurrection of Lazarus is instructive here. Mary meets Jesus after he has finally come to the village where his friend Lazarus has died. Jesus says to Mary, "Your brother will rise again." Mary sounds like she is reciting the proper words of traditional Christian belief, "I know that he will rise again in the resurrection on the last day" (11:23–24). The words sound impersonal or rhetorical. Mary says them, but conviction is lacking. She says them, but they do not seem to help much in the face of her brother's death. Jesus then answers her with one of the "I am" sayings, "I am the resurrection and the life. Those who believe in me, even though they die, will live, and everyone who lives and believes in me will never die" (11:25–26). Then Jesus goes about restoring Lazarus to life. The point of the chapter seems to be that a faith relationship with Christ is resurrection. Resurrection is not some vague hope for something that will happen way out there in the shadowy future. It is a present experience when Christ is present.

More present eschatology is expressed in the assertions concerning eternal life. To live with faith in Christ is already to live eternal life (5:24). The expression "eternal life" is, of course, part of that Johannine dualism we have discussed. It seems to mean the quality of the believer's existence. It is not a future hope (but let us not forget 12:25). It is a present reality accruing from faith in Christ. It is, if you will, the new self-understanding that results from the revelation of God in Christ. To be sure, it may have something to do with the survival of physical death (as chapter 11 affirms), but it is primarily a quality of life. We might say that it is the peculiar quality of life resulting from a proper self-understanding in Christ that cannot be annihilated by death.

This kind of eschatology is new, at least in its radicality. It has affinities with some of the things Paul says about the presence of salvation in the believer's experience. The Fourth Gospel takes those experiences connected with the last day in traditional Christian eschatology and declares, "They are present now in the believer's life!" It reverses the direction of Christian expectation, at least in these passages, turning expectation away from the future and toward the present. Before we explore this any further, we must look at the third kind of eschatology and then try to reconcile the conflict among the three.

Some of the later chapters of the Gospel may express a *heavenly eschatology*. This is an eschatological view that is futuristic, but it is quite different from traditional futuristic eschatology in early Christian thought. There is a heavenly home waiting for the Christians. Christ will take them there (14:2–3). In that heavenly place there will be a perfecting of the relationship among the Christians and between the Christians and God. They will attain a perfect oneness (17:23). Now this heavenly eschatology is not explicitly associated with futuristic eschatology. That is, it is not stated that, following the resurrection and judgment, Christians will be taken to their heavenly home and perfected. It sounds more as if it is something that occurs after the death of the individual Christians, and that this heavenly perfection is simultaneous with the continuance of world history. If this is the case (and there is ample reason for uncertainty that it is), then we have still another radically different view of the promise of salvation. It is not a part of a historical dualism like the futuristic eschatology of the Gospel seems to be. Rather, it suggests a cosmic dualism. There are two realms in the cosmos—the world and heaven. In the heavenly realm Christians have a place, and there they are promised perfection. (Ernst Käsemann is one interpreter who finds this heavenly eschatology in the Gospel. See *The Testament of Jesus According to John 17.*)

How can we come to terms with the presence of these three different forms of eschatological thought in the same Gospel? We have witnessed several cases in which the Gospel's teachings seem to be contradictory. Now in its eschatological views another contradiction cries out for resolution. Again, let me suggest some alternatives before I present my way of resolving the conflict.

1. The *both and* solution is first. It simply affirms that the Gospel of John means all it says. The heavenly eschatology is not to be disassociated from the futuristic one. It is part of what the believer may hope for in the future consummation of God's plan. The Evangelist simply neglects to make that association explicit. There is no cosmic dualism in the heavenly eschatology. The heaven is simply the new age that dawns with the completion of

God's work in Christ. So the events of the heavenly eschatology are to be understood as a further historical sequence of the futuristic eschatological events. Moreover, the split between the future and present eschatologies is not to be exaggerated. Like Paul, all the Evangelist means is that the future blessings of the Christian are already beginning to be available through their relationship with Christ. To have eternal life and resurrection now is simply to have the promise of them. The fulfillment of these blessings still resides in the future. The present holds the taste of the future. It is the down payment and the future will be payment in full. The hors d'oeuvres enable the diner to anticipate the tasty meal that will be coming soon. So, the present eschatology of the Fourth Evangelist means to say that these experiences are a foretaste of things to come.

This view of the eschatology of the Gospel makes the Evangelist look rather orthodox. Perhaps the Gospel does stress the present a bit more than the future, but not to the elimination of the future hope. This alternative would have us take everything the Evangelist says with equal seriousness and see that he or she relates it all in a traditional way.

2. The *spoiler* alternative is quite different. Some (most adamantly, Bultmann) contend that the Fourth Evangelist wrote only the passages espousing a present eschatology. The Evangelist entirely rejected the future eschatology and believed only in the fulfillment of the promises in the present. Bultmann understands, therefore, that the Evangelist in effect demythologized the futuristic eschatology. That is, the author understood all the symbolism about the resurrection at the last day, judgment, and similar matters, in terms of the possibilities of the present relationship with God. When the Evangelist finished the Gospel, there was no futuristic eschatology at all to be found in its pages.

Then along came the "spoilers." Rather orthodox believing Christians got hold of the Gospel, and they did not like all that they read there. So, they took it upon themselves to "repair" the document and make it more congenial to their own views. Among other things, they supplied the Gospel with a futuristic eschatology. It was they who wrote the passages stressing that the promises are yet to be fulfilled. Bultmann argues that these churchly revisers of the Gospel left evidence of their work. Hence, it can be distinguished by means of an analysis of style and content, as well as the way in which their work causes breaks in the flow of the narrative. (Bultmann actually speaks of only one such reviser, but I suggest a group of Christians may have been involved. For Bultmann's views, see both his commentary *The Gospel of John* and part III of *The Theology of the New Testament,* vol. 2.)

The spoiler alternative can also account for the heavenly eschatology in several different ways: First, some argue it is part of the Evangelist's own present eschatology. The believers are in their Father's house in the community of believers. There they are perfected into oneness. Hence, the heavenly eschatology is reduced to a part of the Evangelist's present eschatology. Second, Bultmann insists that the Evangelist maintains that the quality of the believer's present existence will survive the grave. The Evangelist believes in a life beyond death that will continue the faith existence begun in this life. In this way the heavenly eschatology is harmonized with the present eschatology as a part of the work of the Evangelist. Only the futuristic eschatology is the work of the revisers of the Gospel, who in effect spoiled the harmony of the Gospel's position on this question.

3. The *preserver* alternative is different in only one way. Bultmann is correct in saying that in the present eschatology the Evangelist is reinterpreting (demythologizing) futuristic eschatology. But this alternative proposes that the futuristic passages came to the Evangelist in tradition and are preserved in the Gospel. Rather than arguing that a spoiler added the futuristic eschatology, this solution claims that that view of eschatology is there as a result of the Evangelist's concern to preserve traditional materials. As in other aspects of the community's heritage, the Evangelist incorporated traditional eschatological views even though they contradicted his or her own theological stance. This author respected the tradition and honored its place among the members of the community, but also added other dimensions to the older eschatology—namely, the present and heavenly themes—in order to address the community's current needs.

In a sense, what the Fourth Evangelist was trying to do was to take the symbols of the older futuristic eschatology and express their meaning for Christians in the Gospel's day. That she or he did this is evidenced by the proximity of the futuristic and present passages to each other in the text of the Gospel. Perhaps you noted how often the present and future eschatologies are found in the same chapter, for example, 5:24–26 and 5:27–30 (see also 6:39–58). Often (but not always) the author repeats the traditional symbols of the futuristic eschatology near the point at which their new interpretation in present eschatology is expressed. The contradictory views of the Gospel are the result of the Evangelist's persistent effort to be a faithful preserver as well as an interpreter of the community's tradition.

This alternative would agree with Bultmann that the Evangelist espoused a heavenly eschatology that was consistent with his present eschatology. Or, it might argue that heavenly eschatology is intended only as a symbolic expression of the present eschatology. It might be that the cosmic dualism of the heavenly eschatology means only that the present life of the believer is the meeting of the divine and human realms. We suggested in Chapter 2, on Johannine dualism, that the Evangelist's cosmic dualism might be a symbolic articulation of a human polarity. It might be argued too that the heavenly eschatology is a more poetic way of expressing those beliefs having to do with present eschatology. Still again, it might be the case that the heavenly eschatology developed in the community as a supplement to the present eschatology. That is, in light of the death of Johannine Christians, the community began to ask, What happens after death to those who in this life already have eternal life? The conclusion was that they were taken to a heavenly home on their physical demise.

We believe that the preserver solution to the contradictions in Johannine eschatology is the most promising of the three alternatives. Our study has found consistently that the evangelist preserved traditional material even when it contradicted his or her own view of matters. We found, too, that the author often attempted an interpretation of the inherited materials for the Gospel's own day, as in the understanding of faith in the signs source. Therefore, it seems entirely possible that what we have in Johannine eschatology is the same sort of thing. The Evangelist feels that the traditional, futuristic eschatology is no longer meaningful.

It had been nearly fifty years since the early Christians had begun anticipating the Parousia. They had thought that event was near at hand, but it was not. Each succeeding group of Christians had been disappointed. Christ had not returned. "Enough of this!" the Evangelist says. "Let's stop focusing attention on the future and realize that the present holds the fulfillment of those promises!" Let us use our imaginations a bit: The Evangelist may have been raised in a home of Christians who had looked expectantly for the imminent reappearance of Christ. His or her parents had died disappointed that they had not lived to witness the fulfillment of the eschatological expectations. Disillusioned, the Evangelist along with other Christians undertook a study of these eschatological promises. They found that the present experience of the believers is filled with the realities looked for in the future. So they begin teaching that the present is the time of God's fulfillment of God's vows. The believer already lives in the last day. Eternity is now!

This is one of the most drastic revisions of traditional Christian thought the Gospel proposes. It claims that the Christians need not live only by hope, but by the reality of the blessings of their present lives. The future orientation of early Christians had deprived them of the blessedness of the present. The Gospel expands its sensory theology with an experiential eschatology. Not only is faith born out of sensory experiences, but the blessings of the future are already here to be experienced now. This is a radically present orientation—a now orientation.

An analogy might be found in the reaction of many persons to the space program in America. They do not reject that program out of hand. Space exploration is a legitimate and promising pursuit. But they are concerned that so much of our money is spent on the exploration of outer space while the problems of our life here and now in this world increase. They say, "Let's spend more money and energy on the improvement of life on this planet before we devote more to the frontier of outer space." The Fourth Evangelist is saying that too much energy has been spent on the expectation of the future. More must be devoted to the present and the quality of Christian life here and now.

The Fourth Evangelist found that *the present is pregnant with possibility*, and wanted readers to be sensitive to those possibilities and to actualize them. Eternal life? It is yours now as you live a new kind of existence on the basis of the revelation of God in Christ. Resurrection? Being born to a new life as a result of faith in Christ is resurrection. Judgment? You are judging yourself by the kind of response you make to the proclamation of the Christian gospel. Parousia? Christ comes again when you believe in him.

We may have overemphasized the impact of the present eschatology in the Gospel. The truth is that the text of the Gospel contains promises for both the future and the present. The futuristic expectations have been revised and qualified by the assertions of the present eschatology. But they have not been eliminated! They stand there in the text, alongside the claims for the present experience of the Christian. This must mean that the Gospel teaches *both* an acute attention to the way in which the present fulfills God's promises *and* the dimensions of those promises yet to be fulfilled in the future. So, in a real sense the both and solution to the problem is sound. The Evangelist not only preserves the traditional futuristic eschatology but also affirms it by preserving it. That view of the promises of God is still sound! It still merits our trust!

Hence, the result is that the Gospel of John presents us with what we might call a *dialectical eschatology*. That means that the truth is not found in one or the other position, but only in the dynamic interchange between both of them. The true Christian eschatology, the Gospel insists, is not in being exclusively future or exclusively present in our orientation. Rather, it is found in holding firmly to both, embracing both the now and the not yet. There is a sense in which God has already fulfilled the divine promises in our present life. There is a sense, too, in which God has yet to complete that fulfillment in the future. The two must go together, as the old song would have it, like love and marriage, horse and carriage.

We recall the title of our study, "John, the Maverick Gospel." In its dialectical eschatology the Fourth Gospel is indeed a maverick among the early Christian writings. It runs free and unbranded, free of the burden of simply adhering to traditional beliefs. But unlike some mavericks, it respects and honors the past. It preserves the traditional while trying to point it in a new direction. It espouses what is lost to some cultural mavericks in American. It knows that effective change in thought and practice does not totally disregard the past but preserves and reinterprets it. And this is precisely what the Gospel does with its complex eschatology.

THE JOHANNINE VIEW OF THE SPIRIT

We must now begin to consider why the Fourth Gospel could have such high regard for the possibilities of the present life of the Christian believer. Its eschatology is surely the result of convictions the Johannine community had about the quality of Christian experience. One of those convictions involves the presence of the Spirit among believers. Because Johannine Christians valued so highly the presence of the Spirit in the experience of the Christian community, they could declare that the future blessings are already present. Their view of the Spirit is another of the great contributions this Gospel has made to Christian thought.

106

Reader's Preparation: Skim the Gospel, searching for the use of the word "spirit." Then try to determine the meaning of this word as it appears in the Gospel.

We begin our investigation of the Spirit in the Gospel of John by noting the way in which the Greek word *pneuma* is used. It is found approximately twenty-four times in the Gospel, referring most often to the Spirit of God but occasionally to the human spirit. John 11:33 and 13:21 are examples of the latter. However, it is the use of Spirit to refer to God's presence that particularly interests us. In these instances it appears that the Gospel speaks of the Spirit in four distinct but interrelated ways.

First, the Spirit is simply the power and the character of God given to the man, Jesus. This appears to be the case in 1:32 and 33. The Baptizer witnesses to the descent of the Spirit on Jesus. The point is restated in 3:34: The Father has given the son the Spirit without limits. The Fourth Gospel shares this view with the Synoptics (see especially the Gospel of Luke).

The second use of the word "Spirit" is more distinctive, namely, "the pneuma life." The word "Spirit" seems associated with the divine presence that results in the new life of the believer. It is through Christ that this divine presence is given to believers (7:39; 20:22). The narrator's comment in 19:30 is ambiguous. The usual translation is "Then [Jesus] bowed his head and gave up his spirit." The translators obviously take spirit in this case to be Jesus' own life spirit. However, translators are also, inescapably, interpreters! The Greek literally reads simply "gave up [or handed over] the spirit." Hence, the reference could once again be to Jesus' giving of the divine Spirit to believers.

In chapter 4 of the Gospel comes some indication of how the presence of God in the Spirit produces a new kind of life. Verse 23 speaks of the transformation of the believers' worship, and verse 24 makes explicit that the Spirit is God's own presence. This second verse is not so much a definition of God as it is an affirmation of God known to the believer in the Spirit. Spirit is used in all these passages as the divine presence that alters the believers' life. In this way, the Spirit is linked with the revelation of God in Christ. The revelation makes possible a new sense of the presence of God, which in turn transforms human existence.

The third theme in the Johannine concept of the Spirit arises from the second. The transition to this new life accorded by the Spirit is presented as a birth. The pneuma life arises from a "pneuma birth." The believer is born out of water and the Spirit (3:5), and this new birth is distinguished from a physical birth, since its origin is the work of God, not human activity (3:6; 6:63). Because this new birth is the work of God, it is mysterious, like the blowing of the wind (3:8). (*Pneuma* means both wind and spirit.) This idea of the birth by the Spirit is a kind of metaphor to suggest the way in which the life of the believer emerges as a result of being embraced by the presence of God. The Gospel of John does not propose to tell us exactly how this pneuma birth happens, but—quite the opposite—suggests that it is as unpredictable and mysterious as the comings and goings of the wind on a March afternoon. But the Gospel clearly asserts that the Spirit radically reorients human life.

Finally, we find Spirit used in association with a uniquely Johannine expression, the "Advocate" or "Helper." We will need to discuss this more fully in just a moment. But for now, note that the Fourth Evangelist equates the divine Spirit with this Advocate. The Advocate is called the "Spirit of Truth" in 14:17, 15:26, and 16:13. If my hunch is correct, Truth in the Gospel of John means the revelation of God in Christ. Therefore, the Spirit of Truth is the one who communicates that revelation of God. In 14:26 the Advocate is called the "Holy Spirit," a traditional label used when speaking of the mysterious presence of God among Christians.

A few quick conclusions: The Gospel affirms that the Spirit is given to Jesus (1:32), so that he in turn might give it to the believers (20:22). The bestowal of the Spirit on believers is closely tied to the crucifixion and resurrection of Jesus (19:30; 20:22). It appears, then, that the Fourth Gospel takes some of the traditional Christian affirmations about the Spirit and reshapes them. The reshaping results in an emphasis on two points: Jesus himself gives the Spirit to believers, and that gift of the divine presence occasions a radically new life. Yet the most creative contribution of the Gospel of John to Christian thinking about the Spirit lies ahead of us.

> *Reader's Preparation*: Read the following passages in which Jesus speaks of an Advocate: 14:15–17, 25–26; 15:26–27; 16:7–15. Consider these questions: Who is this Advocate? How is the Advocate related to Christ and to the Father? What does the Advocate do and to whom or for whom? What are the major affirmations about the Advocate made in these passages?

The next thing we must do in our investigation of the pneumatology (that is, what is believed and taught about the Spirit) of the Fourth Gospel is to examine the peculiar word that it sometimes uses for the Spirit. That word is Paraclete (*parakletos*). The Fourth Gospel is the only New Testament document that uses this word to describe the Spirit. Its meaning is a bit difficult to define exactly. In effect, there are at least four different shades of meaning and hence four translations of the Greek word. The first two have in common the fact that they both come from the language of the legal court system of the day. Paraclete may mean "one called to the side of another to help." This is one who is called to assist a client in a court case. Hence, the translation "Advocate" is used for the Greek word in the New Revised Standard Version. The second meaning is similar. The Paraclete is "one who intercedes, entreats, or makes appeals for another." Again the context is a legal trial. The Paraclete is the defense attorney (a sort of Perry Mason figure, if you will), who speaks on behalf of the defendant. Therefore, the translation "Intercessor" is sometimes found in the passages you read.

The next two possible meanings of the Greek word *paraklētos* are not legal or court meanings. The first is "one who comforts and consoles another." This meaning of the Greek gave rise to the translation "Comforter." As if this array were not enough, we find that this fascinating Greek word was also used to designate one who "proclaims or exhorts." So the word could also be appropriately translated "Proclaimer."

Obviously the word was a very rich one in our Evangelist's day. It was one with multiple and varied meanings—Advocate, Intercessor, Consoler, and Proclaimer. The Fourth Evangelist seems to combine the meanings in a new way to create a new concept. We know, too, that the word was used in some Jewish circles regarding the functions of the angels. The Gospel of John has taken this rich word and applied it to the Spirit of God. The result is an amazing theology of the Spirit. This should not surprise us. We saw in chapter 1 how the Gospel does essentially the same thing with the word "Logos," which also had wide and varied meanings. By applying it to Christ this Gospel suggests a profound and penetrating view of Christ. Much the same is true of the Spirit. With the word "Paraclete" the Fourth Gospel catches the imagination of a wide range of readers and opens numerous avenues of meaning for the Spirit. It is safe to say that the Fourth Evangelist had a way with words. Much of the genius of this Gospel is rooted in their provocative use. On that score its author has as much in common with a good poet as with a good theologian.

Surely the application of the word "Paraclete" to designate the Spirit means something more. It means that for some reason the Johannine community was not entirely satisfied with the simple title of Spirit. Of course, the Gospel uses that expression without any apparent reservation, as we have seen. But when it comes to the explication of the role of the Holy Spirit in chapters 14 through 16 the Gospel begins to employ the word "Paraclete." Maybe the Evangelist objected to a common idea among the Jews that there was a special angel who functioned as the Paraclete. Perhaps the passage dares to give the Christian concept of the Spirit of God a special designation in order to affirm that Christ alone gives the Spirit, and the Spirit alone is the Paraclete. Dealing with the leaders of the Jewish synagogue, the Johannine Christians needed to speak of the presence of God in their midst in a distinctive way. For whatever reason, the Gospel of John attaches this title to the Spirit and thereby provokes a great deal of thought.

We must try to summarize the nature and function of the Paraclete as the Gospel of John describes it. (Here as elsewhere in this discussion of the Paraclete, I am profoundly indebted to Raymond E. Brown's excellent appendix on the subject in his commentary on John, *The Gospel According to John*, Anchor Bible, vol. 29a.) About the nature of the Paraclete we can say two things:

1. The Paraclete comes from and is related to both the Father and the Son:
   a. The Paraclete comes only if Jesus departs (15:26; 16:7, 8, 13).
   b. The Paraclete comes from the Father (15:26).
   c. The Father gives the Paraclete in response to Jesus' request (14:16).
   d. The Paraclete is sent in Jesus' name (14:26).
   e. Jesus sends the Paraclete from the Father (15:26; 16:7).
2. The Paraclete is identified in a number of different ways:
   a. "Another Paraclete," implying that Jesus is the first (14:16).
   b. The "Spirit of Truth" (14:17; 15:26; 16:13).
   c. The "Holy Spirit" (14:26).

In summary of this evidence, we may say that the Paraclete is a continuation of Christ, even the alter ego of Christ. What is said of the relationship of the Son to the Father throughout the Gospel can be said in large part of the relationship of the Paraclete to the Father. But this mysterious being is dependent on Christ's ministry. The Paraclete is, as it were, "act two" that cannot begin until "act one" (Jesus' ministry) is completed.

We may speak about the function of the Paraclete under two separate categories:

1. The relationship of the Paraclete to the disciples. The Paraclete
   a. Is easily recognized by the disciples (14:17).
   b. Is within and continues to remain with them (14:16–17).
   c. Is their teacher (16:13).
   d. Announces to them things that are to occur in the future (16:13).
   e. Declares what belongs to Christ and what does not (16:14).
   f. Glorifies Christ (16:14).
   g. Witnesses to Christ (15:26).
   h. Reminds the disciples of all that Jesus said (14:26).
   i. Speaks only what is heard (16:13).
2. The relationship of the Paraclete to the world. The world
   a. Cannot accept the Paraclete (14:17).
   b. Cannot see or recognize the Paraclete (14:17).
   c. Rejects the Paraclete (15:26).
   d. But its rejection does not prevent the Paraclete's witness to Christ(15:26).
   e. Is condemned, proven wrong, and pronounced guilty of sin by theParaclete (16:8–11). (John 16:8–11 is a very difficult passage both to translate and to understand. But the summary catches at least some of its basic meaning.)

Obviously, according to the Fourth Gospel, the Paraclete has a twofold function: to communicate Christ to believers and, to put the world on trial and find it guilty as charged.

The Fourth Evangelist is solving two basic problems with this view of the Paraclete. The first is a problem faced by a great deal of New Testament literature, namely, the delay of the Parousia. Christ has not returned as he was expected to do. But, asserts the Evangelist, he has reappeared in the form of the Paraclete. He is present even though it seems that the Parousia never occurred. The Paraclete and Christ are closely identified in the passages we have examined just so this point could be made. The Paraclete is Christ in our midst, claims the Evangelist! The Evangelist is showing readers that the old Christian expectation of the return of Christ was looking in the wrong direction. Don't look into the future for the return of Christ. Look, rather, into the present experience of the community. The Christians' experience of the Spirit is their experience of the reappeared Christ. The Parousia has occurred but not in the rather gross way it was expected. Hence, the view of the Paraclete in the Gospel is part of the eschatology of the book. It is a segment of the present eschatology taught by the Evangelist, and a part of the writer's conviction that the present experience of the believer is pregnant with possibility.

The Gospel of John was also answering a much greater question with its doctrine of the Paraclete. The delay of the Parousia was a peculiarly Christian problem at one stage in the history of that religion. The other problem with which the Fourth Evangelist wrestles is a much more universal concern. It is the problem of historical distance from the time of revelation. If a religion teaches that the Ultimate Reality has been revealed at a particular point in history, a question immediately arises. How can persons avail themselves of that revelation if they live at a later point in history? Christianity was later to solve this problem by the creation of a canon. It said that the historical revelation of God is preserved in these certain writings—the Bible—and one may have access to that revelation through the reading of the Bible. But the Johannine Christians lived in a day before there was a Christian canon. The Gospel's answer to the question of bridging the temporal gap back to the historical revelation is through the person and work of the Paraclete.

The Paraclete takes the revelation once made of God in the person of Jesus and mediates it to persons of a later time. Therefore, the Gospel stresses that the Paraclete does not teach *new* things but only what Christ taught (e.g., 14:26). The Gospel asserts as well that the Paraclete is the witness to the revelation of God in Christ (15:26). In effect the Paraclete is the medium of divine revelation—the divine messenger of revelation (see figure 4–2).

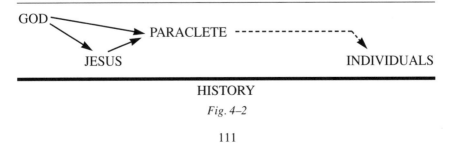

HISTORY

Fig. 4–2

We can understand why the question of revelation was a necessary one for the Evangelist to answer. The Johannine Christians lived in a day when the eyewitnesses to the historical Jesus were dying. There were second- and even third-generation Christians asking how they might have direct access to what happened some fifty years before. The Gospel of John gives them their answer. By virtue of the work of the Paraclete, they have as direct an access to that revelation as did the original disciples. They are not secondhand Christians. Their truth comes from an agent who is nothing less than the alter ego of Christ himself.

There is another way of putting this that is perhaps a more positive way of expressing the same concern. How is it that Christians continue to experience the presence of Christ even after all these years? Why does the revelation of God in Christ continue to grasp the lives of persons and transform them? How do we explain the reality of the presence of Christ for believers? The answer the Fourth Evangelist gives is in this view of the Paraclete. The experience of the Christian can only be accounted for by means of a divine Presence. It is the Paraclete who is the living presence of Christ, and it is the Spirit's work that keeps the revelation of God in Christ readily available to all.

The Paraclete concept is then a stroke of genius! It boldly expands the older concepts of the Spirit of God by using a new word in a new way. It gave the Christians a distinctive way of thinking about the presence of God, answered the nagging question of the delay of the Parousia, and solved the problem of the growing temporal separation from the historical revelation. Occasionally a great thinker comes upon an idea that in a nearly perfect way speaks to his or her age. We might say that Plato, Thomas Aquinas, Hegel, Freud, and many others were such thinkers. I believe the Fourth Evangelist also belongs in that category, at least in terms of the concept of the Paraclete.

In the Paraclete the Fourth Gospel has again affirmed the richness of the Christian's present experience. It declares that in that present—the now— Christ is present. The fullness of the revelation of God in history is at the individual's fingertips in the activity of the Paraclete. Eternity and history touched in the past at the incarnation of God in Christ. Eternity and history may again touch in the future as God brings history to its climactic conclusion. But eternity and history are linked in the believer's present. Eternity is now.

THE JOHANNINE VIEW OF THE CHURCH

The richness of the believers' present is affirmed still further in what the Gospel has to say about the Christian community. It has been claimed that the concept of the church plays a minor role in the Fourth Gospel and even that there is no concept of the church in this Gospel. This is claimed by virtue of the fact that the Fourth Gospel never uses the word "church." However, such a judgment is premature. Without ever using the word "church," the Gospel expresses a very important understanding of the Christian community. This Gospel articulates a view of the church without ever resorting to the use of that word.

> *Reader's Preparation*: Two of Jesus' metaphorical speeches are relevant to the discussion of the Gospel's view of the Christian community: (1) the Good Shepherd and the Door (10:1–18) and (2) the True Vine (15:1–10). Read these and then continue reading through chapters 15, 16, 17, and 20. The heart of the concept of the Christian community is found in what Jesus is made to say in these passages regarding the relationships among the Christian believers and the relationship between them and Christ. See if you can draw up a list of the characteristics of these relationships.

The view of the Christian community in the Fourth Gospel is a far different one from those found elsewhere in the New Testament. That is especially true if we ask about the views of the church found in the New Testament literature written after 70 C.E. From that time on in the history of the early Christian movement there was a prominent concern for the understanding of the church and particularly an interest in the growth of institutional matters and in the question of proper authority. Compare, for example, the passages you have just read with the Gospel of Matthew. In the latter, the nature and structure of the church is highly important. The famous (and controversial) words of Jesus spoken to Peter after the confession at Caesarea Philippi are the Gospel of Matthew's way of understanding the foundation of the church upon apostolic authority (Matthew 16:13–20). The First Gospel's special concern for this matter can be seen when we contrast its telling of the story with those of the Gospels of Mark and Luke (Mark 8:27–33 and Luke 9:18–22).

This concern is not prominent in the Fourth Gospel. The whole point made by the Gospel of Matthew's account of the confession at Caesarea Philippi is entirely missing in the Gospel of John. Our Evangelist does not seem to have been interested in the institutional structure of the church. His or her understanding of the Christian community did not focus on the authority of the church or its leaders. Nor did our author share the First Evangelist's insistence on the apostolic basis of the church. All of this is missing from the Fourth Gospel. Why? I will suggest later that the Fourth Evangelist was not yet confronted with the kind of issues that aroused an interest in institutional questions. The Johannine church is still confronting a serious threat from outside the community of believers. Hence, our Gospel's view of the church is structured around that issue. Only later, when the Johannine church is threatened from within by views that could undermine the community, is there a concern for institutional authority and structure. We see that development not in the Fourth Gospel but in the Johannine Epistles. When the Gospel was written, the question of institutionalization was simply not yet relevant. Institutionalization addresses internal, not external problems, and the

Johannine Christians were consumed with external problems when our Evangelist wrote. But the Fourth Gospel is not really anti-institutional. The Evangelist and first readers had just not yet gotten around to the question of the organizational structure of the church. (See Appendix A, "The Johannine Epistles and the Gospel of John.")

What does the Fourth Evangelist have to say about the Christian community? We offer five generalizations about the community of believers in the Fourth Gospel. These are sweeping generalizations, to be sure, but they capture the essence of the Johannine view.

First, *the community of believers is one because of its oneness with Christ.* This point is summarized in 17:23 as part of the prayer of Jesus, "I in them and you in me, that they may become completely one." The community of believers is one with Christ. Christ is one with the Father. The members of the community are one. Here the Johannine view of the community of believers builds on its view of Christ. As there is identity and individuality between the Father and the Son, so it is with the community. The oneness spoken of in the relationship of the Christian believers with one another and with Christ is modeled on the relationship between Christ and God. The members are united with Christ, yet that does not mean they are absorbed into the being of Christ. This is not a mystical view of the community. The distinctive individuality of the community is maintained in its unity with Christ, just as the individuality of Christ is maintained in his unity with the Father.

If it is true that the relationship of the Father and Son is the model being used here, something else follows. The oneness of the believers is not a unity that abolishes their own individuality. They are one, but they are united as individuals. Individuality is preserved amid their commonality as members of the community. We have then the same kind of tension between individuality and identity that we confronted in Chapter 1 when we wrestled with Johannine Christology. The bonds within the community of believers might be analogous to the modern understanding of marriage. It is a union of two persons—the two shall become one (Genesis 2:24). But the individuality of the spouses is preserved. The union is real while preserving the sacredness of the distinctive persons. The relationship might be represented in a figure eight. If the figure is viewed one way, it is a continuous line unbroken in its unity. Viewed another way, it is two circles. Each circle is independent of the other. Yet they touch one another at one point. Hence, there is unity, but also distinctive individuality. Imagine, if you will, numerous figure eights all composed of one unbroken line, but forming a series of individual circles all touching upon one another. Such an imaginary figure might represent the Johannine concept of the Christian community—unity in diversity.

Second, *the community is one in love.* The theme of love among the believers is best expressed in 15:14–17. The commandment under which the community lives is a simple one, "Love one another" (15:17). Again the model is a christological one. God loves the Son, and the Son loves the Father. The Son in turn loves the believers, and they are to love one another. The quality of the relationship between the Father and the Son and between the Father and the world (3:16) is the kind of thing to which the community is called. It is mutual love. The community of believers is to exemplify the kind of love that exists between God and God's unique Son.

The third generalization brings us to the heart of the Johannine view of the church: *The community is the locus of the manifestation of God.* This point is found in 17:22–23. But it involves a rather complex logic. First, it must be understood that glory is used here in the basic Hebraic sense of *kabod.* That Hebrew word is used in the Hebrew scriptures to designate the manifestation of God. God is revealed, made present, in mighty deeds in history. The presence of God is glory! The logic of the Gospel's view presupposes this foundation in the First Testament, and in chapter 17 it runs like this:

Glory is given to Jesus (17:22, 24).
Jesus gives that glory to the believers (17:22).
Therefore, the believers manifest the glory of God (17:23).

This means that the manifestation of God in Jesus has now been transferred to the community of believers. It is among them that God is made known as once God was made known in mighty deeds in the Hebrew Bible and then in the person and work of Christ.

This is a startling idea! It claims that the revelation of God is present in the community of Christian believers. This means that the community of believers is now what the mighty deeds of God in history and in Jesus were to the world. If the locus of the revelation of God was once in Jesus, it is now among and through the community of believers. If you will, the community of believers displays the continuing incarnation. The Paraclete is active among the believers, and it is in their midst that the presence of God is to be found.

Here is a further reason for the Fourth Gospel to stress as it does the present experience of the Christian. The community of believers is the place of God's revelation, the divine presence. Hence, God is available to the believer in his or her present time through the Paraclete. The believers are invited by the Fourth Evangelist to look at their present experience in the community for the revelation of God. Eternity touches history in the community of Christian believers, the Evangelist boldly proclaims. So, for them, eternity is now.

We may now summarize these three generalizations about the Johannine view of the community of believers. These three points are really one, as shown in figure 4–3.

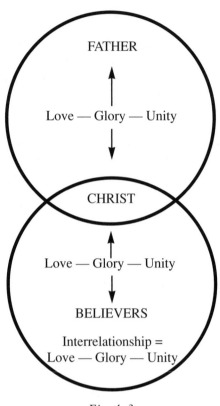

Fig. 4–3

The understanding of the Christian community is shaped in the image of the relationship between the Father and the Son. As the Father loves the Son, so the believers are to love one another. As the Father and Son are united as individual beings, so the community of believers is to be united. As the Father is revealed through the Son, so the Father is revealed in and through the community. I submit that this is a very significant view of the church. It is one that gives a very high place to the role of the community of believers—perhaps even too high a place! It is one that values the community as the ongoing locale of that which was so decisive in the historical revelation of God in Christ.

The fourth generalization about the Johannine view of the church is of a different kind: *The Fourth Evangelist "democratizes" church order*. (Here my dependence on Käsemann's *The Testament of Jesus According to John 17* is explicit. Throughout this section on the church, however, Käsemann's discussion has been a primary source.) The Fourth Evangelist presumably wrote at a time when church organization was rapidly developing. However, the Gospel shows very little interest in the matter. When there is an especially high interest among early Christians in the development of distinctive officers in the church organization, our Evangelist seems to move in the opposite direction. The most striking thing about the Johannine discussion of the community of believers is that there are no distinctions made among the believers that might become a basis for official leadership. There is no distinction made between the role of the apostles (the original twelve disciples) and other believers. The Gospel, as a matter of fact, does not use the expression "apostle" at all. It uses the word "disciples" where we might expect to find "the Twelve." And our Gospel seems to mean by disciple, any believer. For instance, the power to forgive sins and the gift of the Spirit are given to the disciples in general, not exclusively to the Twelve (20:21–23). This led Käsemann to say that the Fourth Gospel has democratized church order. It has de-emphasized the authority of the original followers of Jesus and claims that all believers have an equal authority and equal gifts. This is so, it appears, by virtue of the presence of the Spirit-Paraclete among the believers.

We are brought, then, to the difficult question of the role of Peter in the Fourth Gospel. With that question comes the role of the enigmatic "disciple whom Jesus loved" and the mysterious "other disciple." It is not just a "two for the price of one" problem we face, but a *three* for the price of one"! We cannot solve all the problems connected with these three interrelated questions: What is the role of Peter? Who is the beloved disciple and what is his or her role? Who is the "other disciple" and what is that person's role? Nor can we even take the time to summarize adequately the complexity of the questions and their interrelatedness. The following will have to suffice.

Reader's Preparation: Below are the passages in which the "disciple whom Jesus loved" is mentioned. Also, here is a list of those passages which speak of "another disciple." As you read them, you might ponder a number of questions that bear upon our immediate issue: Who was the beloved disciple? Who is this other disciple? Is the other disciple synonymous with the beloved disciple? Does the beloved disciple seem to you to be a real historical person or a symbolic figure? What is the relationship between the beloved disciple or the other disciple and Peter in those passages in which both appear? 1:37–42; 13:23–26; 18:15–16; 19:25–27; 20:2–10; 21:7, 20–24.

First, a word about the role of Peter in the Fourth Gospel. It is less prominent here than in the Synoptic Gospels. In our Gospel Peter does not emerge as the leader of the original Twelve in the same way as he does in the other Gospels. Nor does he function as the sort of model disciple we are accustomed to find in the pages of the Synoptics. The commissioning of Peter in the context of the confession at Caesarea Philippi in the passages cited above is missing in the Fourth Gospel (although 6:67–69 may be the Johannine parallel). The substitute story centering on Peter in chapter 21 is thought by most scholars not to have been part of the original Gospel. Chapter 21 is understood almost universally as an appendix to the Gospel, added at a later time by another author.

Second, alongside the diminished role of Peter is the prominence of the beloved disciple. This disciple almost seems to take Peter's place at times. It is he or she who is closest to Jesus (e.g., 13:23). Peter seems to rely upon him or her for the meaning of Jesus' words. As Peter and the beloved disciple race to the tomb after hearing that it is empty, it is the latter who arrives there first (20:4). She or he is credited with first believing that Christ has arisen from the dead (20:8).

Does this mean that the Fourth Evangelist wants to depreciate the place of Peter and emphasize the prominence of the beloved disciple? Some have argued that this is the case. They say that the Evangelist is reacting against the importance assigned to Peter in the developing organization of church authority. The Fourth Evangelist is rebelling, they argue, against the authority of Peter and wants to stress that another disciple was closer to Jesus than Peter. Many scholars claim that this beloved and unnamed disciple was none other than John, the apostle, son of Zebedee, upon whose memories the Fourth Gospel is based.

Such an argument has an element of truth in it. The Fourth Gospel does seem to diminish the prominence of Peter in favor of the beloved and unnamed disciple. But I think we need not reach the same conclusions as would some. It is not necessary to assume that the Gospel is caught up in a childish game of arguing about which disciple was the more important. The Fourth Evangelist is not saying to other Christian communities something like, "My father is more important than your father!" It is more likely, I think, that the tradition that the Fourth Evangelist received did not give Peter the same prominence as did the traditions embedded in the Synoptic Gospels. However, the Johannine tradition knew of an anonymous disciple who was highlighted in the accounts of Jesus' ministry. The Evangelist is working with that tradition without consciously trying to depreciate one disciple and appreciate another. To put it another way, if there is an anti-Petrine (anti-Peter) motif in the Fourth Gospel, it is not a deliberate one. I suggest that the Fourth Evangelist was not aware of the growing authority of Peter in some other Christian communities. He or she had not read the recent "best-seller," the Gospel According to Matthew!

Who is this mysterious beloved and unnamed disciple? There are at least four alternative answers: (1) She or he might have been the apostle John who originated the tradition that the Fourth Evangelist used. (2) The beloved disciple might have been Lazarus whom it is said Jesus loved (11:5). The beloved disciple first appears in the Gospel's narrative in chapter 13, after Jesus has rescued Lazarus from the tomb (11:1–44). (3) The disciple whom Jesus loved might be an ideal disciple. That is, perhaps there is no historical person represented in the figure of the beloved disciple, but only a symbol of what true Christian discipleship is all about. (4) Perhaps he or she was a figure in the history of the Johannine community who was a model disciple even though not an eyewitness to the historical Jesus. The beloved disciple was a model in much the same way Abe Lincoln is thought of as part of the spirit of America, even though Lincoln's presidency was nearly a century after the founding of the nation. And, because of the radical democratic nature of the Johannine community, we cannot exclude the possibility that the beloved disciple was a woman. (See Appendix B, "The Women of the Gospel of John.")

We would prefer to leave the mystery of the beloved disciple unsolved—partly because it may not really matter! Perhaps it is best to believe that she or he is a totally anonymous figure. The theory that the beloved disciple is the apostle John, son of Zebedee, is difficult to maintain, I think. And perhaps it is inappropriate to deny all claim to this figure's actual historical existence, thus making him or her a purely symbolic character. However, this figure does *function* in the Gospel as a symbolic ideal. That is, whether or not there was such a historical person is irrelevant. Through the beloved disciple, the Evangelist portrays exemplary discipleship. Thereby the Gospel invites the reader to identify with and emulate the beloved disciple.

Sometimes in a novel one wonders if the hero is based on some actual historical person. Such a question makes for interesting speculation. But finally what is important is the message the novelist communicates through the central character. The question of his or her actual existence becomes insignificant. This is the case with the beloved disciple. The Evangelist either does not want the name of that figure known or assumes everyone already knows that name. So, in this character the Evangelist presents the kind of believer the reader is called to be. Furthermore, so far as church leadership is concerned, the Evangelist claims no special authority of this unnamed disciple. The beloved disciple's authority is not official, not organizational. It is simply that she or he loved Jesus and was loved by him in return. That authority, the Evangelist implies, is available to any believer.

If this view of the unnamed, beloved disciple is correct, we have further evidence that the Fourth Evangelist holds a very democratic view of church structure and authority. The believers are all called on to be the kind of disciple represented in the symbolic figure of the beloved disciple. Through the Paraclete all are equally capable of authoritative access to the revelation of God in Christ. The Gospel's view represents a maverick form of early Christianity, for it has no apparent interest in delegating special authority to special persons in the community. All believers are disciples. All believers may have that kind of relationship with Christ epitomized in the beloved disciple.

The Johannine democratic view of church authority does not take us as far away from our central theme in this chapter as it might appear. The reason, I think, the Johannine Christians could advance such a view of the community of believers is their confidence that the revelation is immediately available in the church. All persons have access through their immediate experience to the presence of God. Therefore, all have equal authority. Because eternity is in the midst of the community's present experience, there is no need for church structure or authority.

Perhaps this view of the church and church structure is naive. Perhaps it is the view of those who have not yet seen all the problems the church must face in the world. The ideas that the community is the locus of the presence of God and that radically democratic leadership should and could prevail are perhaps too idealistic. Did the Johannine Christians forget human sin and brokenness? Did they take into account that the community could not long be as perfectly one as they imagined? Did they overlook the inevitability of splits and differences? Did they not foresee that the community would eventually embrace those who held radically different views—and that those views would need to be controlled by strong leadership? Is their view of the community of believers naive—or, is it an expression of what the community of Christian believers could truly be? Perhaps it is less naive than we think. Perhaps the Johannine conviction is what the church must strive to be regardless of the circumstances it must face.

We come at last to the fifth and final generalization about the Johannine view of the church: *The community is sent into the world.* In the climactic twentieth chapter of the Gospel, the risen Christ unexpectedly appears to the disciples huddled in fear behind locked doors (20:19). Christ greets his followers, shows them his wounds from the crucifixion, and then speaks words pregnant with meaning. Our interest narrows to those attributed to the risen Christ in verse 21, "Peace be with you. As the Father has sent me, so I send you." The sending of the disciples actually completes a series of sendings in the whole of the Gospel. We recall that John, the baptizer, was sent (1:6) and we cannot have escaped the barrage of statements that Jesus was sent by God (most notably 3:16–17 but throughout the Gospel narrative, e.g., 5:24). Then we read how the Holy Spirit would be sent after Jesus' departure (14:26; 15:26; 16:7). Now the disciples are the ones sent.

The impression one gains from the Gospel is of a "sending God." God has an agenda that includes the rescue of the world from its plight (see esp. 3:16–17). Then God dispatches agents into the world in the service of the divine agenda. God's plan is constructed around a series of envoys, each of whom has a specific role to play in the divine scheme. John, the baptizer, as a preparation for Christ, Christ as the supreme revelation of God for the world, and the Holy Spirit as the continued presence of God with the believers. The disciples now take their place among the vital envoys in that scheme. The prelude to this divine sending of the disciples in 20:21 is in 4:38, where the disciples are sent as a harvesting crew into the fields.

The answer to where or to whom the disciples are sent by the risen Christ is tucked away in the final prayer of Jesus in 17:18, "As you have sent

Sent

me into the world, so have I sent them into the world." On first reading, this strikes us as strange. In the Fourth Gospel the world is noted for being the realm of unbelief and evil—the opposite pole from the believing community. (See the discussion of the dualistic symbols of the Gospel in Chapter 2.) Jesus declares without equivocation that the believers do not belong to the world any more than he himself does (e.g., 17:16). One would expect to find the disciples sheltered from the world, sealed off in some hermetically safe cocoon. But, no, they are sent *into* the world, for the divine agenda entails the salvaging of the distorted creation. The disciples' place then is in the world as Christ's agents.

All of this is made clearer by a remarkable feature to the commissioning of the disciples. Christ's sending of the disciples is compared in both 20:21 and 17:18 to God's sending of Christ. The comparison is astonishing, since the absolute uniqueness of Christ would seem to rule out any comparable sending of humans. What might it mean for the Johannine church to understand its mission as analogous to Christ's unique mission? The sending of Christ was motivated by God's love of and determination to save the world (3:16–17). Therefore, as Christ was the crux of God's redemptive plan for the world, the disciples are the continuation of that plan conceived in divine love.

The evidence is conclusive. The Johannine community understood themselves as a commissioned group, sent into the world to continue the divine plan of God inaugurated in Christ. Such a self-understanding is lofty. They are agents sent in the same way and for the same reason as their Lord! There is much in the Gospel of John that betrays the image of an almost sectarian group of Christians, fighting off the attacks of their opponents. We have tended to see an insider-outsider dichotomy through much of the document—a sectarian struggle between "us" and "them." With that sectarian mentality comes a propensity to withdraw from the world. But now our image must be redrawn. True, the internal life of the community portrayed in the Gospel is strong. Equally as strong is the mission consciousness of the community. In this sketch of the Johannine church there are dark lines moving in two opposite but equal directions. One is inward, moving attention to the internal solidarity and mutual love shared within the community. The other line is outward, pointing to the work of the church in the world around it. Yet these opposite-directed lines are paradoxically conceived as pointing in the same direction for the believers. Even the unity of the church (an internal characteristic) is understood to be part of the church's mission in the wider world, for it, Jesus' prayer claims, brings the world to belief (17:21). Compared with other religious traditions of the world, the Johannine self-understanding places it among the type we call evangelical. Convinced of its divine mission, Johannine Christianity must be about the work of aiding its God in the salvation of the world.

Armed with the understanding of this mission dimension of the Johannine church, a number of things about the Gospel narrative become clearer. We are able to see how the Fourth Evangelist wanted readers to find in some of the characters models for their mission in the world. We are able to see how and why witness is important in this Gospel. From among the models for the believers' witness to the world, the Gospel presents three in particular. The first is surely John, the baptizer, whose persistent effort to point beyond himself to Christ (1:19–34) is so vividly presented along with the disclaimer that he was anything more than a witness to Christ (1:6–8). The second is the Samaritan woman in chapter 4. She models the way in which an encounter with Christ elicits testimony to others and her story demonstrates the powerful effect of that testimony (4:39–42). The third model is Mary Magdalene. Before the other disciples are commissioned, Mary is sent by the risen Christ to share the news of his resurrection (20:17–18). (It is not accidental that two of these three models are women. See Appendix B, "The Women of the Gospel of John.")

In summary, the Johannine view of the church includes the community's sense of unity, their mutual love for one another, their conviction that among them God continues to be manifested, their democratic, egalitarian life together, and their mission in the world. Like a giant spider's web, this strand of thought in the Gospel is interlaced with other strands. The view of the church is sustained by the fact that the eschatological blessings of the last day are already present in the community. The Johannine view of the community intersects with the view of the Spirit. The Paraclete in the community of faith produces an environment in which believers are empowered for their life together and their mission beyond.

THE SACRAMENTS IN THE FOURTH GOSPEL

Here our thesis concerning the emphasis upon the believer's present experience hits a stone wall! We would expect that a Christian position like the one we have been sketching in this chapter would emphasize the sacraments, which are generally thought to be the means by which the Christian can immediately experience God's presence. Therefore, given the propensity of the Fourth Evangelist for an experiential and sensory theology, surely the sacraments play an important role in the Gospel. But, alas, such is not the case! At least, that is not what *appears* to be the case. So, we must ask what view the Gospel takes with regard to the sacraments.

Reader's Preparation: Two groups of passages are important for the following discussion: (1) Read 1:29–39. Why does the Baptist not baptize Jesus? Compare 3:22 and 4:2. Read 13:1–20. This is the point in the narrative where one would expect (from the Synoptic pattern) to find the institution of the Lord's Supper. Does the washing of the feet of the disciples function as a substitute for the Last Supper sacrament? Is it a sacrament? (2) The following are passages in the Fourth Gospel that are sometimes understood as references to the sacraments of the Lord's Supper and/or Baptism. Read them and determine for yourself whether or not references to the sacraments are intended: 2:1–11; 3:5; 6:1–13, 51–59; 13:1–17; 15:1–6; and 19:34.

The first thing that strikes one about the Fourth Gospel when the question of the sacraments is posed is one simple fact: The institutions of the sacraments are missing! Jesus himself is not baptized. His baptism has been the traditional sanction for the rite of baptism in Christian practice. Further, from the Fourth Gospel we cannot even discern clearly if Jesus practiced baptism! At one point it is said that he did and at another that he did not (3:22 and 4:2). Neither does Jesus institute the Last Supper, or Eucharist! Such blatant omissions put into question any sort of discussion of sacramentality in the Fourth Gospel. It is like asking if the Wright brothers believed in space travel! There is simply no explicit mention of the sanctions of the two rites of baptism and the Lord's Supper.

However, some scholars find explicit reference to the sacraments at other points in the Gospel. They argue that the transformation of the water into wine in the story of the wedding at Cana implies the wine of the Eucharist. Jesus' assertion that one must be born "of water and spirit" in 3:5 is, some say, a sure allusion to baptism. Moreover, the feeding of the multitude in chapter 6 is understood by many to be the Johannine institution of the Last Supper. In verse 11 Jesus gives thanks and distributes the bread and fish. The Greek word translated "gave thanks" is *eucharistēsas*. That word is the root of the word "Eucharist." The eucharistic meaning of the feeding of the crowd is made explicit, say these interpreters, in the speech of Jesus coming later in the chapter (6:51–58). There Jesus is made to declare, "Unless you eat the flesh of the Son of Man and drink his blood, you have no life in you" (v. 53). Others find the washing of the feet of the disciples in chapter 13 to be a symbolic representation of the meaning of the Eucharist. Perhaps the allegory of the vine (15:1–6) is meant to imply the eucharistic wine. Finally, 19:34 speaks of the blood and water flowing from Jesus' side. The blood may represent the eucharistic cup and the water, baptism, according to some interpreters.

Consequently, in spite of the absence of the institution of the sacraments, some scholars argue that the Fourth Gospel is highly appreciative of the sacraments. The point is, they contend, that it takes for granted the reader's understanding of the institution of the sacraments. Therefore, it focuses upon their meaning, particularly in chapters 6 and 13. This understanding of the Gospel claims that the Fourth Evangelist was a sacramentarian of the highest kind. In this case, silence is understood as profound appreciation rather than neglect. The poet who wishes to celebrate our nation's heritage in a work does not rehearse the history of the founding of these United States. Rather, she or he alludes perhaps subtly to the depths of meaning in the spirit of those founding events. So, too, argue some, did the Fourth Evangelist celebrate the significance of the Lord's Supper and baptism.

There are those who would propose a drastic alternative. Bultmann and others have argued that the Fourth Gospel is anti-sacramental. The argument goes something like this: The Fourth Evangelist knows about the sacraments, but is disgusted by their abuse in the church of the time. So, this author deliberately ignores the sacraments in the Gospel. The Gospel's silence screams a loud protest against the sacraments! The water of baptism and the bread and wine of the Eucharist have come to take the place of Christ himself, the Evangelist thinks. Eventually, however, the Gospel is revised by a rather traditional Christian. That person does not like the omission of any reference to the sacraments. Thus, this unknown editor adds sacramental passages at points such as 3:5 (by inserting the words "water and") and 6:51–58. (This view is part of the spoiler theory described in the first section of this chapter.) The result is that these passages stand out like sore thumbs, according to Bultmann.

A third view interprets the Fourth Gospel as revisionist. That is, it does not oppose the sacraments (as Bultmann would have us believe), nor does it endorse them (as the proponents of the first alternative would counsel). Rather, the Gospel attempts to revise the readers' understanding. So, the bread of life discourse (chapter 6) and the foot washing scene (chapter 13) each interpret the meaning of the Lord's Supper. Baptism is reinterpreted as a meaningful rebirth only through the gift of the Spirit (3:5).

Still a fourth alternative for understanding the sacraments in the Fourth Gospel goes something like this: The Johannine church did not mean to ignore the sacraments in its Gospel. Rather, the Gospel leaves them at an implicit, rather than explicit, level. Gradually, the Gospel undergoes small revisions that seek to make the sacramental references more explicit. Baptism was surely implied in the discussion of chapter 3, so some kindly reviser added the words "water and" to make the meaning of the passage clearer. This view differs from the spoiler theory of Bultmann and his followers in an important way. The revisers who are responsible for many of the sacramental passages are in agreement with, rather than opposition to, the Gospel's original view. They help the Gospel say more clearly what they were confident it wanted to say.

Finally, a bold alternative remains. The Johannine church does not know the tradition of the sacraments. They have no access to the stories of their origin and do not observe them. This is possible because the Johannine church is out of the mainstream of early Christian development (that is, the development known to us through the Pauline epistles and the Synoptic Gospels). It is not sacramental or anti-sacramental, but rather asacramental—meaning the Johannine Christians are ignorant of the sacraments and the traditions concerning them. Such a view is possible only if one takes seriously a couple of assumptions. First, the Johannine community is not tied closely to the other Christian communities of the time. If the Johannine community does not know the Synoptic Gospels and the epistles of Paul, then they are a relatively isolated Christian church. Second, their isolation is due in part to the fact that they had been for years a Christian community within the synagogue. They lived, as it were, within the confines of the Jewish community and were for that reason nonsacramental. The result is, as we have claimed several times, a maverick Christianity. Third, to view the Fourth Gospel as asacramental requires that one entertain the possibility that the sacraments were not a part of the practice of all the Christians of the first century. It is to view the earliest Christian movement as diversified, even on the matters as vital as baptism and the Eucharist.

If this last alternative is indeed the case, then the references that are often argued to be sacramental must be read differently. References to "gave thanks" and "eat flesh" are not eucharistic. Every time the Gospel mentions wine or water it does not allude to the sacraments. (Just because syncopation is typical of popular rock music does not mean that wherever there is syncopation there is rock—quite the contrary!) Thus, without intending sacramental meaning the Gospel could well use words that are elsewhere in the Christian movement associated with the sacraments without meaning to suggest sacramental meaning. Perhaps, too, some of the sacramental-sounding passages were later additions to the Gospel. After the Gospel was in circulation in the wider Christian community, perhaps words and phrases were added to refer to the sacraments. This is especially the case in 3:5, where an argument can be made that the words "water and" were not in the original text. Such additions were not in opposition to the Evangelist's view. Nor were they friendly revisions to make explicit what the Evangelist implied. They were added at points where the Evangelist was neutral.

The problem eludes solution! Still, I believe that another alternative is possible. There is so much of the Gospel that seems to reflect no interest in the sacraments. At those points in the narrative where tradition would have the sacraments, they are missing. Yet the evidence of 3:5 and 6:51–58 is hard to dismiss as later and hostile revisions. If we merge the fourth and last alternatives, something still a bit different emerges. Hence, I propose that, during their time within the synagogue, the Johannine Christians did not employ the sacraments, at least as major experiences in their lives. Hence, their tradition did not feature either baptism or the Eucharist. But with the expulsion from the synagogue and in their search for new Christian self-identity, both sacraments came to play more and more significant roles in their community life. Baptism came to be more appreciated as the mark of their identity. The Lord's Supper became more highly valued as their source of sustenance in their struggles with the world around them. John 3:5 and 6:51–58 may very well have been later interpretations of the earliest Johannine traditions. They were incorporated, I suggest, in one of the earliest of the revisions of the Gospel, not decades later. They were interpretations that were part of the entire revamping of the Johannine tradition by the Fourth Evangelist. Even so, this alternative is as vulnerable as are the others. The question remains perplexing.

However, we have yet to focus on another dimension of the question of the Johannine view of the sacraments. Whatever the Gospel's view of baptism and the Eucharist, there is a fundamental sacramentality about Johannine theology, as I proposed in Chapter 3. The theology of the Gospel is a sensory theology. The suggestion that faith grows out of immediate, everyday physical experiences is precisely what the sacraments in Christian thought are all about. When the Gospel asserts that seeing and hearing are the beginnings of the growth of faith, it proposes a sacramentality, for the sacraments are sensory experiences that epitomize the presence of God in ordinary realities. Bread and wine and water become the sensory experiences through which the Ultimate Reality is communicated to the believer in his or her present situation. So, the Johannine view of the relationship of faith and experience is fundamentally a sacramental view. It makes sense that, if the sacraments had not been known or widely practiced in the community, they would still have risen to prominence. In the context of the theology of the Gospel, baptism and Eucharist could easily have become acts that caught up the whole life experience of the Christians. Even though the Gospel's teachings on the sacraments themselves may be difficult to ascertain, paradoxically its view of normal daily experience is basically sacramental!

Drawn back to the Gospel's view of the relationship of faith and experience, I hope we can see even more clearly how it stresses that the Christian's present experience is ripe with the actualization of God's salvation. The Gospel honors the present as the time of salvation. Eternity touches history in the experience of the believer now.

CONCLUSION

If the exposition just completed is at all true to the Gospel, we have a remarkably consistent picture. The experience of the Paraclete, the understanding of the church, and the Evangelist's view of experience and faith all fit neatly together. They form the foundation upon which the Fourth Gospel asserts its radical present eschatology. They are the axioms of its system. They all lead to one conclusion: God is known now. God's gifts of salvation are immediately available. These elements all feed into the conviction that the present time is the time of salvation. Each one drives the reader toward a radical present eschatology and away from a focus upon the future. (See figure 4–4.)

This approach constitutes a bold solution to the religious problem posed at the beginning of this chapter. Are the benefits of religious salvation available in the believers' present experience or only in the future? The Fourth Gospel confidently asserts that believers know those benefits now. It makes

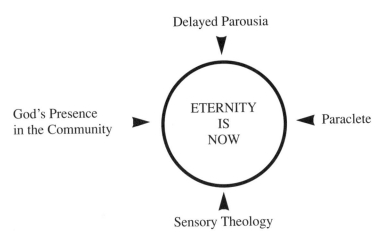

Delayed Parousia

God's Presence
in the Community

ETERNITY
IS
NOW

Paraclete

Sensory Theology

Fig. 4–4

this claim on the basis of the experience of the Johannine community. The Gospel does not deny the future and the hope for what the future will bring. But it teaches that the future holds no surprises for the Christians, for they already experience the future in their present. God's benefits for humanity are not confined to a blessed past. Nor are they only "pie in the sky by and by." Now is the time for the bestowal of those gifts for which all humanity yearns.

The Gospel's view makes some degree of sense the way we have laid it out. Basically, there is a consistency between the community's experience and the Gospel's conclusions. That is admirable. Whether or not the Johannine view of the matter is universally true is a far more difficult task to ascertain. Did the Johannine community correctly understand their experience? Or did they deceive themselves? Did they put too much emphasis on the present? Were they overreacting to Christian futuristic eschatology (as an adolescent might overreact to the views of her or his parents on a particular issue)? These are questions I leave you to ponder and discuss.

It remains only to be said that the Gospel structures a view that made sense of the experience of one religious community centuries ago. That is what all human beings must do as best they can: determine the meaning of their experience and found their religious beliefs (whatever they may be) on that determination. If the Fourth Gospel is wrong in terms of its conclusions about the presence of eternity in the now, at least it is an example of the way in which the task of seeking a religious position must be done.

CONCLUSION
JOHN, THE UNIVERSAL GOSPEL

A few decades ago there was much talk in America about the generation gap and about the rebellion of youth. Gradually what came to our attention was the fact that almost every age in the history of the human race had experienced the same thing to some degree. Young people were separated from their parents by a different view of the world, different priorities, different ideas, and different goals. Communication between parents and their young adult children was strained and problematic. Such a situation, we learned, was not the exclusive property of the twentieth century in America. It could be found as far back as ancient Greece. Youthful rebels are in many ways a universal phenomenon.

I would like us to bring our discussion of the thought and symbolism of the Fourth Gospel to a close with this proposal: The Fourth Gospel is in many ways a maverick piece of first-century Christian literature—a rebel. It strikes out in a drastically different direction from that of the other New Testament writings. At the same time, beneath the basic concerns of the Gospel we have discussed lie some universal religious questions. Those with which the Gospel of John deals are not confined to first-century Chris-tianity. They are questions that many religious traditions have pondered and continue to ponder. The Fourth Gospel viewed in one context is a maverick Gospel, a rebel. However, when viewed in a wider context it is a universal Gospel. Let us conclude our survey by considering these two different views of the work—a maverick Gospel and a universal Gospel.

THE PLACE OF JOHANNINE THOUGHT AND
SYMBOLISM IN EARLY CHRISTIANITY

We have argued from the beginning that the Fourth Gospel represents a peculiar form of first-century Christian thought. This argument is dangerous because it could be made with regard to any piece of New Testament writing. It can be said, for instance, that the Gospel of Luke and the Acts of the Apostles are a form of Christian thought quite different from the Gospels of Mark and Matthew, and that they are clearly distinct from Pauline Christianity. A similar case could be made for other sections of the New Testament. However, the contention of this introduction to the Fourth Gospel is that with Johannine Christianity one is dealing with a more fundamental uniqueness. The Gospels of Matthew and Luke were both dependent on the Gospel of Mark and probably the hypothetical source of sayings called Q. While the Acts of the Apostles may have misunderstood Paul, that work claims to represent the early apostle accurately. The Gospel of John makes no claim of being linked with other forms of early Christianity, and there is good evidence that this was indeed the case.

We may speak of the uniqueness of Johannine Christianity under several categories. The first is the distinctiveness of the *tradition* embedded in the Gospel. As we suggested in the Introduction, that tradition was an independent stream of Christian thought. It must have been rooted in an oral tradition that also eventually gave rise to the Synoptic traditions. But it is distinct both in form and content. The Fourth Gospel faithfully preserves those traditions cherished by the Johannine community. The preservation of traditional materials has struck us again and again in the course of our study. The fact that the Gospel conserved these particular traditions sets it apart from the other early Christian literature by virtue of the fact that the Johannine heritage was unique. The Fourth Gospel alone, so far as we know, informs us of the existence of that non-Synoptic, non-Pauline tradition.

Second, we may speak of the uniqueness of the Johannine *situation*. While all early Christianity may be traced back to Jewish roots, the Fourth Gospel is different. The earliest Christians were all Jewish Christians. They were related to their Jewish heritage while at the same time adhering to their new Christian beliefs. But very soon the Christians stood independent of Judaism. Already in the writings of the apostle Paul that split is well under way. Paul finds his most promising candidates for the Christian faith not among his Jewish colleagues but among the Gentiles. The split of Gentile Christians from the Jewish Christians was advanced by the so-called Jerusalem Council, about 49 C.E. The independence of Christianity from Judaism was surely completed by the early 60s and certainly by the destruction of Jerusalem in 70 C.E.

However, in the Gospel of John we find that the split from the synagogue is a later phenomenon. Everything we have encountered has pointed to the fact that the Fourth Evangelist is dealing with a community recently expelled from the synagogue and engaged in a serious dispute with the Jewish leaders. One is almost tempted to say that the Johannine church was slow in coming out of the womb of Judaism! It had lived peacefully there among the Jewish adherents for years longer than other Christian communities. Dare we say that in comparison with the other Christian communities it was slower in its development? Is the Johannine church like the young people who continue to live with their parents until the age of thirty-five and only then are expelled from their homes? This analogy has limits. It is true that Johannine Christianity continued longer in the safety of the Jewish synagogue. But it does not seem that such safety retarded its development, for the tradition preserved in the Fourth Gospel suggests that it had a long history and had been carefully nurtured. Certainly we cannot say that the Fourth Evangelist was a less mature Christian than other New Testament writers!

However, the Johannine community finds itself cast out of the synagogue. The result, we have suggested, is a serious and traumatic social dislocation.

The crisis affects the identity of the Christians in that community. Who are they if not Jews who embrace Christ? What is their Christianity if not a refined and sophisticated Judaism of a particular kind? Like young adults disowned by their parents, the Johannine community is in the midst of an identity crisis. This situation is made worse by the continuing conflict with the Jewish synagogue and contributes significantly to the distinctiveness of the Fourth Gospel and its thought.

We may speak of the distinctiveness of the Fourth Gospel in terms of its tradition and in terms of its situation. Finally, we may speak of that distinctiveness in terms of its *thought and symbolism*. The uniqueness of Johannine thought and symbolism is a result in part of the first two categories. The traditions employed in the Fourth Gospel make the concepts and symbolism of the document distinctive. The situation in which and for which the Gospel was written likewise contributes to that distinctiveness of thought and language. However, the genius of the Evangelist clearly played a major role in the peculiar form of Christianity articulated in the Gospel. The previous chapters have demonstrated how the mind of the Evangelist worked in a decisively distinct way. To cite but one example, recall the Evangelist's fondness for reshaping pregnant words (such as Logos and Paraclete) for use in the Gospel. This author took rich words and molded them to new Christian uses.

We need rehearse only briefly and generally some of the uniqueness of the thought and symbolism of the Fourth Gospel. First, the view of Christ as the Father's Son stands out. Nowhere in the New Testament do we find a Christology shaped in quite this manner. The Evangelist tried to hold together the unity and individuality of the Father and the Son. The "I am" sayings contribute to the Gospel's Christology and distinguish the Johannine view of Christ from others in the New Testament.

Second, the dualism of the Fourth Gospel is more pronounced than any we can find in the other early Christian literature. The blend of a human dualism and a cosmic dualism is different. Different too is the use of a wide variety of terms to express the poles of the dualism. Similarly, I would maintain that no New Testament writing wrestles so consciously with the question of divine determinism and human freedom as does the Gospel of John. However, I will concede that Paul runs a close second!

Third, the experiential theology of the Gospel stands out. Nowhere in the New Testament can we find a concept of the relationship of faith and experience worked out as thoroughly as in this Gospel. Nowhere is the sensory basis of faith emphasized as it is here. Equally distinct is the insistence of the Fourth Gospel that faith without seeing is the goal of the believer. Faith and knowledge are explicated in a manner unlike other early Christian thinkers.

Fourth, the emphasis upon the presence of salvation in the believers' experience significantly departs from the common themes of other New Testament literature. While the effort to solve the problem of the delay of the Parousia may be beneath the surface of a number of pieces of New Testament literature, the solution they offer is not as radical as that of the Fourth Evangelist. The profound appreciation for the believers' present is clearly unequaled in the New Testament. We could go on to mention the peculiar concept of the Spirit-Paraclete, the church, and the treatment of the sacraments. But we will let this be enough to jog the reader's memory.

The distinctiveness of Johannine thought and symbolism is clear, I hope. Yet it should not be overly stressed. Perhaps that is the danger our discussion has fostered. One may itemize the way in which two siblings are so radically different. They embrace entirely different life-styles. They do not even have a "family resemblance." They have diverse talents and skills. One wonders how they could even be related, yet they are. When the analysis is carried far enough, the family heritage is evident. Different though they are, they are genetically similar. They share the same parents. So, our analysis of the individuality of the Fourth Gospel must recognize that it shares the same genetic structure with other forms of Christianity in the first century. It has the same parentage as other New Testament writings. It too is rooted in the witnesses to the man Jesus of Nazareth and the earliest community of believers gathered around him. Maybe the distinctiveness of the Fourth Gospel results from the environment that shaped it after its birth, even as the difference between the two siblings might be traced to their respective environments.

How then shall we characterize the place of Johannine thought and symbolism in early Christianity? We have used the expression "maverick Gospel." That seems most fitting, for the thought and symbolism of the Gospel do not seem to seek consistency with any other form of early Christian thought. Rather, it freely goes its own way and explores new avenues of expression. It is an adventuresome Christianity, which does not flow with the mainstream of New Testament thought. But still it must be stressed that it is *Christian*. It shares with the rest of the New Testament the basic Christian gospel. So, a maverick it may be in the context of the New Testament, but it shares with the rest of the canonical literature a profound commitment to the belief that God has acted decisively in the person of Jesus for the salvation of humanity.

It is instructive to look ahead in the history of New Testament Christianity, beyond the production of the Gospel itself. The three Epistles that carry the name of John in the canon may help us to understand the place of the Fourth Gospel in relationship to early Christianity. It appears that the Johannine Epistles were all written at a later time than the Gospel. They were composed after Johannine Christianity had become associated more closely with the mainstream of early Christian thought. They were written, at least in part, to stem the tide of a deviant movement in the Johannine church. That movement appears to have been based on the Fourth Gospel! There were some in the later Johannine church who took the Fourth Gospel very seriously—perhaps too seriously. As a result, they were out of step with others of their church. The authors of the three Epistles attempted to identify the errors of this rebellious group. The authors represented and wrote to

Christian communities descended theologically from the Fourth Gospel, but ones which by then had been harmonized with mainstream Christianity. (See Appendix A, "The Johannine Epistles and the Gospel of John.")

Note what it is that the Epistles are concerned about correcting in these heretics. The eschatology of 1 John stresses the nearness of the Parousia (2:18–25; 2:28–3:2). It emphasizes the humanity of Jesus against a Christology that apparently did not take the incarnation as seriously as it should have (1 John 2:22; 4:2; 2 John 7). It stresses human sin because the rebels did not seem sufficiently conscious of their own sin (1 John 1:8ff.). The Epistles were written by those who believed Johannine Christianity to be fully homogeneous with mainstream orthodox Christianity. They wanted these radical thinkers corrected. As J. L. Houlden points out, the Johannine Epistles "are all part of a campaign to put a brake upon those who would 'gnosticize' the johannine tradition of Christian teaching" (*The Johannine Epistles*, p. 18. Houlden does an excellent job of relating the Gospel to the Epistles in his commentary).

The Fourth Gospel was a most likely document to inspire an independent and defiant movement. We do not contend that the group attacked in the Johannine Epistles correctly interpreted the Gospel. The opposite is generally the case. Yet the fact that such a movement grew out of the Johannine community on the basis of the Fourth Gospel is most important. The gnostic movement of the second century within the Christian church found the Gospel of John most congenial to its ideas. This was the case, I suggest, because the Gospel was not a "standard" Christian document. It was different. In several of its themes it allowed for the possibility of heretical interpretations—its dualism, its determinism, and its Christology. This historical fact of the susceptibility of the Fourth Gospel to heretical interpretation makes our point. It is an unusual piece of first-century Christian literature. Ernst Käsemann has called the theology of the Fourth Evangelist a "naïve gnosticism." I do not think that is entirely correct. But there is a sense in which the Fourth Evangelist writes with a naive disregard of how the Gospel's ideas and symbols might fit into the emerging pattern of early Christian thought. The Gospel is unbranded—a maverick. Its author does not seem to care about "fitting in." This Evangelist simply speaks his or her mind—preserving the Johannine traditions and addressing as effectively as possible the Gospel's first readers. There is something refreshing and exciting about that. It is what makes the study of the Fourth Gospel so intriguing.

JOHANNINE THOUGHT AND SYMBOLISM
AS REPRESENTATIVE OF THE RELIGIOUS QUEST

How then can we entitle this conclusion to our study "John, the Universal Gospel"? Its relationship with other early Christian thought seems to lead to the conclusion that it is a very particular Gospel, designed for and written out of a very peculiar situation. Hardly universal!

Yet the other theme of our study has been to show how the Fourth Gospel in its peculiar way deals with some of the basic questions in the religious quest of humans. We have tried to relate the main themes of Johannine thought to major questions that one finds in a number of religions. We have shown that broad, almost universal themes have been addressed in the maverick Gospel. Let us review the ones we have touched on in the course of our study:

First, there is the question of *the nature of the founder of the religious movement*. Every religion must come to some definition of the nature and work of its founder. Each religious tradition gradually works through this question, finally establishing a theological perspective based on some statement about its founder. In its Christology the Fourth Gospel makes a daring effort to do just that with regard to Jesus of Nazareth. In its claim that Jesus was the Father's Son, the Gospel of John reflects on the nature and work of the founder of the Christian movement.

Second, what is *the nature and source of evil*, which opposes and frustrates the will of God? Again, this is a universal question in religion. Every religion poses an answer, some more clearly than others, some more insistently than others. But almost always a religious system takes into account the reality of undesirable aspects of life. The Gospel of John (perhaps unconsciously) does this with its provocative dualism. Whatever the problems may be in understanding the nature of that dualism, it is one answer to the reality of evil. That dualistic split among persons is what the divine will seeks to overcome, and the negative pole of that dualism accounts for the reality of the resistance to belief.

Third, *the relationship of faith to experience* haunts every religious thinker. How is experience to be understood in relation to religious belief? Is faith based on experience? If so, how? Such questions are not limited to Christian thought or even to Western religious mentality. They are universal religious concerns. Our Gospel thoroughly explores and probes those questions. The result is that beneath the surface of this document rests a very profound concept of the relationship of faith and experience.

Fourth, religions promise some sort of salvation—some benefit for humans. The question is whether that benefit is bestowed during the believers' earthly existence or promised for some future age. The religious question of *the relationship of the present and the future in the promise of salvation* is perhaps an expression of a broader philosophical question. Maybe the religious question expresses the philosophical concern for the threefold existence of time—past, present, and future. Regardless, concern for the present and the future bestowal of the benefits of belief smolders in nearly every religious tradition. In its strong effort to highlight the present time of salvation, the Fourth Gospel offers a solution to that universal religious concern. Out of the experience of its community, the Gospel dares to announce that for Christians eternity is now.

The fact that our Gospel deals with these four common religious questions is our reason for claiming that it is a universal Gospel. We do not mean necessarily that the Fourth Gospel offers a religious system of thought and practice that every person in every age can embrace in detail. Certainly a case for that claim could be made, but we are not concerned with it here. The point is that this document shows us how a religious community wrestles with at least four (and doubtless many more) questions that concern every religious person in nearly every age. In that sense this is a universal Gospel.

An illustration from another area of early Christian literature might help. The Book of Revelation and the writings of Karl Marx have a good deal in common. Both the author of Revelation (John of Patmos) and Marx deal with a universal religious question, What is the meaning of history? Each of them proposes a view of history and its meaning. Both try to evoke their readers' belief that their view of history is true. They deal with a basic human question all thoughtful persons ask themselves, What is history all about? Is it just a pointless sequence of occurrences leading nowhere? Is there a pattern to the events of history? Do humans alone determine the course of history? Or, is there some outside force that mandates, or at least shapes, the general direction of history? John of Patmos and Marx give radically different answers to these questions, but both propose solutions. They both respond to a universal yearning of the human mind to understand history. The Fourth Gospel is universal in that it addresses itself to a number of such questions. It reaches beyond its parochial setting to embrace universal inquiries that arise from humans in quest of religious understanding.

Maybe our point could be put this way: What is universal about the thought of the Gospel is not its content but its method. It is the way in which the Gospel addresses these matters. The effort to resolve the issues haunting religious persons is its universal feature. What makes the Gospel universal is not the solutions it offers but the questions it explores. The solutions are perhaps less relevant than the willingness to pose the questions. Its answers may be less applicable than its questions!

Sometimes a teacher is remembered by her pupils for years. Often it is not *what* she taught, but *how* she taught that makes such a lasting impression. The Fourth Evangelist is perhaps a universal thinker not by virtue of *what* she or he thought but *how* she or he thought. In this way the author is an example for every religious person and represents the necessity of facing certain issues honestly and directly.

Some would want to make a much different kind of claim for the universality of the Gospel. I would not deny their appeal and have made just such appeals. But for now I want us to become aware of the first level of universalism in the Gospel—the level of the questions it poses.

Finally, then, the Fourth Gospel is *a maverick Gospel* in the context of early Christianity. Yet it is one that deals with important issues in the lives of religious persons of many different persuasions in many different centuries.

It represents the diversity of early Christian thought and the universality of the basic questions connected with being religious. Thus it is both a maverick and *a universal Gospel*.

It is my understanding that for years after the first performance of Beethoven's Ninth Symphony (*The Choral Symphony*), the finale of that work was a storm center for critics. They hotly debated Beethoven's drastic departure from the usual symphonic form. The theme of the final movement was either judged an utter failure or hailed as a stroke of genius. Critics were widely divided on the question. It appeared that one was convinced of the final movement's artistic failure or of its unprecedented brilliance.

Often genius is hard to distinguish from drastic failure. The genius in his or her own age is often taken for an idiot, and some who are hailed as geniuses are proven by history to have been idiots. So it is with the Fourth Evangelist. We must say that his or her work is either brilliant—a stroke of genius—or a regrettable mistake in early Christian thought. There seems to be little middle ground. The question, I suppose, can only be resolved by each student in the light of his or her own convictions. Still, on this much we can agree: The Fourth Gospel represents an intriguing and provocative piece of religious literature. It is one that bears our study again and again. Whether the work of a genius or a blunderer, the Gospel of John invites our analysis and tantalizes our minds with its ideas and imaginative language. Our Gospel has had this effect on Christians for nearly twenty centuries and will doubtless continue to do so for centuries to come.

APPENDIX A
The Johannine Epistles and the Gospel of John
(With a Note on the Book of Revelation)

Adherents to a religious tradition sometimes take the sacred literature of their religion to be a singular, harmonious, and static expression of the truth. While the history of the origin of a religion may interest the scholars, it often seems (and perhaps is) irrelevant to the believers themselves. Life itself is too complicated without the complexities of historical change and development in one's religion. After all, we want our religion to be the single unchanging dimension of an existence filled to overflowing with ceaseless mutation. Yet the truth is that in nearly every case careful and critical study of sacred literature betrays diversity and change in the origins of a religion. Popular Jewish mentality has wanted to assume that Judaism stretches back to Abraham with immutable consistency. But the scholars of Jewish origins demonstrate tidal waves of change throughout the crucial years of the emergence of normative Judaism.

It is no different with Christianity. In fact, this book is premised on the fact that Johannine Christianity was considerably different from other expressions of Christian faith in the first century of the common era. The glimpse of the faith and life we get through the peepholes in the Gospel of John suggests changes even within that one stream of early Christianity. If we are then privileged to take additional glances at what may have been the same stream of early Christianity, we may gasp at what we see. Johannine Christianity within the first half century of its existence is a paradigm of the way in which a religion mutates. Some of those changes are the subject of this appendage to our visit with the Fourth Gospel.

A study of the Gospel of John invariably raises questions concerning three other documents in the New Testament to which tradition has also attached the name John. What is the relationship between 1, 2, and 3 John and the Fourth Gospel? Are they the work of the Fourth Evangelist? Were they written after or before the Gospel? A brief glance into those three shorter documents known as the Johannine Epistles supplements our study.

Let us first summarize some of the salient information about these three documents before asking about their relationship to the Gospel of John.

THE JOHANNINE EPISTLES

Reader's Preparation: Read 1, 2, and 3 John, looking for their essential teachings.

A brief introduction to the Johannine Epistles requires that we examine authorship, form, setting, and message of each of the three.

The *authorship* of the three books was attributed to "John" because of the obvious similarities between them and the Gospel. We will consider those similarities in the section below. For now it is only necessary to say that these three writings shed little more light on their respective authors than does the Fourth Gospel illumine the identity of the Fourth Evangelist. In 2 and 3 John the author calls himself "the elder" (verse 1 of each), but 1 John nowhere gives us an indication of the identity of the author. (I assume the elder of 2 and 3 John was a man, since *ho presbyteros* in the Greek is masculine. Titus 2:3 is an instance of the feminine form of the word.)

We can conclude little more about the author of 1 John than that this was a person of some authority in the church (or churches), for she or he presumes to direct the community(ies) in matters of faith and life. We may also conclude that this author was gifted with considerable literary skill and theological acumen. We can say little more about that one who calls himself the elder. Obviously, the title claims some authority. However, elder may not identify an established office. Instead it may point to a stage in the formation of the later, widely recognized, position of leadership. It is also possible that the title simply means an elderly person, who by virtue of his age and experience is respected by the community. With such scarce evidence it is no wonder that the church took nearly three centuries to bring these three writings together and to attribute them to the same author, the Fourth Evangelist.

The *form* of 1 John differs markedly from that of 2 and 3 John. The latter two are obviously letters, written in the standard form of correspondence of the Greco-Roman world. As letters they predictably begin with a statement identifying the author and the recipient: "The elder to the elect lady and her children" (2 John 1); and: "The elder to the beloved Gaius" (3 John 1). In typical letter form this is followed by the greeting we see in 2 John 3 and 3 John 2. Then come some of the formalities often found in contemporary letters: "How are you? I am fine" (see 2 John 4 and 3 John 3–4). The author next gets down to the substance of the letters, which conclude with greetings and pronouncements of peace (2 John 12–13 and 3 John 13–15).

The determination of the form of 2 and 3 John is easy! The tough part comes when we ask about 1 John. How are we to take it? A general letter, a sermon, a tract, or what? It has none of the usual features of a letter. Scholars have suggested almost as many different forms as there are scholars! So, we are left with some generalizations. The document appears to be a series of loosely related admonitions and consolations, each written in what we would judge to be a rather rambling and almost stream of consciousness style. It is difficult to create an outline of 1 John, because it is nearly impossible to discern logical breaks in the flow of the discussion. The discussion does, however, finally yield up some central themes to which we will attend.

It appears that 1 John is some sort of anthology of fragments that thematically hang together, however indeterminately. The fragments may be bits of sermons, extracted from their original setting and strung together into written form. This anthology was compiled, I propose, to circulate among a number of churches. Such a view is only a stab into the darkness of the structure of 1 John, but it may be a beginning point.

What is clearer in 1 John are a few clues as to the *setting* out of which and for which it was written. Here is a quick summary of these clues: A group once within a church (or churches) has voluntarily withdrawn and its members—in the view of the Johannine author—were never full participants nor even authentic Christians (2:19). According to the author, those of the separating group:

- do not practice love, at least in relationships with the readers of 1 John (2:9–11; 4:20–21);
- deny the humanity of Christ (2:22, 4:2–3; 5:5–6);
- are allied with forces at odds with the faith of the church (2:15–16; 4:5–6);
- are weapons of evil (3:8) and even the antichrists of the last days (2:18–23), for they do not hold to the teachings of the main church (4:6);
- claim to know and love God and to practice their faith but in fact do not (1:6; 2:9);
- are then guilty of "mortal sin" (5:16), even though they claim to be free of sin (1:6–10; 3:3–6);
- live without moral restrictions (3:4–10).

The author is doubtless prejudiced in the assessment of these rebels, and the reader gets nothing approaching a fair and objective description of them and their faith. Efforts to identify the group of dissidents generally reach into the second century to grasp on to the Gnostic Christians. That later group generally denied the humanity of Christ in favor of a purely spiritual being and were inclined to think that their Christian faith freed them from any moral law. Such attempts to name the rebels described in 1 John have limited value. We are probably on safer ground if we say only that the separatists of 1 and 2 John were likely the precursors of the Gnostic Christians of a later time. But certainly 1 John was written to address a situation resulting from a schism in a congregation or a series of congregations. Further, the difference between the author of 1 John and his or her opponents centered on proper views of Christ, sin, and morality.

The document was written then to strengthen the confidence of the original churches. First John alternates between assurance (e.g., 3:19–24) and exhortation (e.g., 2:15–17). The author wants to cement the readers into a coherent group around a single understanding of Christian life and belief. This writer is also pastoral enough to know that readers have been shaken by this trauma in the congregation(s). The departure of former brothers and sisters in faith has caused doubts and uncertainties—"Maybe the dissenters are right, and we are wrong!" So, they need to be reassured that their understanding of Christianity is true. This author has the task of quieting a dis-ease in the congregation(s), preventing further disintegration among its members, and articulating the central identity of the community in order to purge the body of a deadly disease. Such seems a likely setting for and purpose of the writing of 1 John.

The setting for 2 John may be related to the one proposed for 1 John. Like 1 John, 2 John urges the readers to lead moral lives, perhaps in contrast to some others (vs. 5–6). It too counsels a view of Christ as a fleshly being, against "deceivers" who teach otherwise (v. 7). Such false Christians, it is urged, should be denied hospitality when they come into the readers' village (v. 10). It is not hard to imagine that something like the same setting proposed for 1 John lurks in the historical shadows behind 2 John. The dissenters are propagating their views in the surrounding villages, and the "elder" tries to defuse their influence.

Third John is harder to relate to the setting of schism. A certain Diotrephes has proven himself a disturber of the peace in the congregation in which Gaius (to whom the letter is addressed) is a leader. This disrupter is accused of putting himself first and of assuming more authority than he deserves (v. 9). He refuses to recognize the authority of the elder and fuels gossip about the leader (v. 10). He has even driven off those who disagree with him (v. 10). Most serious, perhaps, is the fact that he does not welcome Christian visitors (v. 10). The elder in this case tries to win the loyalty of Gaius and thereby strengthen the author's influence in the congregation.

That much is pretty clear. Whether or not the situation of 3 John is related to the one perceived behind 1 and 2 John is less clear. Possibly 3 John is linked with 2 John only through the author's title ("the elder") and originally had no connection with the communities addressed in the other two Johannine Epistles. But it is also possible that Diotrephes has reacted to the confusion caused by the split in the churches by advocating isolationism. Confused by the dispute between the main church body and those who have separated themselves from it, he in effect declares, "A plague on both their houses. We will have nothing to do with either the so-called dissenters or the elder!" Such a connection requires some imagination, to be sure, but is feasible nonetheless. In any case, in 3 John we witness a power struggle between claimants to authority within a congregation.

The *message* of 1 John (shared in part by 2 John) is by far the most important of the three. Although the structure of 1 John remains obscure, the themes of the writing can be handily condensed around five themes. The first is the fleshly humanity of Christ (e.g., 1 John 4:2; see also 2 John 7). The second is the saving work of Christ (1 John 1:7b, 9; 2:2; 3:5; 4:10). The understanding of sin comprises the third theme (1 John 1:8, 10; 3:4, 8, 9; 5:16–17). Fourth, all three of these documents stress the importance of moral living for the Christian (e.g., 1 John 1:7; 2:3, 4, 6, 24; 3:7, 14; 4:5, 7, 16; 2 John 5–6; 3 John 11). No less than five times the commandment to "love one another" occurs in these three (1 John 3:11, 23; 4:7, 11–12; 2 John 5).

Finally, the "last days" occupy an important place in 1 and 2 John (1 John 2:18, 28; 3:2; 4:17, 18; 2 John 7–8).

These three documents are important in the New Testament and our grasp of early Christian history, for they give us a snapshot of the early church struggling to maintain its unity and integrity. They take us behind the scenes, as it were, to let us see some of the dirty laundry of early Christianity. The church is not one big happy family after all. There are divisions, quarrels, accusations, condemnations, and power struggles. Yet, these letters are more than an exposé of the unseemly side of early Christian history. They demonstrate the earliest Christians' challenge to define their identity. What is crucially important to Christian faith? Can one believe just anything about Christ, or is there a true view that makes all the others false? In other words, the Johannine Epistles show us the battle over establishing a single, true theology—an orthodoxy. They give us a peek into the combat between doctrinal and ethical purity, on the one hand, and tolerance on the other. Moreover, they provide us with a knothole in a wall nearly two thousand years old through which to watch the game of authority being played out. What is the authority of the leaders of the church? How far does their authority extend?

These twin issues of orthodoxy (in faith and practice) and authority are paramount in the emergence of the church. The Johannine Epistles afford us the opportunity to stop the action in one place at one time in order to witness the struggle with these issues. Most important is that they enable us to put flesh and blood on those issues, to view them through the agonized eyes and pained hearts of some of the participants, and to witness the trauma of the church's maturation process toward the end of the first century.

THE RELATIONSHIP OF THE JOHANNINE EPISTLES AND THE GOSPEL OF JOHN

Reader's Preparation: Read once again 1, 2, and 3 John, this time looking for comparisons and contrasts with the Gospel of John.

We now have at least some vague sense of the central concerns of the Johannine Epistles. Hence, we are ready to ask how they relate to our maverick Gospel. The vital queries are these: (1) Were the Epistles written by the Fourth Evangelist? (2) When and under what conditions were they written in relationship to the Gospel of John? (3) How do they differ from the Fourth Gospel in their understanding of Christian faith and life?

The authorship question is plagued with difficulty. The traditional identification of the author of the Johannine Epistles with the Fourth Evangelist has fallen victim to critical study and is no longer as widely held as it once was. Still, as you read the Epistles you are doubtless struck by how often there is a familiar ring about the language and style. The Epistles do indeed exhibit an impressive number of similarities with the Gospel. These are most frequent in

1 John. A few examples must suffice: the use of the words or phrases such as "life" (3:15), "eternal life" (5:11), "truth" (5:6), "Father"/ "Son" (4:14), and "new commandment" (2:7–8). Moreover, as one reads 1 John the comparison with some of Jesus' speeches in the Gospel is inescapable. The styles are similar—spiral-like in their development, with word association used to link sentences and subjects. The similarities are less frequent in 2 John: "Truth" (vs. 1, 2, 3, 4), "abide in" (vs. 2, 9), "Father"/"Son" (vs. 3, 9), and "new commandment" (v. 5). In 3 John the similarity of vocabulary is found only in the use of the word "truth" (vs. 1, 3, 4, 8, and 12). However, since 2 and 3 John are so very short and are letters (a very different literary genre from that of a Gospel), we should not expect to find the same impressive array of parallels.

Yet one may also notice differences, especially thematic ones, between the Gospel and the Epistles. In 1 John, for instance, a reader is struck by the emphasis on the futuristic eschatology (e.g., 2:18) with little, if any, evidence of the present, realized eschatology we have come to know in the Fourth Gospel. The word "doctrine" (*didachē*) in 2 John (vs. 9–10, RSV) has a different connotation than in the Fourth Gospel (cf. John 7:16, 17; 18:19). "The elect lady" of 2 John 1 is foreign to the reader of the Gospel of John. The emphasis on hospitality to strangers in 3 John (vs. 5–8), as well as the use of the word "church" (*ekklēsia*) in verse 9, are at best additions to the Johannine repertoire.

This brief portrayal of the relationship between the Johannine Gospel and Epistles is sufficient to suggest that we have a problem. How shall we explain both the similarities of vocabulary and the dissimilarities? If we allow our minds to play freely with this problem, a couple of options dawn. First, we might conclude that the same author wrote the Gospel and the Epistles but at different periods of time and for different situations. That would account for the likenesses as well as the dissimilarities. Second, different authors might have been sufficiently influenced by the Gospel of John to have imitated its vocabulary without necessarily being wholly consistent with its thought. Think about, for instance, the way a novelist might be influenced by the works of a previous literary figure. Finally, we might combine the first two options and supplement them in a way that imagines a slightly different scenario. Suppose this author (or authors) was part of the Johannine community at either an earlier or a later time than that of the writing of the Gospel. The Johannine vocabulary would be natural, even while circumstances were different.

This third option commends itself—at least to me. Might it not be the case that the Johannine Epistles (or at least 1 and 2 John) were written out of and for the Johannine community when its situation was markedly different from the setting of the Gospel? This proposal would explain the similarities without requiring that the author(s) be entirely consistent with the Gospel. It prevents our having to explain the reasons for the variations between a single author's thought in one document and the other. Furthermore, this proposal allows for the possibility that each of the three Epistles need not have come from the same hand. Surely, 2 and 3 John are from the same hand, that of the "elder." But the author of 1 John might well have been another leader in the community. This proposal necessitates that we think about when and under what conditions the Epistles were written.

The question of date is more easily handled if one agrees to the proposal that the Epistles come from different authors than the Gospel but from the same community. The issue then becomes whether they might be later or earlier than the Gospel. The nature of the questions with which the community is struggling in the Johannine Epistles is the key to the puzzle. They seem to reflect a later stage in the Christian church—certainly one later than the stage that gave birth to the Gospel. Specifically, the concerns for proper Christian belief and practice and ecclesiastical authority smack of a later time.

The Johannine church at the time of the writing of the Gospel was preoccupied with the dispute with the synagogue. Its life task was to get its own identity squared away over against Judaism. Its concern for proper doctrine is related solely to the messianic confession—Jesus is the Christ in spite of what the synagogue may say. There seems to be little or no interest in differing views of Christ within the Christian community itself. Moreover, the church reflected through the lens of the Fourth Gospel had little interest in the authority of its leaders. Rather, the Johannine church at the time of the Gospel conceived of itself as ruled by the authority of the Spirit (see chapter 4, the sections on the Spirit and the church). A religious community acutely sensitive to the immediate guidance of the divine Spirit has no need for official human leaders. Its leaders arise unofficially (charismatically, we would say today) and convincingly proclaim the guidance of the Spirit.

By the time of the writing of the Epistles, the Johannine church has moved on to intra-Christian problems. Attention has shifted from the antagonist outside the church to the one within. What kind of messianic confession is proper and true? The relationship with the synagogue is no longer relevant, but the relationship among different Christian groups is given top billing. Furthermore, the leadership of the Spirit is now understood to be mediated through church officials. The sense of the immediacy of the guidance of the Spirit, that we think we see in the Gospel of John, has given way to mediated guidance. The mediators are those who have been sanctioned by the community through some sort of official process. This procedure is not yet universally accepted, it would seem, since 3 John suggests that there are those Christians who feel free to challenge the authority of the "elder."

Therefore, it is feasible that the Gospel of John was written at an earlier time, and the Epistles later. If we must put dates to these writings, it might look something like this. The Gospel was written perhaps within a decade of the destruction of the Temple in Jerusalem (70 C.E.—see the discussion of the date of the Gospel in the Introduction). At least another decade passes after the composition of the Gospel and before the Epistles are penned. Hence, the Gospel was written about 75–85 and the Epistles about 90–95. Of course, these are approximations and the result of a good deal of imagination. Yet there is still more in the way of comparison between the Johannine literary siblings to be considered.

The question of Christian perspective must be addressed. Ample evidence suggests that by the time of the writing of the Epistles the Johannine community has made some important shifts away from the tradition articulated in the Gospel. While still clinging to that tradition, the community has been influenced by other streams of Christian thought. If we put the best reading on it, the Johannine tradition has been "enriched" by other traditions and has adjusted as the result of other Christian perspectives.

A number of examples of such shifts in perspective are evident. We have already mentioned the fact that the futuristic eschatology of the Epistles seems to have crowded the present eschatology of the Gospel into the corner. The delicate balance between the present and the future so effectively achieved by the writing of the Fourth Evangelist has tilted toward the future. Additionally, the understanding of the saving work of Christ articulated in 1 John is considerably different (shall we say more mature?) than that of the Gospel. The death of Jesus is an "atoning sacrifice" (*hilasmos*, 2:2; 4:10) that cleanses (*katharizō*) sin by the shedding of blood. Jesus is now the "paraclete" who takes away sin (2:1)—a very different use of the word from that in the Gospel (see Chapter 4, the section on the Spirit). Soteriology is also involved in the "anointing" (*chrisma*—a word alien to the vocabulary of the Fourth Evangelist) spoken of in 2:20 and 27. While the Gospel has little in the way of ethical teachings, 1 John speaks of the dangers of "lawlessness" in morality (3:4). For the Fourth Evangelist sin is simply unbelief, but the author of 1 John finds it necessary to distinguish between "mortal" and "immortal sin" (5:16–17).

These differences are not blatant contradictions but subtle shifts. Each point of contrast may be explained in terms of roots in the Gospel, but something new has been added or subtracted. Could it not be that the Johannine community has learned from and is in the process of adapting itself to other (and probably more predominant) forms of Christian thought? Many, but not all, of the differences in the Christian perspectives of the Gospel and the Epistles could be explained on this premise. The community out of which the Gospel was written, I have argued, was one relatively isolated from other streams of Christian thought, such as the Pauline. However, the community from which the Epistles emerged betrays evidence of having had some intercourse with those traditions (for example, an eschatology leaning toward the future expectation and an understanding of Jesus' death expressed through metaphors drawn from Jewish sacrificial worship). The result is a new brand of Johannine Christianity much more compatible with other Christian churches. Still, such a proposed source of the innovations in the Epistles does not diminish the fact that the author (or authors) and the community were creative (for example, the concept of the "anointing" mentioned above has no exact parallel in any other New Testament literature).

A diagram might help us see more plainly the history of the Johannine community in its relationship with other Christian communities of the first century. Figure A–1 suggests that there was an exchange among Christian traditions before the writing of either the Synoptic or Johannine Gospels (see the discussion of the relationship of the Synoptics and the Gospel of John in the Introduction) but that the influence of other Christian groups on the Johannine church was minimal during its life within the synagogue. After the expulsion from the synagogue, however, relationships with other churches were established and had an impact on the Johannine understanding of Christianity. Perhaps the lines of influence went the other way, as well—that is, the Johannine church affected other churches.

THE MAVERICK IS BEING TAMED!

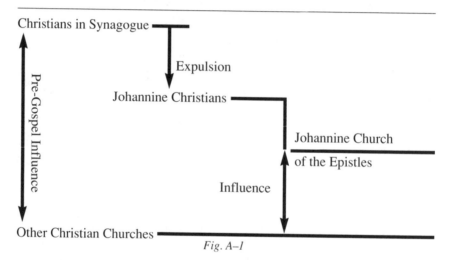

Fig. A–1

A NOTE ON THE BOOK OF REVELATION

Because the author of Revelation identified himself as "John" (1:1, 4, 9, 22:8), the last book of the New Testament has sometimes been aligned with the Gospel of John and 1, 2, and 3 John. Especially since the authority and value of Revelation was questioned for a time in the early church, its attribution to the Fourth Evangelist was a way of authenticating its place in the Christian canon. Therefore, the question of the relationship of Revelation to the Gospel of John is worthy of at least a note.

Some students of Revelation have noted similarities between it and the Fourth Gospel. Two very different kinds of proposed resemblances enable us to gain a feel for what some understand to be the connection between the two documents. The first is a vocabulary association, namely, the use of the title

"Lamb" for Christ. The Gospel of John explicitly uses that title only twice (1:29, 36). However, the Gospel's dating of the crucifixion on the day lambs were slain for the Passover feast may imply the title (see the Introduction on the relationship of the Synoptics to the Gospel of John). In Revelation "Lamb" is the most frequent title for Christ (e.g., 5:6, 8; 12:11; 13:8; 17:14; 21:9). A second exemplary similarity is sometimes perceived in the style of Revelation and the Fourth Gospel. Both are poetic and occasionally even burst forth in actual poetry (e.g., John 1:1–8; Revelation 18:21–24; 19:1–3). The hymnic passages, furthermore, are the kind that might well have originated and been used in early Christian worship. (For a thorough discussion of the issue, see the introduction to R. H. Charles's classic commentary, *Revelation*.)

Beneath the apparent similarities, however, lies a fundamental difference. Revelation is a peculiar type of literature, known as apocalyptic (see the opening discussion in Chapter 4). Therefore, its entire perspective invites the reader to consider God's promises for the future. The Gospel of John, we have noted, is careful to supplement that kind of futuristic perspective with attention to the present. It may even counsel against the dangers of an apocalyptic mentality. However, to state the difference in this way may be superficial. The Apocalypse of John is clearly designed to change the reader's perception of the present by showing its relationship with the future. Because God has promised the Christians ultimate victory over their oppressors, the experience of oppression is radically transformed. Therefore, we cannot easily dismiss Revelation as entirely oriented toward the future. In fact, one might argue that the apocalyptic eschatology of Revelation seeks in a different way the same goal the Gospel of John seeks with its careful articulation of the present and futuristic eschatologies. The genre of the two are radically different—an apocalypse and a gospel. Hence, each treats the issue of the future in a different way.

However, given the similarities and the tenuous nature of the major difference, the issue is still fraught with difficulties. The language and style of the two documents is radically different, as are the theologies (cf. their theologies of the cross). Even a casual reading of the two back-to-back makes it difficult to believe they are the products of the same author.

Let us suppose however that Revelation did arise from the Johannine community and perhaps even from the hand of the Fourth Evangelist. How might the two of them be related in the history of the community? Two very different patterns are possible. The first would conceive of Revelation as arising early in the history of the community before the writing of the Gospel (and the expulsion of the Johannine Christians from the synagogue) and before the Johannine Epistles. The carefully balanced present and futuristic eschatologies of the Gospel would, then, have to be understood as another way of expressing the promises of God articulated in Revelation. Such a hypothesis would require that we date Revelation fairly early. Since most think that it was written at a time when Christians were seriously at odds with the Roman Empire, a date in the 60s would be the only possibility.

The other pattern reverses the order. The Gospel, then the Epistles were written, followed by Revelation. In this case, the trajectory would suppose more and more concentration on the futuristic eschatology. The Gospel balanced the present and the future. First John stressed more firmly the future dimension of the promises of God. Revelation concentrated attention exclusively on the future. In this proposed relationship, Revelation would have been written soon after the Epistles, during the time the Christians were suffering persecution at the hands of Emperor Domitian (or as John anticipated that persecution) in the last decade of the first century.

While such speculation is most interesting, it seems far better not to squeeze Revelation into the already speculative construction of the history of the Johannine community. Both patterns sketched above smack of forcing Revelation into a slot for which it was never intended. Surely there were many "Johns" in the early Christian church. That the author of Revelation calls himself John and tradition has named the Fourth Evangelist John is hardly a basis for attributing both to the same author. My own suggestion is, therefore, that Revelation be treated on its own merit without recourse to the so-called Johannine literature in an attempt to penetrate its mysteries.

Revelation is a maverick of its own kind in New Testament literature. It runs free, even as we have suggested the Gospel of John does. It is better to allow each of these mavericks to be itself rather than trying to argue that they are different offspring of the same parents.

APPENDIX B
The Women of the Gospel of John

It is not unusual for a religion to formulate norms for societal life and specify roles for groups within a community. Examples of such efforts are found in those New Testament passages known as "household codes" (e.g., Ephesians 5:21–6:9). In the 1990s in Islamic culture the place of women, dictated by the Koran, captured the attention of the Western world when a group of Muslim women protested the prohibition that prevented their driving cars. Like Christianity, Islam struggles with an ancient view of women amid the increasing pressures of modern life to adjust that view. Indeed, the place and role of women is one of the crucial issues facing nearly all of the major religions of the world.

For a first-century document our intriguing maverick Gospel presents us with a unique portrayal of women, though it is not unusual to find women represented in the narratives of the Synoptic Gospels. Indeed, they play a prominent role in all four of the New Testament Gospels. One need only remember the persistent faith of the Canaanite woman in Matthew 15:21–28 (see also Mark 7:24–30). Jesus marvels at the degree of her faith. Or, recall the woman who had suffered the flow of blood for twelve years and wriggled her way into the crowd to touch the hem of Jesus' garment (Mark 5:25–34; see also Matthew 9:18–22 and Luke 8:43–48). Jesus says her faith has made her well. These are only two of the many women who appear in the Synoptic Gospels as examples of faith. Women are far from second-class citizens in the Synoptic stories of Jesus.

Even so, the Gospel of John is remarkable for its intentional presentation of women as models of faith. We can quickly comprehend that extraordinary quality by examining, first, the place of women in the structure of the whole of the Gospel, then, by glancing at each of the female characters who encounter Jesus, and, finally, by drawing some conclusions from this mini-survey.

WOMEN IN THE STRUCTURE OF THE GOSPEL OF JOHN

Reader's Preparation: Skim the whole Gospel once again and jot down the chapter numbers in which female characters appear.

This Evangelist is sly and clever in the presentation of women. The whole of the narrative appears to be arranged in such a way as to slip some subtle messages into the reader's mind. Like subliminal messages, the author of the Gospel packs meaning between the lines—or in this case between the scenes—of the story. One of the literary techniques of the Fourth Evangelist is to sneak up behind the unsuspecting reader and implant a suggestion of which the reader is at first only vaguely aware. After the Evangelist has cunningly done this several times, the reader begins to get the point. Such is the case with the topic of women.

When we ask where in the Johannine story of Jesus the author presents the female characters of the drama, it occurs to us that they pop up at all the crucial places. If you have done your reader's preparation, you will not be surprised to learn that women appear in chapters 2; 4; 11; 12; 19; and 20. How important those chapters are! Women are found early in the narrative of Jesus' ministry, beginning with his mother's role in his first public act (2:1–11). Following close on the heels of that figure appears the Samaritan woman in chapter 4. Then for six chapters the story is dominated by men. But at the crucial point of the raising of Lazarus, Mary and Martha step onto the stage. Martha takes the leading female role in chapter 11 and Mary in 12. These two chapters are the grand turning point of the story. (See the Introduction, the section on the literary structure of the Gospel.) Jesus' wondrous act in chapter 11 evokes the plan to have him put to death (11:45–54) which is put into action in chapter 18. Mary's anointing of Jesus (12:1–8) prepares him for his death and opens the chapter that constitutes Jesus' final public appearance before his passion. At the apex of his passion a group of women are present at the foot of the cross, including his mother, Mary Magdalene, and others (19:25). Their presence is highlighted by the conspicuous absence of all but one of the male followers (the beloved disciple, if this person was a male). Finally, the climax of the entire Gospel is found in the stories of the resurrection appearances, and who should be the first to discover the empty tomb and meet the risen Christ but a woman—Mary Magdalene!

Women then are involved in the beginning, the middle, and the conclusion of the Johannine story as figure A–2 demonstrates.

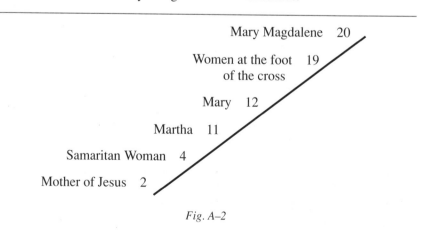

Fig. A–2

What is the subliminal message in this design? First, women were among Jesus' disciples—of that this Gospel allows no doubt. They are the equals of the male disciples. Second, their discipleship is central to the Jesus story. Without them it would be hard to tell the Johannine version of Jesus' ministry. Finally, the reader is directed to female (as well as male) figures to witness the models of faith. This conclusion, however, requires that we briefly examine each of the prominent women of the Gospel.

FEMALE CHARACTERS IN THE GOSPEL OF JOHN

Reader's Preparation: Read the stories of the following women: the Mother of Jesus (2:1–11; 19:25–27), the Samaritan Woman (4:1–42), Mary and Martha (11:1–12:8), and Mary Magdalene (19:25–27; 20:1–18).

Before beginning our discussion of each of the women in the Gospel, it is necessary to make a few observations about the Evangelist's use of characters in general. First, none of them is fully developed and all play a supporting role. Their places in the narrative are always in relationship to the main character, Jesus. They remain undeveloped in order to keep attention focused on him. Second, they share a single function. Each represents a kind of response to Jesus. Some are portrayed as examples of a negative reaction, such as the paralyzed man in chapter 5, who is healed by Jesus, and perhaps Pontius Pilate. Others give a positive response of faith, and still others an ambiguous reaction (e.g., Nicodemus). Those assigned a positive role invariably represent some degree or dimension of faith, as we shall see in the following discussion. In other words, the characters of the Gospel are used to provoke the reader's faith. They are instruments in the hands of the deft surgeon, who cuts out the tissue of unbelief. Finally, we observe that each of the female characters in the story is cast in a positive role. None is portrayed as ambiguous or negative in her response to Jesus. Each exemplifies some measure or some characteristic of faith.

The mother of Jesus appears only twice in this Gospel—once in the narrative of Jesus' first public appearance and again in the crucifixion scene. Much has been made of the symbolic role she may play in the Gospel, but we are concerned with more mundane matters. We first meet her at a wedding party, where she informs Jesus of the embarrassing depletion of the supply of wine. When he claims that this is not a concern of theirs, she quietly tells the servants, "Do whatever he tells you" (2:5). Her part appears to be minor in setting up Jesus' first wondrous act, but she demonstrates a quiet confidence in her son. It is the confidence and trust that foreshadow faith. The first woman character in the drama is an example of the way faith is first experienced and expressed.

More significant, perhaps, is the appearance of Jesus' mother at his crucifixion. There with the other women, she shares in the mysterious exaltation of Christ. But she is also the beneficiary of a distinct honor. Jesus' word makes her the mother of the beloved disciple, and the beloved disciple becomes her son. Thus out of the tiny company gathered at the foot of the cross a new community is formed with the mother of Jesus as its matriarch. Of this incident Alan Culpepper has written:

> The impact of this scene has been tremendous. Here are the man and "woman," the ideal disciple and the mother he is called to receive, standing under the cross of the giver of life. There is the beginning of a new family for the children of God. (*Anatomy of the Fourth Gospel*, p. 134)

As the prologue promised, those who believe in the Word made flesh receive a power to become children of God (1:12), and a new family is created. This new family takes as its earthly parents the one whose only name derives from Jesus' love for him, and Jesus' own mother. The church is comprised equally of men and women of faith who witness the cross.

The Samaritan woman is a different sort of figure. A member of the antiestablishment, nonconformist Samaritans—and a woman at that—engages Jesus in a discussion of religious tradition and law (4:12, 20, 25). In the discussion she holds her own admirably well. To be sure, she misunderstands Jesus in humorous ways—she misinterprets the meaning of the "living water" of which he speaks (4:15). But the Evangelist hardly makes fun of her. (Remember, the male disciples also blunder badly in their efforts to understand Jesus, for instance, 16:29–33.) Nor does the Evangelist necessarily represent her as an immoral person. We are never told why she has had five husbands and now lives with a man who is not her husband, and Jesus shows no interest in giving her a little lesson in proper morality. On the contrary, she is a perceptive and bright woman who sees in Jesus' knowledge of her an indication that he is a prophet (4:19). Moreover, she demonstrates trustful acceptance of Jesus' declaration of his true identity (4:25–29). We would hardly expect this lowly Samaritan to believe what only puzzled Nicodemus (3:1–14), but she does. The contrast with Nicodemus is evident. He is part of the religious establishment but cannot bring himself to believe in Jesus (at least publicly). The Samaritan woman, on the other hand, is cut off from the established religion, rejected and hated, but she comes to belief. She represents the way in which Christ is accepted among the outcast and despised, even while he is rejected by the learned and pious. When the Samaritan woman is coupled with the Gentile nobleman at the end of chapter 4 (vs. 46–54), the reader encounters a pair of believing outcasts. One is a poor Samaritan woman; the other a wealthy Gentile man.

But the role of this woman is still greater. Not only does she believe, she witnesses to her faith. Forgetting her water pots, she runs back to share her newfound faith with her village. With joyful exaggeration she invites her neighbors to "Come and see a man who told me everything I have ever done!" and then entices them with the question she knows very well is going to pique their curiosity, "He cannot be the Messiah, can he?" (4:29). Her witness reminds us immediately of Jesus' invitation to the first disciples and of their invitation to others to "come and see" (1:39, 46). The first witness to Christ in the Gospel of John is John, the baptizer (1:29–34). The Samaritan woman is the baptizer's female counterpart. And what an effective witness she proves to be. Her budding faith and enthusiasm result in many of the villagers believing in Jesus (4:39). Because of her witness the believers of the village proclaim Jesus the "Savior of the world" (4:42)—a confession that captures the essence of 3:16. This Christ is for the salvation of the "world," including the outcast and forgotten.

In the Gospel's narrative the Samaritan woman is the first of the people living on the margins of society to believe. She is the model of how one's encounter with Jesus' word provokes faith, and an example of the way faith bubbles over into witness. Because of her the reader of the Gospel knows that no matter who you are—no matter what your status in society may be—the revelation of God in Christ is for you!

Mary and Martha enter abruptly on stage to play their roles in two scenes and then disappear. We are told that with their brother, Lazarus, they share a special relationship with Jesus (11:3, 21; 12:1–2). Martha is featured in the first scene—the wake for Lazarus. Her trust in Jesus is evident in the first words she speaks to him, "Lord, if you had been here, my brother would not have died. But even now I know that God will give you whatever you ask of him" (11:21–22). But Martha still doesn't comprehend what is in store for her. There ensues a brief conversation of the hope for Lazarus' resurrection. Martha dutifully recites the creed—memorized from catechetical class, no doubt, "I know that he will rise again in the resurrection on the last day" (11:24). She then learns that Jesus himself is the resurrection, and his appearance is the last day.

Martha is a provocative representation of faith's growing edge, of a maturing faith discovering the full significance of the one who is the object of belief. She is the Evangelist's medium for a message that faith can never be stagnant, for it will always be stretched beyond its own limits.

Mary plays a far different role. By the act of anointing the feet of Jesus she prepares him for his burial (12:1–7). Hers is a simple act of love and gratitude for the one who rescued her brother from the jaws of the tomb. She demonstrates that faith is rooted in grateful recognition of the giver of life. But her act is more than an expression of thankfulness. Hers is a prophetic gesture—one that says more than she knows—for it is the anticipation of the grand exaltation of Jesus.

Together this feminine pair delineate the contours of faith. Founded in confidence and trust, expanded in maturation, and shaped by gratitude and love, their faith is a means by which God accomplishes the divine plan in the world.

Mary Magdalene is the final woman to appear in the Johannine drama, and the best is saved for last. If the reader has not yet gotten the picture, the

Evangelist will draw it sharply in this female paradigm of faith. In Mary all the features of faithful believers are represented. Playing the supporting role in the first of the climactic scenes, Mary Magdalene crowns the major roles assigned to women in the entire narrative. She comes to the tomb that supposedly holds Jesus in order to express her affection for him. Discovering that it is empty, she cannot repress her tears. Her devotion and love remind us of Mary of Bethany. But when the risen Christ appears to her, she receives him with joy, reminding us of the receptivity of Martha. Her role is expanded still further when Jesus asks her to go and share the news of his resurrection with the other disciples. Mary immediately goes and does just that, and the image of the witness of the Samaritan woman comes to mind. Devotion, love, receptivity, and witness. These are the features of discipleship, all embodied in a single female figure.

Mary Magdalene is the personification of all that it means to be a disciple. But she is still more. She is cast in the eminent role as the first to discover the empty tomb, the first to witness the risen Christ, and the first to announce the good news of the resurrection. Not even Peter or the beloved disciple is so privileged. As Raymond E. Brown has pointed out, Mary Magdalene is the first apostle—one who witnesses the risen Christ and is sent forth to announce his resurrection. In fact, she is the apostle to the apostles (*The Community of the Beloved Disciple*, pp. 189–190).

CONCLUSIONS

What shall we make of the prominence of women in the Gospel of John? Two drastically different alternatives come to mind. The first is that the Fourth Evangelist feels it is necessary to reaffirm the place and role of women in the ministry of Jesus because the church of the time is in danger of forgetting those vital facts. We can imagine the possibility that the Evangelist's church has fallen into the grips of male dominance, a victim of the masculine propensity to assert superiority over women. Alarmed by this turn of events, the Evangelist writes a corrective message to call the church back to its original grasp of the fact that in Christ "there is no longer male and female" (Galatians 3:28).

Yet we sense nothing polemical about the presentation of women in the Gospel. There is no haranguing the reader to throw off the chains of sexism. The tone is much different. The portrayal is much more matter of fact, casual, and natural. Christ remains the central message, not gender inclusiveness. Certainly, there are some subtle contrasts of male and female figures. For instance, there seems to be a subtle contrasting of Nicodemus to the Samaritan woman. Perhaps, too, the portrayal of Mary Magdalene is meant to contrast with Peter and the beloved disciple. But these contrasts do not constitute a polemic.

The second option, then, is for us to suppose that the church for which and out of which the Fourth Evangelist writes is one in which the equality of the place and role of women and men is taken for granted. It is an egalitarian community in which both genders occupy prominent places and in which the gifts of both are valued. The story of the belief of the Samaritans suggests that the Johannine community knows that the outcasts and marginalized persons of the society are equal participants in the benefits of Christ and share communion with all others. That inclusivity may also be the backdrop for the portrayal of women in this Gospel. The Fourth Evangelist knows no other tradition—no other way of telling the Jesus story—than in the context of the equality of women and men in Christ.

Dare we ask, then, one other question that spins off this discussion? Could it be that the Fourth Evangelist is a woman? The strong role of women in the Gospel certainly allows for that possibility. Nothing in the Gospel precludes it. However, that conspicuous role of women also allows for the prospect of a male author sensitive to and appreciative of his sisters in the faith. The Gospel's emphasis on relationships is another feature to be considered. All the discussion of the relationship of the Father and the Son, of the Father and believers, of the Son and believers, and of believers with one another (see chapter 17) may be suggestive of a feminine consciousness. But, alas, such a suggestion I fear arises more from our twentieth- than first-century mentality and may be only another stereotype of the genders. Ultimately, the task of determining the gender of an unnamed author is impossible. There are no clear and acknowledged criteria for deducing gender from literary (much less theological) works. The argument invariably becomes sexist by the very generalizations it assumes.

However, one vital issue confronts us when we suggest that the Fourth Evangelist may have been a woman. That issue is the dominance of the male image of God portrayed in the Fourth Gospel, most especially by the common title "Father." We cannot speak of God as Father in our culture without raising the question of sexist language. This image of God as a male parent conjures up masculine associations and attributes them to the Ultimate. Must we then conclude that the Gospel of John is the most sexist in its image of God in the New Testament literature? Is it impossible for a feminist to make her or his peace with this excessively masculine portrayal of God? Therefore, is it impossible to believe that a woman is responsible for the God-language of the Gospel?

I think not. The male parental title for God appears to be rooted in the tradition out of which Jesus spoke of God as "Abba, Father" (Mark 14:36, see also Romans 8:15 and Galatians 4:6). Consequently, we are bound to inquire about the context and motivation of that tradition. The most persuasive of the explanations for its origin, I believe, is the one offered by Elisabeth Schüssler Fiorenza. She argues that Jesus does not refer to God as Father because he thinks God is male. He does not desire, above all, to teach that the Christian disciple must image God as masculine and thereby attribute all the features of that gender to God. Rather, suggests Fiorenza, almost the opposite is the case. Jesus' naming God Father arises from his

153

attempt to loose the grip of masculine superiority and authority over women and children. There is but one authority, and that is God. There is but one father who claims absolute obedience, and that is God. Indeed, "Call no one your father on earth, for you have one Father—the one in heaven" (Matthew 23:9). By imaging God as Father, the authority of males is subverted. The masculine reign over women and children in the family structure of the day is annihilated. (See Elisabeth Schüssler Fiorenza, *In Memory of Her: A Feminist Theological Reconstruction of Christian Origins*, pp. 150–151.)

If this theory of the origin of the tradition wherein Jesus named God as Father is sound, some conclusions follow about the prominence of the Father title in the Gospel of John. Among all New Testament literature, this Gospel most radically concentrates authority outside of societal structures. The Fourth Evangelist develops the early tradition about Jesus' language for God still further by concentrating God language in the parental representation. Far from tightening the noose of masculine supremacy and authority around the throats of women and children, it shreds the rope entirely. Consequently, I believe the egalitarian character of the Johannine community extended into family relationships. There it minimized and democratized the role of the man. For that reason the abundant use of the male image of God as Father does not necessarily undermine the prospect that the Gospel of John was authored by a woman. Rather, the opposite may be the case. Because the Gospel arises from a feminist perspective and within an egalitarian community, the God-language may be further evidence of the dissolution of patriarchal authority, along with all other human authority.

This much we may conclude, and probably no more: There is no convincing evidence that requires us to reject the possibility that the Fourth Evangelist was in fact a woman. She may have been a prominent leader in the Johannine community, who (if she had been denied the opportunity to learn to write) dictated the Gospel to a scribe. If our conclusions about the egalitarian nature of the Johannine church are viable (see Chapter 4, the section on the church), the implication is that a woman might well have been held in such esteem and have assumed such leadership that she was inspired to write for her Christian community. It is only a possibility, but one that the evidence of the Gospel compels us to entertain.

Be that as it may, our maverick Gospel goes its way without regard for the social customs of the time. It honors female characters with major roles in the narrative and through them tantalizes the reader with a variety of models of true faith. There is mounting evidence that women were prominent in the ministry of Jesus and the leadership of the earliest church, and the witness of the Gospel of John is significant among that evidence. The tragedy is that this maverick Gospel became domesticated in due time—a victim of the cultural roles dominated by men. In our continued quest for a more authentic societal pattern for gender roles, the Gospel of John speaks a clear and commanding word.

BIBLIOGRAPHY

The works listed have been chosen for two reasons: First, they are the ones upon which this book depends most heavily. Second, they are works to which the reader should go to pursue issues raised in this book.

Commentaries

Barrett, C. K. *The Gospel According to St. John.* 2nd ed. Philadelphia: Westminster Press, 1978.

Beasley-Murray, George R. *John.* Word Biblical Commentary, vol. 36. Waco, Tex.: Word Inc., 1987.

Brown, Raymond E. *The Gospel According to John.* Anchor Bible, vols. 29 and 29a. Garden City, N.Y.: Doubleday & Co., 1966, 1970. After all these years, perhaps still the best commentary on the Fourth Gospel.

Bultmann, Rudolf. *The Gospel of John.* Philadelphia: Westminster Press, 1971. An idiosyncratic classic!

Carson, D. A. *The Gospel According to John.* Grand Rapids: Wm. B. Eerdmans Publishing Co., 1991.

Haenchen, Ernst. *John.* 2 vols. Hermeneia. Philadelphia: Fortress Press, 1984.

Kysar, Robert. *John.* Augsburg Commentary on the New Testament. Minneapolis: Augsburg Publishing House, 1986.

Lindars, Barnabas. *The Gospel of John.* New Century Bible Commentary. Grand Rapids: Wm. B. Eerdmans Publishing Co., 1972.

Schnackenburg, Rudolf. *The Gospel According to St. John.* 3 vols. New York: Seabury Press, 1982. A most thorough commentary with helpful excursuses.

Sloyan, Gerard. *John.* Interpretation. Atlanta: John Knox Press, 1988. A commentary for teachers and preachers.

Studies

Ashton, John, ed. *The Interpretation of John.* Issues in Religion and Theology, no. 9. Philadelphia: Fortress Press, 1986. See especially the articles by Borgen, Martyn, and Meeks.

Beasley-Murray, G. R. *Gospel of Life: Theology in the Fourth Gospel.* Peabody, Mass.: Hendrickson Publishers, 1991.

Brown, Raymond E. *The Community of the Beloved Disciple.* New York: Paulist Press, 1979. Best for the relationship between the Gospel and the Johannine Epistles.

Bultmann, Rudolf. *The Theology of the New Testament*. Vol. 2. New York: Charles Scribner's Sons, 1955.

Culpepper, Alan R. *Anatomy of the Fourth Gospel: A Study in Literary Design*. Philadelphia: Fortress Press, 1983. Excellent on the literary features of the Gospel.

Dodd, C. H. *The Interpretation of the Fourth Gospel*. Cambridge: Cambridge University Press, 1953.

_____. *Historical Tradition in the Fourth Gospel*. Cambridge: Cambridge University Press, 1963. Dodd's works are classics in the field.

Fiorenza, Elisabeth Schüssler. *In Memory of Her: A Feminist Theological Reconstruction of Christian Origins*. New York: Crossroad, 1984.

Fortna, Robert T. *The Gospel of Signs*. Society for New Testament Studies Monograph Series, no. 11. Cambridge: Cambridge University Press, 1970.

_____. *The Fourth Gospel and Its Predecessor*. Philadelphia: Fortress Press, 1988. In these two volumes the author attempts to establish and defend a source theory for the Gospel.

Fuller, Reginald H. *The Foundations of New Testament Christology*. New York: Charles Scribner's Sons, 1965.

Harner, Philip B. *The "I Am" of the Fourth Gospel*. Biblical Series, no. 26. Philadelphia: Fortress Press, 1970.

Käsemann, Ernst. *The Testament of Jesus According to John 17*. Philadelphia: Fortress Press, 1968. A theological classic!

Kee, Howard Clark. *The Origins of Christianity: Sources and Documents*. Englewood Cliffs, N.J.: Prentice-Hall, 1973.

King, Winston L. *Introduction to Religion: A Phenomenological Approach*. New York: Harper & Row, 1968.

Kysar, Robert. *The Fourth Evangelist and His Gospel: An Examination of Contemporary Scholarship*. Minneapolis: Augsburg Publishing House, 1975.

_____. *John's Story of Jesus*. Philadelphia: Fortress Press, 1984.

_____. "Anti-Semitism in the Gospel of John." In *Faith and Polemic: Studies in Anti-Semitism and Early Christianity*, ed. Craig A. Evans and Donald A. Hagner. Minneapolis: Fortress Press, 1993.

Martyn, J. Louis. *History and Theology in the Fourth Gospel*. Rev. ed. Nashville: Abingdon Press, 1979. A pivotal work in contemporary Johannine studies.

O'Day, Gail R. *Revelation in the Fourth Gospel*. Philadelphia: Fortress Press, 1987. Treats irony with all of its theological significance.

Perrin, Norman. *The New Testament: An Introduction*. New York: Harcourt Brace Jovanovich, 1974.

Robinson, J. A. T. "The Most Primitive Christology of All?" In his *Twelve New Testament Studies*. Naperville, Ill.: Alec R. Allenson, 1962.

Segovia, Fernando F. *The Farewell of the Word: The Johannine Call to Abide*. Minneapolis: Fortress Press, 1991. A literary commentary on the farewell discourses.

Smith, D. Moody. *John*. Proclamation Commentaries. 2nd ed. Philadelphia: Fortress Press, 1986.

_____. *John Among the Gospels: The Relationship in Twentieth-Century Research*. Minneapolis: Fortress Press, 1992. A survey of scholarship on the issue of the relationship between the Fourth Gospel and the Synoptics.

Thompson, Marianne Meye. *The Humanity of Jesus in the Fourth Gospel*. Philadelphia: Fortress Press, 1988. A response to Käsemann.

The Johannine Epistles

Brown, Raymond E. *The Epistles of John*. Anchor Bible, vol. 30. Garden City, N.Y.: Doubleday & Co., 1982. The best commentary on the Johannine epistles.

Houlden, J. L. *The Johannine Epistles*. Harper's New Testament Commentary. New York: Harper & Row, 1973.

Kysar, Robert. *1, 2, 3 John*. Augsburg Commentary on the New Testament. Minneapolis: Augsburg Publishing House, 1986.

The Revelation

Charles, R. H. *Revelation*. 2 vols. International Critical Commentary. Edinburgh: T. & T. Clark, 1920. A classic commentary!

Fiorenza, Elisabeth Schüssler. *The Book of Revelation: Justice and Judgment*. Philadelphia: Fortress Press, 1985.

_____. *Revelation: Vision of a Just World*, Proclamation Commentaries. Minneapolis: Fortress Press, 1991. Fiorenza's books exemplify one of the newer approaches to Revelation.

Krodel, Gerhard A. *Revelation*. Augsburg Commentary on the New Testament. Minneapolis: Augsburg Publishing House, 1989.